D0004262

Data Structures and C Programs

Christopher J. Van Wyk

AT&T Bell Laboratories
Murray Hill, New Jersey

ADDISON-WESLEY PUBLISHING COMPANY

Reading, Massachusetts • Menlo Park, California • New York
Don Mills, Ontario • Wokingham, England • Amsterdam • Bonn
Sydney • Singapore • Tokyo • Madrid • San Juan

To Claudia

This book is in the **Addison-Wesley Series in Computer Science**

Michael A. Harrison
Consulting Editor

Library of Congress Cataloging-in-Publication Data

Van Wyk, Christopher J.
   Data structures and C programs/Christopher J. Van Wyk.
      p.   cm. — (Addison-Wesley series in computer science)
   Includes bibliographical references and index.
   ISBN 0-201-53985-3
   1. C (Computer program language)   2. Data structures (Computer
science)   I. Title.   II. Series.
QA76.73.C15V36   1990
005.7'3—dc20   90-699
                                                                 CIP

This book was typeset in Palatino, Helvetica, and Courier by the author, on an Auto-logic APS-5 phototypesetter and a DEC VAX® 8550 running the 9th Edition of the UNIX® operating system.

Special Printing: all programs coded in ANSI C.

AT&T

Copyright © 1990, 1988 by Bell Telephone Laboratories, Incorporated.

All rights reserved. No part of this publication may be reproduced, stored in a retrieval system, or transmitted, in any form or by any means, electronic, mechanical, photocopying, recording, or otherwise, without the prior written permission of the publisher. Printed in the United States of America.

UNIX is a registered trademark of AT&T.

ABCDEFGHIJ—MA—943210

Preface

One of the best things about computer science is that it offers the chance to build programs that do something, and at the same time to use interesting mathematics with which to study properties of those programs. This book is about some of the important tools that computer scientists use to study problems and to propose and choose among solutions.

Outline of the Book

Part I presents several fundamental ideas. These include abstractions like algorithm, data type, and complexity, and also programming tools like pointers, dynamic memory, and linked data structures. Chapter 6 presents a simple model of computer memory; the concrete details in this chapter suggest the origins of some of the abstractions that appear in Chapters 1 through 5.

Part II presents techniques to solve several general and important problems, especially searching and sorting. Chapter 12 shows how one might apply the material in Chapters 7 through 11 to solve a real-world problem; the emphasis is on building a program that can readily be changed to use different data structures and algorithms.

Part III surveys some advanced material about graphs and graph algorithms. The two chapters cover a lot of topics at a faster pace than Chapters 1 through 12, yet they offer only a hint of what lies beyond the scope of this book.

Each chapter concludes with a section called "Summary and Perspective," which highlights the chapter's important ideas and offers some thoughts on how they fit into the larger scheme of things.

How to Read this Book

It would be good to read this book with pencil and paper in hand. Pause at each problem as it is presented in the text; sketch your own solution before you see the one in the book. This will help you to appreciate the obstacles that any solution to the problem must face.

You can add even more to your reading by using a nearby computer to try your own solutions, and to test, modify, and experiment with the programs that are included in the text. Waiting for a slow program to finish can give you a visceral appreciation of what it means for running time to grow linearly or quadratically with input size.

Finally, your reading will be incomplete unless you do some of the exercises at the ends of each chapter. Many of the exercises reinforce the ideas in the text. Others ask you to extend results in the chapter to solve a new problem. Appendix D contains solutions to about one-fifth of the exercises.

C Programs

The programs in this book are written in C. Programmers who are new to C can consult Appendixes A and B, which contain a brief introduction to the C language and common C library functions; the programs in Chapters 1 through 3 should help you to pick up the essentials of the language.

Since C is a high-level language, it supports most of the abstractions that are important to writing good programs. At the same time, C reflects the architecture of contemporary computers and lets programmers take advantage of it, so a C programmer has a reassuring familiarity with the way a data structure is stored in computer memory. When I taught from an earlier version of this material at Stevens Institute of Technology, students who wrote in C generally understood the material better than those who wrote in Pascal, even though I used Pascal in lectures and sample solutions.

Anything in the text that is labelled "Program" was included directly from the source file of a computer program that was compiled and tested (under the 9th Edition of the UNIX operating system) before it could appear in the book. These programs are meant to illustrate computational methods, not to serve as models for software engineering. In general, they use global variables for simplicity, and contain few comments since they lie near text that explains them.

Some Perspective on Theory

Mathematical techniques figure prominently in the analysis of data structures and algorithms. Careful proofs of correctness give us confidence that our solutions do what they should, while asymptotic methods let us compare the running time and memory utilization of different solutions to the same problem. But mathematical methods are *means* with which to study, not ends in their own right. The programs in this book are meant to counteract the view that the mathematical analysis of data structures and algorithms is paramount.

Of course, some people believe that students of data structures and algorithms do not need to see programs at all. They contend that once you understand clearly the idea for a data structure or algorithm, you can easily write a computer program that uses it. They prefer to write problem solutions in high-level pseudo-code that omits many details. A few even go so far as to claim that "programming has no intellectual content."

I take strong exception to this dismissal of the importance of programming, which is, after all, the source of many interesting problems. I was surprised at how much I learned when I wrote the programs in this book. Sometimes, the final program bore little resemblance to the pseudo-code with which I had started; the program handled all of the details glossed over by the pseudo-code, however, and many times it was also more elegant. Seeing data structures and algorithms implemented also gives a better idea of how simple or complicated they are.

Another advantage of writing programs is that we can run them. This can give us insight into the performance of a particular technique. It can show us errors in our logical and mathematical analysis, or confirm it and give us more feeling for the practical importance of that analysis. Finally, by analyzing statistics gathered from programs, many researchers have been led to discover new data structures and algorithms.

ANSI C

In this printing of the book, all of the programs have been revised to reflect the ANSI standard for C that was adopted in late 1989. The required revisions were quite minor. Besides changing all function declarations to use the new style encouraged by the standard, the principal differences arise from the change in the type of the generic pointer and the demise of function `gets()`.

While I was making the necessary changes to the programs and the text, I tried to smooth out infelicitous prose, added a few recent references, and corrected the mistakes that I found. To my chagrin, the algorithms in Chapter 14 included both errors and parts that were needlessly unclear; most egregiously, Algorithm 14.2 was completely wrong. Since Chapter 14 is the only chapter that does not include any C programs, this experience only reinforces my opinion that the book needs to include programs, not just high-level descriptions.

Acknowledgements

I am grateful to many people who have influenced this book in some way. I learned a lot about putting theory into practice when I worked on projects with Brian Kernighan and Tom Szymanski. Al Aho and Jeff Ullman offered encouragement and advice when I conceived this book and started writing. Doug McIlroy and Rob Pike gave me thoughtful comments on early drafts of several chapters. Jon Bentley and Brian Kernighan read the whole manuscript carefully; in fact, Brian waded through several versions.

I also offer thanks to the following people, whom Addison-Wesley recruited to review parts of the manuscript: Andrew Appel (Princeton University), Paul Hilfinger (University of California, Berkeley), Glen Keeney (Michigan State University), John Rasure (University of New Mexico), Richard Reid (Michigan State University), Henry Ruston (Polytechnic University of New York), and Charles M. Williams (Georgia State University); and to these people, who taught classes from the manuscript: Michael Clancy (University of California, Berkeley), Don Hush (University of New Mexico), and Harley Myler and Greg Heileman (University of Central Florida).

I am happy also to acknowledge the following diligent readers who reported errors in earlier printings: M. Berstein, James H. Davenport (University of Bath), David Levine (Williams College), Bill Pugh (University of Maryland), and Paul A. Sand (University of New Hampshire).

Murray Hill, New Jersey   *C.J.V.W.*

Contents

Part II: Efficient Algorithms

Part III: Advanced Topics

Appendixes

Part I

Fundamental Ideas

1

Charting Our Course

The questions we ask when we study data structures and algorithms have their roots in practice: someone needs a program that does a job, and does it efficiently. The techniques we shall see in the chapters to come were discovered in the quest to create or improve a solution to some practical problem. To give some idea of the circumstances that often surround such discoveries, in this chapter we shall solve a simple, practical, problem.

The two solutions we shall see use only rudimentary programming techniques. Both solutions work, which is an important and good property. But both solutions also have serious limitations: the first is inconvenient for users, while the second takes longer and longer to run as its input grows. These limitations can be overcome only by using more sophisticated data structures and algorithms. Our reflections on these solutions offer glimpses of some important issues in the study of data structures and algorithms.

1.1
PROBLEM: SUMMARIZING DATA

The problem is to write a program with which to keep track of money in a checking account. We want to know both how money is spent on different expense categories (food, rent, books, etc.), and how money comes into the checking account from different sources (salary, gifts, interest, etc.). Following standard bookkeeping practice, we call both expense categories and sources of income *accounts*.

At this point we shall leave the exact details of the input unspecified; instead, we say merely that the data is presented as a sequence of lines, with each line specifying a *transaction*, an account together with an amount to be added to or subtracted from the balance in that account. Each line has the form

account amount

Different solutions can use different ways to designate accounts, tailoring the choice to the programmer's or the user's convenience. We do specify, however, that the output should have the same form as the input, with one line for each distinct account designation, and the amount on that line equal to the sum of the amounts on all input lines containing that designation.

For example, given as input the following six transactions:

```
salary 275.31
rent -250
salary 125.43
food -23.59
books -60.42
food -18.07
```

the program should produce the following output summary:

```
salary 400.74
rent -250
food -41.66
books -60.42
```

As a matter of fact, neither of the programs presented in this chapter accepts exactly this input, although Solution II comes close.

Problems like this arise in many situations. A solution to this problem could be used to maintain the balances in customers' charge accounts at a store; the output reports the amount owed in each account. It could also be used to follow inventories, with each account corresponding to a particular product, perhaps a dish served in a restaurant or a tool stocked by a hardware store.

The requirement that output be acceptable as input leaves fewer decisions for us to make, but it also underscores an important point about program design: A program is often more useful if it can process what it produces. For example, given a program that solves this problem, we might use it to summarize checking account activity by the month; to arrive at an overall summary for the year, we would simply run the monthly summaries through the same program that produced them. The same idea applies to inventory control for a large corporation: if each restaurant or store in a region sends its summarized sales data to regional headquarters, and the summaries are in the appropriate format, then regional headquarters can use the same program to summarize the data from all franchisees in the region and send the results to national headquarters.

1.2
SOLUTION I

In our first solution we adopt an input format expressly chosen to make our programming job simple: each account is designated by a non-negative integer less than n, where n is to be specified in advance. (Although this choice makes it simple to write the program, it is inconvenient for users, as mentioned in the chapter introduction.) For example, if n were five or larger, the following input would be acceptable:

```
0  275.31
1  -250
0  125.43
3  -23.59
4  -60.42
3  -18.07
```

This method for designating accounts suggests a natural data structure to use in a C program, since the first position in a C array is at index zero. We declare *balance*[ ] to be an array of length n, then store the balance of account i in *balance*[i].

We present our solution in a top-down fashion, beginning with a high-level view and refining the details to simpler steps until we reach a working program. We begin with the following outline:

(1) read and process each transaction line
(2) print a summary table

We elaborate Step (1) more fully as follows:

on each line,
    (1a) read two numbers—the account number and the transaction amount
    (1b) update the appropriate element of balance[ ]

```
#include "ourhdr.h"

#define N 5
float balance[N];

void getlines(void) /* read and process each line */
{
    int account;
    float amount;
    while (scanf("%d %f", &account, &amount) != EOF)
        balance[account] += amount;
}

void printsummary(void) /* produce a summary table */
{
    int i;
    for (i = 0; i < N; i++)
        printf("%d %g\n", i, balance[i]);
}

main()
{
    getlines();
    printsummary();
    exit(0);
}
```

PROGRAM 1.1

Solution I to the problem in Section 1.1. See Appendix A for a brief introduction to the C language, Appendix B for a description of the library functions exit(), printf(), and scanf(), and Appendix C for the contents of the header file ourhdr.h.

Step (2) is simpler:

> *as i goes from 0 through n − 1,*
> *print i and balance[i]*

The outline is now detailed enough that we can write Program 1.1. Program 1.1 uses N to denote the size of array balance[], so if we need to change that size, we can simply redefine N. To keep the program simple, array balance[] contains floats; if we were dealing with real money (especially money that belonged to other people) we would want to be more careful about the precision with which amounts of money are stored.

Program 1.1 could be improved in many ways. It would be a good idea for getlines() to check for account numbers that lie outside the bounds of array balance[]. It might be useful to print out only nonzero balances in printsummary(). The exercises suggest some other ideas. Instead of pursuing such elaborations, however, we shall leave Program 1.1 as it stands and do the natural thing: run it.

If we run the sample input presented at the beginning of this section through Program 1.1, we get the following output:

```
0  400.74
1  -250
2  0
3  -41.66
4  -60.42
```

Evidently Program 1.1 works, and it is an adequate solution to our simple version of the problem. Still, the restriction to small integers as account names, and the storage of balances as consecutive elements of an array, make Program 1.1 seriously deficient as a solution to the original problem. Even for a small job, such as balancing a personal checkbook, it would be inconvenient to remember accounts by number. For a very large job, such as maintaining data on credit card customers, storing balances in an array is impractical. Some credit card numbers are 16 digits long: try getting Program 1.1 to work with N defined to be 10^{16}.

1.3
SOLUTION II

Our second solution permits accounts to be designated by character strings of some fixed length. If that fixed length were four, for example, then the program should accept the following input:

```
earn  275.31
rent  -250
earn  125.43
food  -23.59
book  -60.42
food  -18.07
```

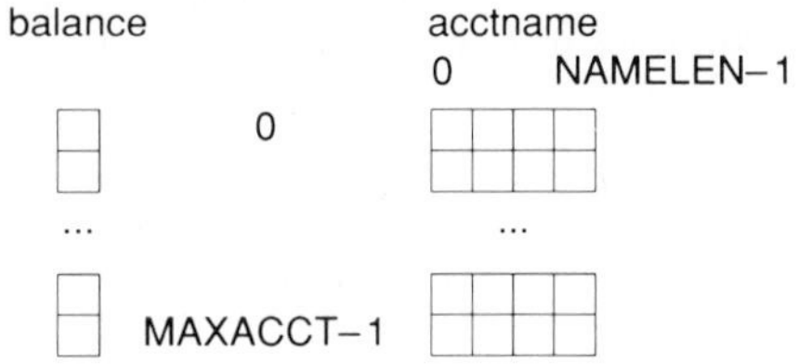

FIGURE 1.1

Parallel arrays for Solution II.

In our solution, we shall store the data in two parallel arrays: acctname[i], which contains the name of an account, and balance[i], which contains the balance in the account named by acctname[i]; Figure 1.1 depicts the arrangement. The C declarations shown in Program 1.2a create these data structures with room for 100 accounts with four-character names; variable numaccts is the index of the first unfilled entry in the array.

Our top-down program development follows lines very similar to those in Section 1.2. The basic steps are the same:

(1) read and process each line
(2) print a summary table

In fact, we can use the same function main() as in Program 1.1.

Because accounts are named by more than a single integer, we need to change both functions getlines() and printsummary(). The change to printsummary() is easier, so we do it first.

The new printsummary() must print an alphabetic account name instead of an account number. We can make the new function resemble the old by having it call another new function, writename(), to

```
#define MAXACCT 100
#define NAMELEN 4
char acctname[MAXACCT][NAMELEN];
float balance[MAXACCT];
int numaccts;
```

PROGRAM 1.2a

Data structure declarations for Solution II. (Program 1.2 is the combination of these declarations with the contents of Programs 1.2b through Program 1.2e.)

```
void writename(int n)  /* print acctname[n] */
{
    int i;
    for (i = 0; i < NAMELEN; i++)
        putchar(acctname[n][i]);
}

void printsummary(void)  /* produce a summary table */
{
    int i;
    for (i = 0; i < numaccts; i++) {
        writename(i);
        printf(" %g\n", balance[i]);
    }
}
```

PROGRAM 1.2b

Functions `writename()` and `printsummary()` for Solution II.

print an account name, as shown in Program 1.2b. Incidentally, note how easy it would be to supply a version of `writename()` that would make `printsummary()` in Program 1.2 work in Program 1.1; maybe the simple form of input in Section 1.2 caused our top-down decomposition to end too early.

It remains for us to rewrite `getlines()`. The control structure is almost the same as it was for Solution I,

> *on each line,*
>   *(1a) read the account designation and the transaction amount*
>   *(1b) update the appropriate element of the balance array*

but the substeps are more complicated. In step (1a), we must extract an account name from each input line. In (1b), we must find the location of the extracted name in array `acctname[]`, inserting the name if it is not already there. Of course, Program 1.1 also does steps (1a) and (1b), but the work is done implicitly because the account names are numbers. In the version of `getlines()` shown as Program 1.2c, each line is read into a character buffer `buf[]` that is global to the whole program; array `buf[]` is declared to be long enough to contain any reasonable line of input. Like `printsummary()`, `getlines()` encapsulates operations specific to processing names in a function; in this case, `findacct()` finds an account with matching name in array `acctname[]`.

```
#define BUFLEN 100
char buf[BUFLEN];

void getlines(void) /* read and process each line */
{
    int n;
    float amt;
    while (fgets(buf, BUFLEN, stdin)) {
        n = findacct();
        sscanf(&buf[NAMELEN+1], "%f", &amt);
        balance[n] += amt;
    }
}
```

PROGRAM 1.2c

Function getlines() and declaration of buf[] in Solution II.

Function findacct(), shown as Program 1.2d, searches array acctname[] for the name that occupies the first NAMELEN places in array buf. It does this using a loop from the 0th through the (numaccts−1)th entry of array acctname. If the name has not been

```
int findacct(void) /* find the account whose name is in
                      the first NAMELEN characters of buf */
{
    int i;
    for (i = 0; i < numaccts; i++) {
        if (samename(i))
            return i;
    }
    if (i >= MAXACCT) {
        printf("too many accounts\n");
        abort();
    }
    /* at this point, i == numaccts */
    copyname(numaccts);
    return numaccts++;
}
```

PROGRAM 1.2d

Function findacct() of Solution II.

```
int samename(int n)  /* 0 if acctname[n] differs from
                         the first NAMELEN characters of buf */
{
    int i;
    for (i = 0; i < NAMELEN; i++)
        if (acctname[n][i] != buf[i])
            return 0;
    return 1;
}

void copyname(int n)  /* copy name from buf into acctname[n] */
{
    int i;
    for (i = 0; i < NAMELEN; i++)
        acctname[n][i] = buf[i];
}
```

PROGRAM 1.2e

Functions samename() and copyname() of Solution II.

seen before, no step of this loop will find it, and findacct() will install the name (if there is room) at the numacctsth place, then increment numaccts.

Function findacct() also uses functions that compare and copy names to encapsulate the processing of account names; Program 1.2e shows the functions needed by findacct().

Program 1.2 produces the following output when given the example input at the beginning of this section:

```
earn  400.74
rent  -250
food  -41.66
book  -60.42
```

So Program 1.2 works. Now we can discuss some of its strong and weak points.

Observations About Solution II

Users are almost sure to find the input accepted by Program 1.2 more convenient than that accepted by Program 1.1. Even though it can be challenging to invent four-character account names, it is still easier to remember the name "rent" than that the number 1 is associated with the rent account. In at least one respect, Program 1.2 is also more robust than Program 1.1: if it runs out of room to store accounts, it terminates processing and issues an error message.

An obvious weakness of Program 1.2 is that the functions that operate on account names are specific to the arrays `acctname[]` and `buf[]`. If we were to use this approach in a program that used several arrays of names, we would have to write separate functions to manipulate the names in each array. It would be better to write name-processing functions that accept one or two character arrays as arguments. Chapter 3 shows how to do this.

If we stored names in strings, we could use functions in the C library to read and write names, and it would be easy to permit account names of different lengths. Section 3.2 discusses strings.

Parallel arrays are not a bad solution to this problem. Were the number of related items were to increase, however, a program that used more parallel arrays would become increasingly complicated and difficult to understand and maintain. Structures, discussed in Section 3.3, would be a better answer.

These examples of weak programming practice, as real and important as they are, would matter only to someone responsible for maintaining the program. A user of the program might be more concerned about the built-in fixed sizes MAXACCT and NAMELEN. Section 3.4 and Chapter 5 explain ways to avoid imposing such *a priori* size limitations on users.

Beyond matters of style and convenience, most users are likely to be concerned about the program's *performance*—how much it costs to run. The "cost" here can be many things, from time spent waiting for the program to finish to dollars demanded by the administration of a computer center. Methods for estimating and improving the performance of programs are central to the study of data structures and algorithms. In the next section we shall study the performance of Program 1.2. Chapters 7 through 9 present several techniques that we could use to improve its performance.

1.4

MEASURING PERFORMANCE

One of the most commonly used indicators of program performance is *running time*: how long the program takes to process its input. In general, to measure running time we need several sets of input data. If we have a suitable variety of test data on hand, we can proceed

```
void randname(int poss)
{
    int j;
    for (j = 0; j < NAMELEN; j++)
        printf("%c", 'a' + nrand(poss));
}
```

PROGRAM 1.3

A function to create a name that is NAMELEN characters long, with one of poss possible characters at each position.

immediately to measure the program. If we do not have enough test data, however, we must construct it.

It is common to construct data sets by hand to see whether a program works correctly. We saw examples of such test data in Sections 1.2 and 1.3. For performance measurement, however, we often need large data sets that are inconvenient to create by hand, so we write programs that generate test data.

Generating Test Data

The key to generating test data for Program 1.2 is a function that generates account names. Function randname(), shown as Program 1.3, uses the random number generator function nrand() to create a name that is NAMELEN characters long, with poss different possibilities in each character position of the name. For example, if we call randname(2) five times with NAMELEN equal to 4, it might print the following five account names:

    baaa baab babb aaab aabb

whereas five calls to randname(10) might produce these five names:

    hgia jgaf hibj aeaf aabb

(Since randname() calls a random number generator, if you run it five times you probably would get different results from those shown here.) When NAMELEN is 4, the call randname(2) can generate one of $2^4 = 16$ different names, whereas the call randname(10) can generate one of $10^4 = 10,000$ different names. In general, the call randname(poss) generates one of $poss^{NAMELEN}$ different names. Given this function to create account names, we can easily create a test data set of any number of transactions that affect up to poss^{NAMELEN} accounts.

Deciding What to Measure

Now that we can generate test data, we want to measure the time the program takes to process it. If we look at a clock during the run, we can obtain a crude measurement of how long the program takes, which is often called *wall-clock* time. This easy method has a couple of disadvantages. If other users share the system on which we time the program, the load that their work imposes on the system makes this measurement unreliable. More important, the measurement of wall-clock time tells us nothing about *why* the program uses the time it does.

If our system has an *execution profiler* available, we can use it to find the time a program spends executing each function. For example, on many UNIX systems we can compile Program 1.2 with the −p option. After we run it on 1000 transactions on accounts whose names are chosen from 10,000 possible different names, executing the prof command produces the following chart:

```
%time   cumsecs   #call   ms/call   name
 59.0      2.40  467489      0.01   _samename
 27.6      3.52    1000      1.12   _findacct
  5.3      3.74                     mcount
  4.0      3.90     950      0.17   _writename
  1.6      3.97                     __doprnt
  1.2      4.02                     __innum
  0.4      4.04                     _doscan
  0.4      4.05                     _creat
  0.4      4.07                     _write
  0.0      4.07     950      0.00   _copyname
  0.0      4.07       1      0.00   _getlines
  0.0      4.07       1      0.00   _main
  0.0      4.07       1      0.00   _printsummary
```

Each line of the chart gives timing data about the function named in the right-hand column; from left to right, the columns show the percent of total execution time spent in the named function, the cumulative number of compute-seconds that time represents, the number of calls to the function, and the number of compute-milliseconds per call. The chart shows that Program 1.2 spends almost three-fifths of its execution time in samename(), and another quarter in findacct(); this suggests that we can speed up the program substantially if we can improve the performance of these two functions.

Although execution profilers can be valuable when we need to find the places in a program that are consuming large amounts of time, there is no single standard profiler that we can discuss here. However, we are always free to add to a program *instrumentation* that measures quantities that we believe are related to running time. Such instrumentation can be useful even if a profiler is available, as when we need to gather program statistics at a more detailed level than that defined by function calls.

To measure Program 1.2, we shall count the number of calls to functions `samename()` and `findacct()`. This is an obvious choice in light of the results from the profiler. Even if we had no profiler available, however, we probably would have decided to measure these quantities. One reason is the common rule of thumb that programs spend most of their execution time in loops. In Program 1.2, almost every function uses loops, but the loop in `findacct()` is unique: its number of iterations is bounded only by the number of accounts, and it is performed once for every transaction.

Obtaining Empirical Results

Program 1.4 shows a modified version of Program 1.2. Variable `numfind` counts calls to `findacct()` and `numseen` counts calls to `samename()`; thus `numseen` divided by `numfind` is the average number of names seen during the search for a name. We measure these quantities by declaring global counter variables and adding statements that increment them to `findacct()`. We also modify `main()` to report the accumulated statistics. To illustrate how the modified program works, suppose we generate 50 transactions with three possible values at each character position. When we use this data as input to Program 1.4, it reports:

```
50 checks on 38 accounts; total seen 853
```

Two things can vary as we examine the performance of Program 1.2: the number of items in the data set and the number of possibilities at each character position in an account name. We begin our study by fixing the variation in account names. By calling `randname(2)`, we can generate at most 16 different account names (composed of the letters *a* and *b*). Figure 1.2 presents the results for eight data sets whose number of transactions is a power of two between 8 and 1024, along with a plot of `numseen` against `numfind`, using a logarithmic scale on both axes. The plot begs us to fit a straight line (numseen = $m \times$numfind$^\mu + b$) to the data points. If we make the simple assumption that $\mu = 1$, linear regression suggests that $m = 8.7$.

```
int numfind, numseen;

int findacct(void) /* find the account whose name is in buf */
{
    int i;
    numfind++;
    for (i = 0; i < numaccts; i++) {
        numseen++;
        if (samename(i))
            return i;
    }
    if (i >= MAXACCT) {
        printf("too many accounts\n");
        abort();
    }
    /* at this point, i == numaccts */
    copyname(numaccts);
    return numaccts++;
}

main()
{
    getlines();
    printsummary();
    fprintf(stderr,
        "%d checks on %d accounts; total seen %d\n",
        numfind, numaccts, numseen);
    exit(0);
}
```

PROGRAM 1.4

Modifications to findacct() and main() of Program 1.2 to measure statistics related to its performance.

Before we run more test data, perhaps we can form a hypothesis about why the slope is 8.7. In the larger data sets (those with 64 or more transactions), the program output shows that numaccts attains its maximum possible value of 16. This is much less than numfind, so most of the searches performed by findacct() actually find the account name they seek, and do not need to install it. Consider what happens once all 16 account names are in the table: each transaction that arrives is equally likely to contain any one of the 16 account names; thus the average search examines $(1+2+\cdots+16)/16 = 8.5$

```
8 checks on 7 accounts; total seen 27
16 checks on 11 accounts; total seen 85
32 checks on 14 accounts; total seen 191
64 checks on 16 accounts; total seen 448
128 checks on 16 accounts; total seen 1004
256 checks on 16 accounts; total seen 2184
512 checks on 16 accounts; total seen 4343
1024 checks on 16 accounts; total seen 8859
```

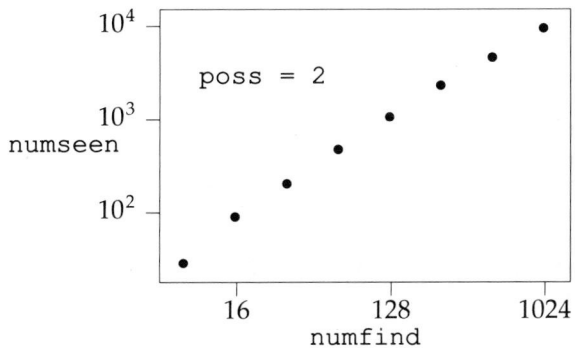

FIGURE 1.2

Output from Program 1.4, together with a plot showing the total number of account names seen during searches as a function of the number of transactions, when poss = 2.

entries in the table. The observed value (8.7) is reasonably close to this predicted value.

Based on this reasoning, we shall formulate the more general prediction that

$$\text{numseen} \approx \frac{\text{numfind} \times (\text{numaccts} + 1)}{2}. \tag{1.1}$$

Figure 1.3 shows that the values predicted by Equation (1.1) agree closely with the actual observed values.

Next let us see what happens when we increase the possible variation in account names. Figure 1.4 shows data generated by running the program on eight data sets of the same sizes as above, but with account names that have 32 possibilities at each character position. Although the graph looks similar to the one for poss = 2, the printed output tells a different story. In each test run, there are as many dif-

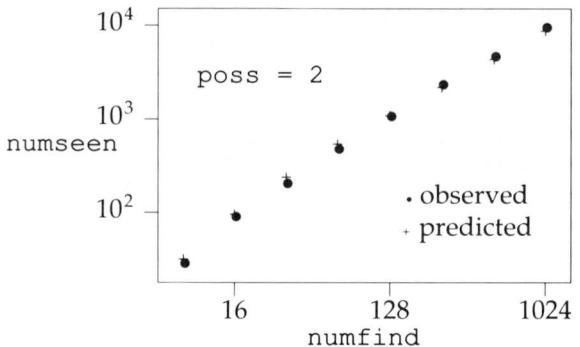

FIGURE 1.3

Predicted and observed values of the number of account names seen during searches as a function of the number of transactions, when `poss` = 2.

ferent accounts as there are transactions: in terms of program variables, `numaccts` = `numfind`. But we need not run the program to know exactly how it behaves in this situation. Each search examines all names already in the table, then installs the new name. Thus, the ith search examines $i - 1$ names, and

$$\text{numseen} = \sum_{i=1}^{\text{numaccts}} (i-1) = \frac{\text{numaccts}(\text{numaccts}-1)}{2}. \quad (1.2)$$

These two data sets test the program in two extreme situations—when there are many more transactions than different accounts, and when the number of transactions and accounts is the same. Equations (1.1) and (1.2) predict the number of names that will be examined in these two cases. Let us use them to predict how many names will be examined in some intermediate situation.

Formulating and Testing a Prediction

Consider the behavior of Equations (1.1) and (1.2). Equation (1.1) arose when `numaccts` was much less than `numfind`, and seems to offer a good prediction in that situation. Equation (1.2) is an exact solution when `numaccts` is the same as `numfind`; note that in this situation, Equations (1.1) and (1.2) are almost the same. Perhaps Equation (1.1) will predict program performance well in general.

To test the predictive power of Equation (1.1) on an intermediate situation, we might produce the output in Figure 1.5 with `poss` = 10.

```
8 checks on 8 accounts; total seen 28
16 checks on 16 accounts; total seen 120
32 checks on 32 accounts; total seen 496
64 checks on 64 accounts; total seen 2016
128 checks on 128 accounts; total seen 8128
256 checks on 256 accounts; total seen 32640
512 checks on 512 accounts; total seen 130816
1024 checks on 1024 accounts; total seen 523776
```

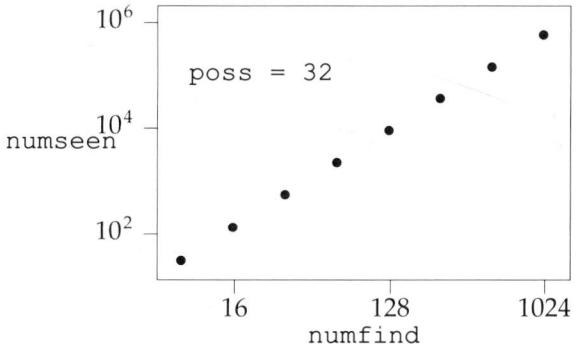

FIGURE 1.4

The total number of account names seen during searches, as a function of the number of transactions, when `poss` = 32.

The remarkably close agreement between observed and predicted values suggests that Equation (1.1) offers a reasonable estimate of the relationship among `numseen`, `numfind`, and `numaccts`.

Equation (1.1) is more than an abstract relationship among several program quantities. It allows us to predict program performance based on parameters of the application. Suppose the program was working acceptably in some application: it offered the flexibility we needed, and it processed data reasonably fast, say in about one minute. If both the number of accounts and the number of transactions were to increase by a factor of ten, Equation (1.1) predicts that the required processing time would increase by a factor of 100, to more than an hour and a half. This might well be unacceptable, and we would have to change the program to meet the new demands.

```
8 checks on 8 accounts; total seen 28
16 checks on 16 accounts; total seen 120
32 checks on 32 accounts; total seen 496
64 checks on 64 accounts; total seen 2016
128 checks on 128 accounts; total seen 8128
256 checks on 254 accounts; total seen 32337
512 checks on 500 accounts; total seen 127017
1024 checks on 969 accounts; total seen 487931
```

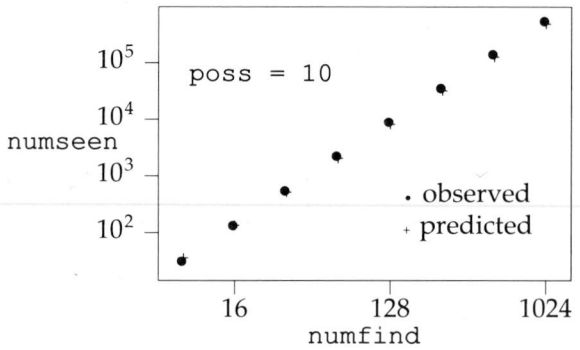

FIGURE 1.5

Observed and predicted number of account names seen during searches, as a function of the number of transactions, when poss = 10.

1.5
SUMMARY AND PERSPECTIVE

In this chapter we saw two solutions to a simple problem. Program 1.1 meets the letter of the problem specification, and is about the simplest way one could do so. Program 1.2 offers a more convenient input format; the increased flexibility brings with it non-trivial questions about the program's structure and performance.

There are many ways to improve the way Program 1.2 is written. However, the stylistic imperfections of that program should not obscure an important point: it works, probably well enough for some purposes. If we are in this happy situation, it might well not be worth improving the program's style or ease of use. Should we need to improve either of these aspects of the program, Part I shows how to use strings, structures, and dynamic storage allocation.

In general, to the extent that we are concerned with programs at all, we are more interested in their performance than their style. The real focus of our interest, however, is the *ideas* on which a program is based, rather than the details of a particular implementation. These ideas are algorithms and data structures. Roughly speaking, an *algorithm* describes the steps one takes to do something, while a *data structure* describes how data is arranged for access by an algorithm. (Note that a "data structure" does not describe the structure of the input data; we usually use the term *format* for this notion.)

For example, Program 1.2 uses a fixed-size table as its data structure, and simple-minded (or *brute-force*) sequential search as its algorithm. Many different programs could have been written using the same idea, but in a different style or even a different language. And if we ran the same program on different computers, the wall-clock time would vary depending on the processing speed of each machine and the distribution of the input data.

For all that variety, however, there is a sense in which we can say that Equation (1.1) governs the performance of any program that uses sequential search for this problem: if we increase either the number of accounts or the number of transactions in the input by a factor of k, the program's running time is apt to increase by a factor of k. In general, when we study data structures and algorithms, we aim to make statements like this, relating properties of the data to the performance of a program based on an idea. Such general statements can help us both to design and to improve programs.

Theory and Practice

To enable us to make such general statements, we shall develop terminology and a mathematical framework in which to describe and analyze data structures and algorithms. Although these formal tools offer many opportunities for the elegant expression of ideas and for intricate analyses of program performance, we should never let them conceal the practical importance of the ideas that led to their development in the first place. To avoid losing sight of the practical side of our subject, we shall implement many of the ideas as programs.

Indeed, sometimes we shall study some properties of an idea by measuring statistics about a program, as we did in Section 1.4. When we do this, we need to remember two points. First, it is not easy to choose which program statistics, and what values of application parameters, will reveal the most about an idea; both careful thought and many experiments go into useful empirical studies of data structures and algorithms. Second, an execution profiler is vital to deciding what to measure about a large program; experience shows that people are almost always wrong about where their programs are spending their time.

EXERCISES

1 Give a persuasive argument that Program 1.1 is correct.

2 Modify Program 1.1 to check that the account number is valid before it posts a change to the account.

3 How many accounts does Program 1.1 examine to find the one that corresponds to the input? In other words, what value of "numseen" should we report for Program 1.1 given the value of numfound?

4 Modify Program 1.1 so it does not produce output for accounts with a balance of zero. Discuss the good and bad points of the resulting program. Can you modify Program 1.1 to output all *active* accounts—those whose balance was non-zero at some time during program execution—even if an active account has zero balance at the end of the program?

5 Give a persuasive argument that Program 1.2 is correct.

6 Describe some input that could cause Program 1.2 to crash for a reason other than i >= MAXACCT. For example, what happens if an account name in the input is preceded by spaces?

7 Modify Programs 1.1 and 1.2 to print account balances using %f instead of %g. How does this change affect the output? What does it suggest about the accuracy of the program?

8 Modify Programs 1.1 and 1.2 to store account balances in integers instead of floating-point numbers. Try to do this so that the old input (including decimal points) is still acceptable.

9 Modify Programs 1.1 and 1.2 to compute a cumulative balance over all accounts.

10 What does Program 1.1 do on the following input?

```
0 275.31 1 -250 0 125.43 3 -23.59 4 -60.42
```

Why?

11 What does Program 1.2 do on the following input?

```
earn 275.31 rent -250 earn 125.43 food -23.59 book -60.42
```

Why?

12 Program 1.5 contains another function to compare account names. How does it differ from Program 1.2e? Predict whether it would

```
int samename(int n)  /* 0 if acctname[n] differs from
                  the first NAMELEN characters of buf */
{
    int i, same;
    same = 1;
    for (i = 0; i < NAMELEN; i++)
        if (acctname[n][i] != buf[i])
            same = 0;
    return same;
}
```

PROGRAM 1.5

An alternative version of samename().

make Program 1.2 run faster or slower. How much of a difference would it make?

13 Find out what execution profilers are available on your system. Use them to test your prediction about Program 1.5 in Exercise 12. How reproducible are execution profiles?

14 Program 1.6 contains another version of findacct(). How does it work? Is there any input that would work correctly with Program 1.2 but would fail if Program 1.2 used this version of findacct()?

```
int findacct(void)  /* find the account whose name is in buf */
{
    int i = 0;
    if (numaccts < MAXACCT)
        copyname(numaccts);
    else {
        printf("too many accounts\n");
        abort();
    }
    while (!samename(i))
        i++;
    if (i == numaccts)
        numaccts++;
    return i;
}
```

PROGRAM 1.6

An alternative version of findacct().

15 There is a weakness in the problem specification of Section 1. Since each distinct account designation is assumed to be valid, it can be difficult to detect errors. For example, if the input contained boot 18.99, we might prefer to hear about it (and correct the error in spelling "book") than have a new account established for footwear. Suggest ways to remedy this weakness.

16 How many different names can be printed as a result of the function call randname(1)?

17 Write a program to generate test data for Program 1.2 using Program 1.3. What would be a good choice for the amounts in each transaction?

18 Some programmers are reluctant to add instrumentation to their programs because it requires effort to remove the relevant statements from the program after they have served their purpose. Suggest some ways to make it easier to find and delete instrumentation from a program.

19 Show that $\sum_{i=1}^{n} i = n(n+1)/2$ for $n \geq 1$.

20 Why are numbers of the form $n(n+1)/2$ called "triangular numbers"?

21 How different are the values given by Equations (1.1) and (1.2)?

REFERENCES

An important book about the top-down structured design of programs is

O.-J. Dahl, E. W. Dijkstra, and C. A. R. Hoare. *Structured Programming*. London and New York: Academic Press, 1972.

The December, 1974, issue of the journal *Computing Surveys* contains several papers about programming:

P. J. Brown. "Programming and documenting software projects." *Computing Surveys* 6 (1974): 213–220.

B. W. Kernighan and P. J. Plauger. "Programming style: examples and counterexamples." *Computing Surveys* 6 (1974): 303–319.

D. E. Knuth. "Structured programming with go to statements." *Computing Surveys* 6 (1974): 261–301.

N. Wirth. "On the composition of well-structured programs." *Computing Surveys* 6 (1974): 247–259.

J. M. Yohe. "An overview of programming practices." *Computing Surveys* 6 (1974): 221–245.

This book is related to the above article by the same authors:

B. W. Kernighan and P. J. Plauger. *The Elements of Programming Style*. 2d ed. New York: McGraw-Hill, 1978.

2

The Complexity of Algorithms

In this chapter we shall discuss what an algorithm is, see how to analyze an algorithm's performance, and develop some mathematical tools with which to express facts about an algorithm. As an example we consider two algorithms to solve an arithmetic problem, examining their correctness, their efficiency, and some of the issues to consider in implementing them as C programs.

2.1
THE IDEA OF AN ALGORITHM

An *algorithm* is a sequence of well understood steps that one takes to do something.

Daily life abounds with algorithms in the form of directions. Friends give directions for driving to their homes. The government gives directions for filing tax returns. Recipes in cookbooks are frequently cited as examples of algorithms. Even most household products are labeled with simple "algorithms" for their use. Each of these homely illustrations shares some features with algorithms in computer programs.

First, the level at which we present an algorithm depends on the audience. When you tell someone how to get to your home, the directions you give depend on how familiar the person is with your neighborhood. Similarly, our explanation of an algorithm to someone already well-versed in its basic ideas would be more terse than an explanation to a group largely unacquainted with the algorithm's underpinnings.

Second, once the algorithm for doing one job is understood, it can be used as a step in another algorithm. Basic cookbooks include many recipes for foods that are not likely to be served alone, but are frequently used in other recipes. Examples are recipes for beaten egg whites or browned ground beef. The idea of using algorithms as steps in other algorithms should be no surprise to programmers. A function (sometimes called a procedure or subroutine) is just a way of packaging a useful piece of program so that it can be used as a step in another function.

Third, the notion of "well understood steps" includes common sense. Some shampoo bottles include these terse directions: "Lather. Rinse. Repeat." The literal-minded will point to this as an infinite loop. They imagine the obedient consumer thinking: "Let's see. First I apply shampoo and lather, then I rinse; now it says 'Repeat,' so I apply shampoo and lather, then rinse; now it says 'Repeat,' so I . . . ," until the shampoo or the consumer's patience runs out. But of course real consumers don't interpret the directions like this: they take "Repeat" to mean "Repeat once" or "Repeat as often as necessary."

This last idea, that we use common sense to interpret an algorithm, tells us immediately that algorithms are *not* computer programs. Even brief experience with programming is enough to convince most people that computers interpret their instructions *very* literally, and that the appropriate response to every unusual condition must be spelled out in excruciating detail, even when it seems painfully obvious to a human reader. An algorithm is an abstract idea, independent of any machine that might execute it. Conversely, a computer program is an *implementation* (or concrete realization) of an algorithm in a language particular to the computing environment available to its author.

Pseudo-Code

In Chapter 1 we sketched our solutions in a kind of stylized English that could be translated more or less readily into a program. We shall continue to express algorithms in such *pseudo-code*. Our pseudo-code language uses C operators freely, and its programming constructs are similar to those of C. But because pseudo-code is for communicating among people, we generally omit syntactic features of C designed mainly to make it easier for machines to read. For instance, we shall not bother to end every statement with a semicolon, we may not always enclose the conditions on if and while statements in parentheses, and we use indentation rather than curly braces ("{ }") to indicate groups of statements.

Using pseudo-code emphasizes the difference between algorithms and programs. It is also good practice for understanding algorithms in the published literature, which are almost never presented as working programs. In general we use pseudo-code as we are developing an algorithm to express the basic ideas behind it to a human reader. Then, as we turn it into a program, we replace English with code that spells out precisely how to handle all of the special cases that an intelligent reader fills in almost automatically. Real C programs are presented in a typewriter-like font (`like this`). Pseudo-code algorithms appear in a variety of fonts.

2.2
ALGORITHMS FOR EXPONENTIATION

In this section we shall consider two algorithms for raising a number x to a positive integer power n. Since x^n is defined to be the product of n copies of x, these algorithms use multiplications to compute it. We require only that the multiplication operation be associative; thus, x could be an integer, a real number, or a matrix. We define the cost of an exponentiation algorithm to be the number of multiplications it uses to compute x^n.

There are many reasons we might need such an algorithm. As a mundane example, many computer languages lack the operation of exponentiation, so we must write a program if we need to raise an integer or floating-point number to a power. Some methods for encrypting secret messages offer a more exotic application of exponentiation. The message x is encrypted by computing $x^a \bmod b$, where a and b are both about 100 digits long. Obviously we need to use an efficient exponentiation algorithm for such large a.

Solution I

One way to compute x^n is to translate the definition of exponentiation directly into a function $power_1(\ )$, shown as Algorithm 2.1. Besides the looseness of its punctuation, Algorithm 2.1 departs from C in its use of type $number$, which is not a valid type in C. We use it here to avoid specifying the kind of number to which $power_1(\ )$ is applied; of course, $*$ must be interpreted as the multiplication operation appropriate for x.

```
number power₁(number x, int n)
/* Compute xⁿ; n > 0. */
      int i
      number y
      i = n
      y = 1
      while i > 0
            /* ASSERT:  y == xⁿ⁻ⁱ */
A           y = y*x
B           i = i-1
      return y
```

ALGORITHM 2.1

Brute-force algorithm for exponentiation.

Analysis of Solution I

Algorithm $power_1(\ )$ sets y to the value one, then performs n multiplications of y by x. What could be simpler? Nevertheless, we ask about $power_1(\ )$ an important question that we ask about all algorithms: is it correct? (We did not discuss the issue of correctness in Chapter 1, but certainly it is at least as important that an algorithm work correctly as that it run in a certain amount of time.)

To prove the correctness of an algorithm we often use the idea of an *invariant assertion*: a condition whose truth is asserted at some point during execution of the algorithm. In $power_1(\ )$, the comment labeled *ASSERT* says that at the top of the *while*-loop—in fact, before the test $(i > 0)$ is made—the values of y, x, n, and i are related by the equation $y = x^{n-i}$. We call this particular assertion a *loop invariant*, since it lies inside a loop. We can use mathematical induction to verify the loop invariant in Algorithm 2.1 as follows.

When the loop is entered for the first time, $i = n$; thus $y = 1 = x^0 = x^{n-i}$, and the invariant assertion is true. Now suppose that at the top of some later execution of the loop we have $y = Y$, $i = I$, and $Y = x^{n-I}$ (the loop invariant). Let Y' and I' be the values of y and i after statements A and B are executed; by statement A, $Y' = xY$, and by statement B, $I' = I-1$. Recall that $Y = x^{n-I}$; we can multiply both sides of this equation by x, giving $xY = x^{n-I}x$. The right hand side is $x^{n-I+1} = x^{n-(I-1)} = x^{n-I'}$; the left hand side is Y'. Thus we have $Y' = x^{n-I'}$, and the loop invariant is true the next time we enter the loop. When the loop terminates, we have $i = 0$; since the loop invariant holds, $y = x^n$, and the algorithm is correct.

Now that we know that Algorithm 2.1 is correct, we ask how fast it does its job. Let $mult_1(n)$ be the number of multiplications that $power_1(\ )$ uses to compute x^n. The only multiplication in $power_1(\ )$ occurs at line A, and that line is executed n times in computing x^n. Therefore it is simple to express the number of multiplications used by $power_1(\ )$:

$$mult_1(n) \ = \ n. \tag{2.1}$$

Solution II

If we were using $power_1(\ )$ to compute powers by hand, we would get tired quickly, and we might begin to take shortcuts to reduce our labor. For example, to compute x^{50}, we could compute x^{25} and square the result. In general, if n is even and positive, we can use the following algorithm to compute x^n:

number y
y = power$_1$*(x, n/2)*
*return y*y*

This algorithm uses $1 + mult_1(n/2) \ = \ n/2 + 1$ multiplications to compute x^n. It is easy to modify this algorithm to use $(n-1)/2 + 2$ multiplications when n is odd; for example, $x^{51} \ = \ x \times (x^{25})^2$. Furthermore, if n were a multiple of four, it would be clear how to compute x^n using $n/4 + 2$ multiplications; for example, $x^{52} \ = \ ((x^{13})^2)^2$.

To express the general idea for a better algorithm, we use a mathematical notation that rounds fractions to integers. The notation $\lfloor x \rfloor$ is read "floor of x"; it means the largest integer that is not larger than x. For example, $\lfloor 3.1 \rfloor \ = \ 3$ and $\lfloor -3.1 \rfloor \ = \ -4$. The similar notation $\lceil x \rceil$ is read "ceiling of x"; it means the smallest integer that is not smaller than x. For example, $\lceil 3.1 \rceil \ = \ 4$ and $\lceil -3.1 \rceil \ = \ -3$. When n is an integer, $\lfloor n \rfloor \ = \ \lceil n \rceil \ = \ n$.

Our improved exponentiation algorithm is to compute x^n by squaring $x^{\lfloor n/2 \rfloor}$ and multiplying the result by x if n is odd. This is an example of a *recursive* strategy. To compute x^n, we need the value of $x^{\lfloor n/2 \rfloor}$. But computing $x^{\lfloor n/2 \rfloor}$ is another instance of an exponentiation problem, so we use the same algorithm to solve it. In turn, that requires computing $x^{\lfloor \lfloor n/2 \rfloor/2 \rfloor}$. Each time the exponentiation algorithm calls itself, it does so with a smaller exponent, so eventually it reaches a power of x that is trivial to compute.

Function $power_2(\ )$, shown as Algorithm 2.2, implements this idea in general. Since it calls itself to compute its result, we say that $power_2(\ )$ is a *recursive* algorithm. Line A contains $power_2(\ )$'s recursive call on

```
number power₂(number x, int n)
/* Compute xⁿ; n > 0. */
      number y
      if (n == 1)
            return x
A     y = power₂(x, ⌊n/2⌋)
      if n is odd
            /* ASSERT: y == x^((n-1)/2) */
B           return x*y*y
      else
            /* ASSERT: y == x^(n/2) */
C           return y*y
```

ALGORITHM 2.2

Recursive algorithm for exponentiation.

itself. Notice that the second argument—the power to which the first argument is raised—becomes smaller with each succeeding recursive call; when it becomes small enough, the *base case* (when n is 1) is invoked. Figure 2.1 illustrates recursive calls and the base case by showing the steps used by $power_2(3, 5)$.

Analysis of Solution II

The proof that $power_2(\ )$ is correct also uses mathematical induction. We can see directly that $power_2(\ )$ returns the correct value when $n = 1$. Next we assume as an inductive hypothesis that $power_2(\ )$ works correctly for all k, $1 \le k < n$, and prove that it computes x^n correctly. The inductive hypothesis implies that the invariant assertions preceding lines B and C are correct when $k < n$, so there remain two cases to verify that x^n is computed correctly. If n is odd, we execute line B, returning $x \times (x^{(n-1)/2})^2 = x \times x^{n-1} = x^n$, which is correct. If n is even, we execute line C, returning $(x^{n/2})^2 = x^n$, which is also correct.

It is possible to derive an explicit expression for the number of multiplications used by $power_2(\ )$. Instead, we shall get an idea of how $power_2(\ )$ performs by implementing it with statements that count each multiplication. Program 2.1 does this job, and reports the number of multiplications used for $1 \le n \le 50$. The output of Program 2.1 starts out like this:

call power$_2$(3, 5)
5 ≠ 1, so don't return
y = power$_2$(3, 2)
    call power$_2$(3, 2) recursively
    2 ≠ 1, so don't return
    y = power$_2$(3, 1) recursively
        call power$_2$(3, 1)
        1 == 1, so return 3
    y = 3
    *2 is even, so return y*y = 9*
y = 9
*5 is odd, so return y*y*x = 243*

FIGURE 2.1

Steps used to compute *power$_2$*(3, 5) = 3^5.

```
1.1 ** 1  = 1.1 using 0 multiplications
1.1 ** 2  = 1.21 using 1 multiplications
1.1 ** 3  = 1.331 using 2 multiplications
1.1 ** 4  = 1.4641 using 2 multiplications
1.1 ** 5  = 1.61051 using 3 multiplications
1.1 ** 6  = 1.77156 using 3 multiplications
1.1 ** 7  = 1.94872 using 4 multiplications
1.1 ** 8  = 2.14359 using 3 multiplications
1.1 ** 9  = 2.35795 using 4 multiplications
1.1 ** 10 = 2.59374 using 4 multiplications
```

Let $mult_2(n)$ be the number of multiplications used by *power$_2$*( ) to compute x^n.

Figure 2.2 contains a plot of the data generated by Program 2.1, showing $mult_2(n)$ as a function of n. Unlike $mult_1(n)$, $mult_2(n)$ does not appear to be a nice, simple, smooth function of n. However, its value in some special cases reveals much about its behavior.

First, when $n > 1$ is a power of two, the algorithm computes x^n by repeated squaring. If $n = 2^k$ and $k > 0$, then $x^n = x^{2^k}$ is computed by squaring $x^{n/2} = x^{2^{k-1}}$. Therefore we can write the following relation among values of $mult_2(2^k)$:

$$mult_2(1) = 0;$$
$$mult_2(2^k) = 1 + mult_2(2^{k-1}), \text{ for } k > 0. \tag{2.2}$$

```
#include "ourhdr.h"

int mulcount;

double power2(double x, int n)
/* Compute x**n; n>0. */
{
    double y;
    if (n == 1)
        return x;
    y = power2(x, n/2);
    if (n%2 == 1) {
        mulcount += 2;
        /* ASSERT:  y = x ** (n-1)/2 */
        return x * y * y;
    } else {
        mulcount++;
        /* ASSERT:  y = x ** n/2 */
        return y * y;
    }
}

main()
{
    int i;
    double constant = 1.1, result;
    for (i = 1; i <= 50; i++) {
        mulcount = 0;
        result = power2(constant, i);
        printf("%g ** %d = %g using %d multiplications\n",
            constant, i, result, mulcount);
    }
    exit(0);
}
```

PROGRAM 2.1

Recursive solution to the exponentiation problem, augmented with statements to count multiplications.

Equation (2.2) is called a *recurrence relation*, because it defines the value of $mult_2(2^k)$ in terms of its value at a smaller argument, 2^{k-1}. We can use it repeatedly to find the value of $mult_2(2^k)$ for any $k > 0$. For example,

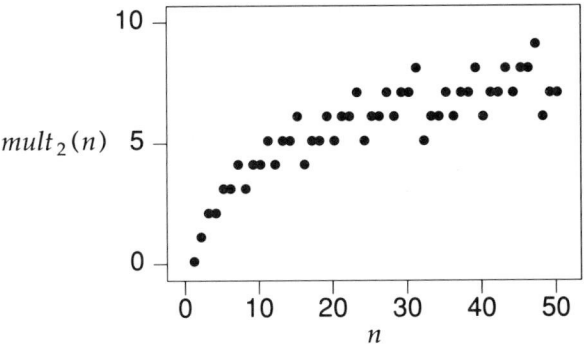

FIGURE 2.2

Plot of $mult_2(n)$ against n for $1 \le n \le 50$.

$$mult_2(8) = 1 + mult_2(4)$$

$$= 1 + 1 + mult_2(2)$$

$$= 1 + 1 + 1 + mult_2(1)$$

$$= 3.$$

The pattern $mult_2(2^0) = 0$, $mult_2(2^1) = 1$, $mult_2(2^2) = 2$, $mult_2(2^3) = 3$ suggests the following explicit solution to Equation (2.2):

$$mult_2(2^k) = k, \text{ for } k \ge 0. \tag{2.3}$$

We can verify by induction that Equation (2.3) solves Equation (2.2). In the base case, $k = 0$, so $2^k = 1$, and Equation (2.3) agrees with Equation (2.2). Assume as induction hypothesis that Equation (2.3) is correct for $k - 1$. By Equation (2.2),

$$mult_2(2^k) = 1 + mult_2(2^{k-1}).$$

By the induction hypothesis,

$$mult_2(2^{k-1}) = k - 1.$$

Combining these equations, we find that $mult_2(2^k) = k$, and the proof of Equation (2.3) is complete. We could also write that $mult_2(n) = \log_2 n$ when $n = 2^k$ and $k \ge 0$.

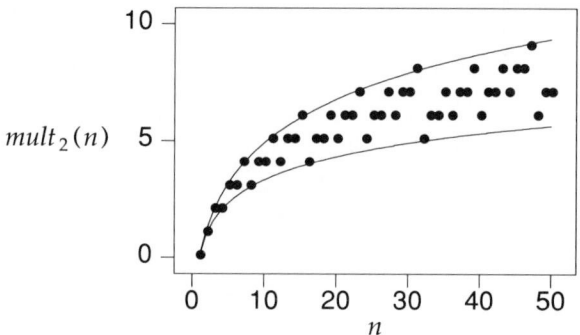

FIGURE 2.3

Graph of Figure 2.2, with curves superimposed to show $\log_2 n$ and $2(\log_2(n+1)-1)$.

A second interesting case occurs when $n > 1$ is one less than a power of two: If $n = 2^k - 1$ and $k > 1$, Algorithm 2.2 squares $x^{(2^k-2)/2} = x^{2^{k-1}-1}$ and multiplies the result by x. Thus we have

$$mult_2(1) \quad = 0;$$
$$mult_2(2^k - 1) = 2 + mult_2(2^{k-1} - 1), \text{ for } k > 1. \tag{2.4}$$

The solution to Equation (2.4) is

$$mult_2(2^k - 1) = 2(k - 1), \text{ for } k > 0. \tag{2.5}$$

We have $mult_2(n) = 2(\log_2(n+1)-1)$ when $n = 2^k - 1$ and $k > 0$.

Figure 2.3 shows the data of Figure 2.2 together with two curves that show Equations (2.3) and (2.5). Even though we have no explicit expression for $mult_2(n)$, this graph suggests strongly that its value always lies between $\log_2 n$ and $2(\log_2(n+1)-1)$.

In fact, if we look again at algorithm $power_2()$, we can see why $mult_2(n)$ behaves this way. Algorithm $power_2()$ calls itself recursively until n is one, each time halving n; since n becomes one after $\lfloor \log_2 n \rfloor$ halvings, $power_2()$ makes at most $\lfloor \log_2 n \rfloor$ recursive calls. Each recursive call of $power_2()$ uses one or two multiplications (at lines C and B, respectively). We can conclude from this that

$$\lfloor \log_2 n \rfloor \leq mult_2(n) \leq 2\lfloor \log_2 n \rfloor. \tag{2.6}$$

These upper and lower bounds on $mult_2(n)$ are about the strongest statement we can make about $mult_2(n)$ without calculating its value explicitly. Equation (2.6) contains the important information that the value of $mult_2(n)$ is bounded above and below by constant multiples of $\log_2 n$.

To see the importance of Equation (2.6), try plotting $mult_1(n)$ on the graph in Figure 2.3: the line goes right off the page! What does this mean about the two algorithms? When n is around 50, $mult_1(n)$ is also around 50, while $mult_2(n)$ is no larger than 10; $power_1(x,50)$ does around five times as much work as $power_2(x,50)$. As n becomes larger, the difference between the algorithms becomes more pronounced. When n is around 1000, $mult_1(n)$ is also around 1000, while $mult_2(n)$ is no larger than 20; $power_1(x,1000)$ does about 50 times as much work as $power_2(x,1000)$.

The graphs of $mult_2(n)$ show that it is not a simple proportionality relationship like $mult_1(n)$ (Equation (2.1)). Nevertheless there is a sense in which we can say that $mult_2(n)$ grows like $\log_2 n$. The next section presents a convenient way to make this notion formal.

2.3
ASYMPTOTIC ANALYSIS

To relate a peculiar function like $mult_2(n)$ to the more familiar logarithm function, we use some ideas from asymptotic analysis. The notations introduced here are pervasive in the study of data structures and algorithms.

Upper Bounds

Suppose f and g are two real-valued functions defined on real numbers. We write $f = O(g)$ when there are constants c and N such that $f(n) \leq cg(n)$ for all $n \geq N$. The equation "$f = O(g)$" is read "f is big-oh of g." It means that when n is large enough, some constant multiple of $g(n)$ is an upper bound on the size of $f(n)$. This idea is important enough to merit several examples.

When $f(n) \leq g(n)$ for all n, then $f = O(g)$ is trivially true. For example, let $f_1(t) =$ your age at time t, and $g_1(t) =$ your mother's age at time t, with both functions measured in years; we have $f_1 = O(g_1)$.

A slightly less obvious example in which $f = O(g)$ occurs when $g(n) > f(n)$ after some point N. Consider the functions $f_2(x) = x$ and $g_2(x) = x^2$. When $0 < x < 1$, $f_2(x) > g_2(x)$. But when $x > 1$, $f_2(x) < g_2(x)$. Therefore, $f_2 = O(g_2)$, even though in the interval $0 < x < 1$ no constant multiple of g_2 bounds f_2 from above.

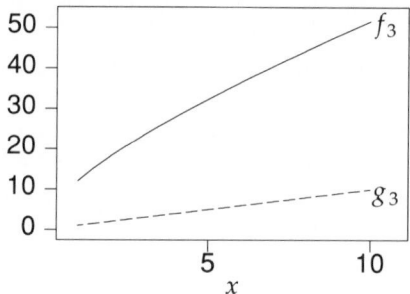

FIGURE 2.4

Functions $f_3(x) = 2x + 10\sqrt{x}$ and $g_3(x) = x$.

Because it deals with the *growth rate* of functions, rather than just their values, the definition of $O(\ )$ applies to a much broader class of examples than the preceding two. For example, let $f_3(x) = 2x + 10\sqrt{x}$ and $g_3(x) = x$; a plot of the two functions appears in Figure 2.4. Even though f_3 is always larger than g_3, we can show that $f_3 = O(g_3)$ by taking $c = 3$ and $N = 100$ in the definition of $O(\ )$. This example illustrates that, speaking asymptotically, only the term of highest order is important, and the size of its coefficient does not matter.

In the examples above, we also have $g_1 = O(f_1)$ and $g_3 = O(f_3)$. (The first equation is true because your mother's age is only a constant amount more than your age, and both ages are growing at the same rate.) It is not true, however, that $g_2 = O(f_2)$. No matter what the coefficients are, a quadratic function eventually grows and remains larger than a linear function. The next pair of functions exhibits an even more striking asymmetry: $f_4(x) = x^3$ and $g_4(x) = 2^x$. By taking $N = 11$ and $c = 1$ in the definition, we can see that $f_4 = O(g_4)$. Figure 2.5 gives a glimpse of how fast exponential functions (like $g(n)$) grow. Since the vertical axis is depicted on a log-scale, 2^x becomes a straight line; meanwhile the lowly polynomial x^3 is compressed against the horizontal axis.

Application to $mult_1(n)$ and $mult_2(n)$

Equation (2.1) means we can write the following asymptotic relation:

$$mult_1(n) = O(n). \tag{2.7}$$

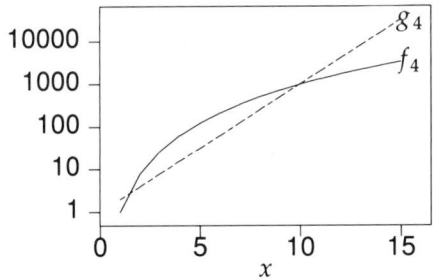

FIGURE 2.5

Functions $f_4(x) = x^3$ and $g_4(x) = 2^x$.

The right hand inequality of Equation (2.6) implies the following asymptotic relation:

$$mult_2(n) = O(\log_2 n). \tag{2.8}$$

We might be tempted to stop here, since the function $\log_2 n$ grows much more slowly than n, and declare that $power_2(\ )$ uses many fewer multiplications than $power_1(\ )$. But Equations (2.7) and (2.8) do not justify this conclusion, because big-oh statements only give *upper* bounds on functions. For example, it is trivially true that $mult_2(n) = O(n^2)$; nevertheless, we would hardly want to conclude from this and Equation (2.7) that $power_1(\ )$ uses fewer multiplications than $power_2(\ )$. In order to assert the superiority of $power_2(\ )$ over $power_1(\ )$, we need to say that the expression in the $O(\ )$-brackets is the best one possible.

Lower Bounds

We write $f = \Omega(g)$ if and only if $g = O(f)$. The equation $f = \Omega(g)$ is read "f is big-omega of g." It means that when n is large enough, some constant multiple of $g(n)$ is a lower bound on the value of $f(n)$. The definition implies immediately that in all four of the preceding examples, $g = \Omega(f)$. We also have $f_1 = \Omega(g_1)$ (some multiple of your age is an asymptotic lower bound on your mother's age) and $f_3 = \Omega(g_3)$ (as shown in Figure 2.4).

When g is both an asymptotic upper and lower bound on f, we write $f = \Theta(g)$. Formally, we say $f = \Theta(g)$ if and only if both $f = O(g)$ and $f = \Omega(g)$. The equation $f = \Theta(g)$ is read "f is big-theta of g." It means that f grows asymptotically at the same rate as g. Of our examples, $f_1 = \Theta(g_1)$ and $f_3 = \Theta(g_3)$.

```
double power1(double x, int n)
/* Compute x**n; n>0. */
{
    double y = 1.0;
    while (n-- > 0)
        /* ASSERT:  y * x**n is desired result */
        y *= x;
    return y;
}
```

PROGRAM 2.2

A C implementation of Algorithm 2.1.

Application to $mult_1(n)$ and $mult_2(n)$, Revisited

Equation (2.1) shows that $mult_1(n) = \Theta(n)$, and Equation (2.6) shows that $mult_2(n) = \Theta(\log_2 n)$. From this pair of relationships, it is correct to conclude that for sufficiently large n, $power_2(\,)$ uses many fewer multiplications than $power_1(\,)$ to compute x^n.

2.4
IMPLEMENTATION CONSIDERATIONS

To illustrate implementations of $power_1(\,)$ and $power_2(\,)$, we use variables of type double, which hold the largest values of all of C's built-in types. Program 2.2 shows an implementation of $power_1(\,)$ in C. Notice that because Program 2.2 changes n during the loop, we need to reword the invariant assertion: we might read the assertion that appears in Program 2.2 as "at this point, there are n multiplications left to perform."

Program 2.1 contains an implementation of $power_2(\,)$ that includes statements to count multiplications. We could remove this instrumentation without prejudice to most applications.

From Algorithms to Robust Programs

Programs 2.1 and 2.2 undoubtedly represent implementations of the algorithms in Section 2.2. From a programming standpoint, however, they share at least one serious flaw. If n is not positive, they fail in strange ways: power1() always returns one, and power2() enters a recursive infinite loop. This does not mean that there is anything

```
double power2(double x, int n)
/* Compute x**n; n>0. */
{
    double y;
    demand(n>0, exponent to power2 must be positive);
    if (n == 1)
        return x;
    y = power2(x, n/2);
    if (n%2 != 0)
        /* ASSERT:  y == x**((n-1)/2) */
        return x * y * y;
    else
        /* ASSERT:  y == x**(n/2) */
        return y * y;
}
```

PROGRAM 2.3

An implementation of *power*$_2$() that rejects nonpositive powers.

wrong with the algorithms of Section 2.2, because the specification of
the problem requires that n be positive. Indeed, the functions begin
with comments that n must be positive; unfortunately, compilers
ignore comments, so this is no help.

The easiest way to correct this flaw is to write power2() as shown
in Program 2.3, so that it fails when n is not positive. Program 2.3
uses the demand() macro from Appendix C; if the logical condition
expressed in its first argument is false, the program prints its second
argument as an error message and stops executing. As the name of
the macro suggests, this logical condition is a requirement for the
correct functioning of the program. In contrast to the invariant assertions of Section 2.2, a demand() expresses a part of the definition of
the problem that is solved by the algorithm, or some other condition
that we know must hold at the point in the program where the
demand() appears; such requirements are sometimes called *necessary
preconditions*.

Granted that Program 2.3 solves the original definition of the problem, it still seems a bit harsh to terminate program execution whenever
the second argument to power2() is not positive. A gentler approach
is to write another function that copes sensibly with unexpected
parameters, as illustrated in Program 2.4. Notice the demand(), which
could be considered a *necessary postcondition* to the preceding

```
double power(double x, int n)
/* Compute x**n. */
{
    if (n == 0)
        return 1.0;
    if (n < 0) {
        x = 1.0/x;
        n = -n;
    }
    demand(n>0, power failed);
    return power2(x, n);
}
```

PROGRAM 2.4

A power function that treats nonpositive powers sensibly.

if-statements, as well as a necessary precondition to the call on power2().

Since power() never calls power2() with a non-positive exponent, it is tempting to remove the demand() that enforces this requirement in power2(). We would be wise to resist this temptation, however, and leave the demand()s in both places. The small amount of redundancy is not very expensive, and it could save us time in finding our mistake in case we ever forget and call power2() directly instead of through power().

The programs in this section also fail when the result of exponentiation does not fit into a variable of type double. It is much harder to repair these functions to work sensibly when this happens. If the result of a double operation is too large to fit into a double variable, the functions probably will cause an error that terminates the program; but if the result of a double operation is too small, many systems simply set the result to zero and continue. Thus, we might not even know that there has been a problem with the exponentiation function. Since neither algorithm overflows or underflows unless the true result is too large or too small to fit into a double variable, the only way to remedy such a failure is to write a much more complicated program that performs multiplications in pieces small enough to fit into a double variable. If we were to do this, the saving in multiplications from using $power_2()$ instead of $power_1()$ would probably be even more important than it is when we use built-in multiplication, because the multiplications would be much more expensive.

2.5
SUMMARY AND PERSPECTIVE

In this chapter we saw that an algorithm represents at an abstract level the steps that a computer program takes to do a job. We required only that the steps of an algorithm be well understood, and stipulated that the expression of an algorithm may vary with the level of understanding of its audience. Sometimes algorithms are also required to halt. Although this might seem always to be a reasonable expectation, it means that certain natural, well defined computational sequences cannot be algorithms. For example, this requirement means that there can be no algorithm to generate all of the digits of π, or all prime numbers, or to control operations at a bank or public utility that is supposed to work all the time. Of course, when we do expect an algorithm to terminate, we often include in its proof of correctness a demonstration that it terminates.

Correctness of Algorithms and Programs

We use many tools to examine the correctness of an algorithm. Prominent among these are conditions that hold at certain points during the execution of the algorithm. This useful idea appears in many guises. We have seen invariant assertions, necessary preconditions, and necessary postconditions. A related tool is the "sanity check," whose violation means that something has happened that the programmer did not expect. When possible we use the demand() macro to test in our programs whether these conditions hold, because we know that something is seriously wrong if they do not.

None of these tools guarantees that our programs will work the first time. Indeed, it is usually not clear just what assertions and demands are necessary, sufficient, or useful to a program's correct operation. In practice, we sometimes add assertions to programs only after their violation causes a problem.

Models of Computation

The appropriate way to define the cost of an algorithm depends on many considerations. Whenever we evaluate an algorithm we adopt a *model of computation* that tells which of the resources used by the algorithm are important to its performance. The resource *complexity* of an algorithm under a model of computation is the amount of resource the algorithm uses. For example, in Chapter 1 we counted how many account names were examined during the search for the account named in each transaction; in this chapter we counted the multiplications used to exponentiate a number. Thus, we measured the name-comparison complexity of Program 1.2, and the multiplication complexity of Programs 2.1 and 2.2.

The general *random-access machine* (or *RAM*) is the most common model of computation used to evaluate algorithms. In the RAM model, we assume that each primitive step—such as addition, multiplication, accessing a variable, or testing the truth of a condition—takes a constant amount of time, and we count the number of primitive steps used by the algorithm to solve a problem of a certain size. The result is the *time complexity* of the algorithm, often called simply its *running time*. Our hope is always that the time complexity does not depend on the details of particular hardware and software, yet remains close enough to reality to predict the performance of programs that are based on the algorithms.

The model of computation in this chapter assumes that numbers are real and arithmetic on them is exact. The more advanced study of algorithms requires a more restricted model of computation, because such infinitely precise arithmetic is unrealistically powerful. We shall not let such scruples trouble us: to do otherwise would require complicating our pseudo-code with notions of the "largest representable number," and would require that we write all algorithms with this limitation in mind.

Limitations of Asymptotic Complexity Measures

We saw in this chapter that $power_1(\ )$ uses $\Theta(n)$ multiplications and $power_2(\ )$ uses $\Theta(\log_2 n)$ multiplications to compute x^n, and we concluded from this that for sufficiently large n, $power_2(\ )$ uses many fewer multiplications than $power_1(\ )$. It is tempting to state the difference more simply: "$power_2(\ )$ is a better algorithm than $power_1(\ )$." But we should be careful in general about drawing such a conclusion based simply on a difference in asymptotic complexities.

First, an algorithm's time complexity is only one fact about it. Sometimes an asymptotically cheaper algorithm is much more difficult to implement than a simpler algorithm whose time complexity is larger, or the asymptotic expression for running time hides a huge constant (c in the definition of $O(\ )$). Second, it is important to remember that asymptotic superiority is evident only when the problems are sufficiently large. If we needed squares and cubes of numbers, it would be silly to spend time implementing $power_2(\ )$. Indeed, on a particular computer $power_1(\ )$ might be cheaper than $power_2(\ )$ even for several larger values of n. Asymptotic analysis tells us only that at some point

N, $power_2(\ )$ should be cheaper than $power_1$ on any machine (the N in the definition of $O(\ )$ will depend on the particular machine).

Importance of Asymptotic Analysis

The independence of asymptotic analysis from particular computers and languages is at once its weakness and its strength. Asymptotic analysis of algorithms offers a way to compare the merits of different fundamental ideas for performing a computation. Thus, even though the same idea can be realized as an algorithm in different ways (for example, the exercises show how to write $power_1(\ )$ as a recursive function, and $power_2(\ )$ as an iterative function), corresponding algorithms will exhibit the same asymptotic multiplication complexity.

As the above discussion suggests, we should not base a choice between algorithms solely on their asymptotic complexities: we need to know how complicated competing algorithms are, and to have some idea of the size of the constant (c) and the crossover point (N) in the asymptotic relationship. One application in which we would expect algorithm $power_2(\ )$ to outshine $power_1(\ )$ clearly is the encryption schemes mentioned at the beginning of Section 2.2. If n were around 10^{100}, and multiplication modulo an integer required a millisecond, function $power_2(\ )$ would use less than half a second to compute $x^{10^{100}}$, while function $power_1(\ )$ would take over 10^{97} years. Even a computer one trillion times faster would not reduce the time required by $power_1(\ )$ to an acceptable value.

A few ways of dealing with asymptotic expressions arise so often that they might be called idioms.

- Since logarithms can be transformed among bases using the relation $\log_a x \log_b a = \log_b x$, we usually write logarithms within $O(\ )$-brackets without specifying a base. (In effect, we fold $\log_b a$ into the constant implicit in the $O(\ )$.)

- If $f(n) = c$ for some constant c, it is common to write $f = O(1)$; the terms "constant" and "$O(1)$" are interchangeable.

- As a general rule, if $f(x) = O(p(x))$ and $g(x) = O(q(x))$, and $p(x) = O(q(x))$, then

$$f(x) + g(x) = O(q(x)).$$

As an application of the latter two rules, we usually write only the highest-order term of an asymptotic expression, with a coefficient of one.

EXERCISES

1 Why does Algorithm 2.2 store $x^{\lfloor n/2 \rfloor}$ in variable y, instead of calling $power_2(\ )$ twice at each recursive call?

2 Function `power()` in Program 2.4 can still cause a program to abort: if x is zero and n is negative, `power(x, n)` divides by zero. Modify `power()` to avoid this problem.

3 Algorithm 2.2 is sometimes called "logarithmic exponentiation," but may be referred to as the "Russian peasant's algorithm." You might well wonder what occasion Russian peasants had to take large integer powers of numbers; actually, they used a simple variant of this algorithm that accomplishes the multiplication $x \times n$ by repeatedly doubling x and halving n. Write a true Russian peasant's algorithm that multiplies a real number by an integer using repeated doubling and halving.

4 In *prefix notation*, an operator applies to the two operands that follow it. For example, '+ 1 2' means the sum of 1 and 2. The definition is recursive, so that each operand can involve operators with operands of their own. For example, '× + 1 2 − 3 4' is written more familiarly as '$(1+2) \times (3-4)$'. Write a function to evaluate an expression in prefix notation composed of single digits and operator symbols.

5 The algorithms in this chapter include two kinds of computation: the multiplications used to compute the answer and "bookkeeping" to keep track of how far along we are toward the answer. Show that the amount of bookkeeping used by $power_1(\ )$ and $power_2(\ )$ is asymptotically the same as the number of multiplications they use.

6 Use induction to verify that Equation (2.5) is a correct solution to Equation (2.4).

7 Show that Equation (2.6) is consistent with Equation (2.4). Show that neither inequality in Equation (2.6) can be replaced by a strict inequality (<).

8 Explain the following recurrence for $mult_2(n)$:

$$mult_2(n) = \begin{cases} 0, & n = 1; \\ 1 + mult_2(n/2), & \text{even } n > 1; \\ 2 + mult_2(\lfloor n/2 \rfloor), & \text{odd } n > 1. \end{cases}$$

Show that this recurrence has the solution $mult_2(n) = \beta(n) - 1 + \lfloor \log_2 n \rfloor$, where $\beta(n)$ is the number of one-bits in the binary representation of n, its "population count." Show that $mult_2(n) = \Theta(\log n)$.

9 What is the asymptotic multiplication complexity of the variants of $power_1(\ )$ that first take the square or the fourth power of x?

10 In the *logarithmic-cost* model of computation, the cost of multiplying x by y is $\Theta(\log x + \log y)$. Derive expressions for the time complexity of multiplication of functions $power_1()$ and $power_2()$ in this model.

11 Suppose we use $power_1()$ and $power_2()$ to find powers of polynomials. A more realistic model of computation might set the cost of multiplying two polynomials p and q at $O(\deg p \times \deg q)$, where $\deg p$ is the degree of p (the largest exponent it contains). What is the time complexity of $power_1()$ and $power_2()$ in this model?

12 Which of the following asymptotic derivations is correct?

$$\sum_{i=1}^{n} i = \sum_{i=1}^{n} O(1) = O(n);$$

$$\sum_{i=1}^{n} i = \sum_{i=1}^{n} O(n) = O(n^2).$$

13 We know from Chapter 1 that $\sum_{i=1}^{n} i = \Theta(n^2)$. Show that $\sum_{i=1}^{n} i^k = \Theta(n^{k+1})$.

14 Show that $\lfloor \lfloor n/2 \rfloor /2 \rfloor = \lfloor n/4 \rfloor$. Generalize.

15 Consider the recursive version of $power_1()$ shown as Algorithm 2.3. Show that $mult_1'(n) = n-1, n > 0$. Implement both $power_1()$ and $power_1'()$ and compare their running times for exponents of modest size.

16 Consider the iterative version of $power_2()$ shown as Algorithm 2.4. Show that

$$mult_2'(n) = \begin{cases} \log_2 n + 2, & n = 2^k; \\ \lceil \log_2 n \rceil + \beta(n), & \text{other } n > 0. \end{cases}$$

Modify $power_2'()$ so that it will not cause an overflow or underflow unless the result would also cause such a problem.

```
power'₁(number x, int n)
/* Compute xⁿ; n > 0. */
    if n == 1
        return x
    return x*power'₁(x, n-1)
```

ALGORITHM 2.3

A recursive version of Solution I.

```
power'₂(number x, int n)
/* Compute xⁿ; n > 0. */
    int i
    number y, z
    i = n
    y = 1
    z = x
    while i > 0
        /* ASSERT:  xⁿ == y*zⁱ */
        if i is odd
            y = y*z
        z = z*z
        i = ⌊i/2⌋
    return y
```

ALGORITHM 2.4

An iterative version of Solution II.

---

17 *Horner's rule* for evaluating the polynomial $p(x) = \sum_{i=0}^{n} c_i x^i$ uses Algorithm 2.5. What is the multiplication complexity of Horner's rule? Suggest a loop invariant to verify the correctness of Horner's rule.

The asymptotic expressions in Section 2.3 offer no way to state that the order of magnitude of one function is strictly larger than that of another. To remedy this lacuna, we can define $f = o(g)$ to mean that $\lim_{n\to\infty} \dfrac{f(n)}{g(n)} = 0$. The equation is read "$f$ is little-oh of g."

18 Show that $\log n = o(n^\varepsilon)$ for any $\varepsilon > 0$.
19 Show that $\log^k n = o(n^\varepsilon)$ for any positive integer k and any $\varepsilon > 0$.
20 Show that $k^n = o(n!)$ for any k.

```
p = 0
for (i = n; i > 0; i--)
    p = x*(p+cᵢ)
return p+c₀
```

ALGORITHM 2.5

Horner's rule to evaluate $\sum_{i=0}^{n} c_i x^i$.

This book always presents the solutions to recurrence equations, though it sometimes leaves the verification to you. The next two exercises illustrate a basic way to solve some recurrences.

21 Consider the recurrence equation

$$f(0) = a,$$

$$f(n) = b \times f(n-1), \; n > 0.$$

Show that the solution is $f(n) = ab^n$.

22 The recurrence equation

$$f(0) = a,$$

$$f(1) = b,$$

$$f(n) = c \times f(n-1) + d \times f(n-2), \; n > 1,$$

has the general solution

$$f(n) = p \times q^n + r \times s^n,$$

where p, q, r, and s depend on a, b, c, and d.
(a) Suppose that $a = b = c = d = 1$; then $f(n)$ is the nth Fibonacci number. Show that in the solution to this recurrence, $p = r = 1/\sqrt{5}$, $q = (1+\sqrt{5})/2$ and $s = (1-\sqrt{5})/2$.
(b) Can you generalize the above rule to solve recurrences in which $f(n)$ depends on $f(n-1)$, $f(n-2)$, and $f(n-3)$?

REFERENCES

The following works are the first two volumes of an encyclopedia of lore about algorithms. Volume 1 traces the origin of the word "algorithm" to the name of the Persian mathematician *Abu Ja'far Mohammed ibn Mûsâ al-Khowârizmî*, and discusses $O(\;)$ notation. Volume 2 considers powering by repeated squaring (Algorithm 2.2).

D. E. Knuth. *Fundamental Algorithms*. Vol. 1, *The Art of Computer Programming*. 2d ed. Reading, Mass.: Addison-Wesley, 1973.

D. E. Knuth. *Seminumerical Algorithms*. Vol. 2, *The Art of Computer Programming*. 2d ed. Reading, Mass.: Addison-Wesley, 1981.

These two books contain carefully reasoned proofs of program correctness:

E. W. Dijkstra. *A Discipline of Programming*. Englewood Cliffs, N.J.: Prentice-Hall, 1976.

D. Gries. *The Science of Programming*. New York: Springer-Verlag, 1981.

On the other hand, the following articles include some interesting ideas about the practical importance of formal proofs of correctness. The letters to the editor in issues of the *Communications of the ACM* subsequent to the publication of both articles contain a lively debate.

R. A. DeMillo, R. J. Lipton, and A. J. Perlis. "Social processes and proofs of theorems and programs." *Communications of the ACM* 22 (1979): 271–280.

J. H. Fetzer. "Program verification: the very idea." *Communications of the ACM* 31 (1988): 1048–1063.

Many textbooks on combinatorics treat recurrence relations and their solution. The following sources have particular relevance to the analysis of algorithms.

D. H. Greene and D. E. Knuth. *Mathematics for the Analysis of Algorithms*. 2d ed. Boston: Birkhauser, 1982.

G. S. Lueker. "Some techniques for solving recurrences." *Computing Surveys* 12 (1980): 419–436.

E. M. Reingold, J. Nievergelt, and N. Deo. *Combinatorial Algorithms: Theory and Practice*. Englewood Cliffs, N.J.: Prentice-Hall, 1977.

Some of our notations for asymptotic analysis are standard in mathematics; others are newer developments to meet the needs of computer science. The notation we use follows that proposed in

D. E. Knuth. "Big omicron and big omega and big theta." *SIGACT News* 8 (1976): 18–24.

There is some debate about the proper definition of $\Omega(\ )$.

P. M. B. Vitanyi and L. Meertens. "Big omega versus the wild functions." *SIGACT News* 16 (1985): 56–59.

G. Brassard. "Crusade for a better notation." *SIGACT News* 17 (1985): 60–64.

3

Pointers and Dynamic Storage

Chapter 1 contains several simple programs. Since they use only elementary programming tools like variables, iteration, and conditional execution, we could take their ideas—the data structures and algorithms they use—and implement them in another imperative programming language like Basic, Fortran, or Pascal. The resulting programs would exhibit little more than syntactic differences from the C programs in Chapter 1.

This chapter introduces some more advanced programming tools that are not found in all imperative programming languages: pointers, structures, and dynamic storage allocation. These tools are fundamental to many of the data structures and algorithms we shall see in later chapters. The chapter also shows how to use these tools in C programs.

3.1
VARIABLES AND POINTERS

We begin our discussion of variables and pointers with a simple model of computer memory. Our model is too simple in some ways, and is more specific to C than a real computer would be, but it contains enough details for now.

Think of computer memory as a huge array of identical cells numbered from zero, as depicted in Figure 3.1. Each cell has room for an integer that is large enough to represent the value of any character; the *address* of the cell is its index in the memory cell array.

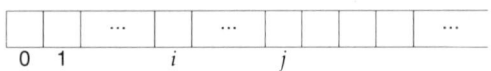

FIGURE 3.1

Memory as a long array of identical cells.

We can store a char variable in a single cell of memory. The char variable's address is the address of the cell where it is stored. For example, we could store a char variable in cell i of the memory shown in Figure 3.1.

When a scalar variable needs to contain more than the character-sized memory cell can hold, it occupies a contiguous set of memory cells. For example, if we needed four cells to store an int variable, we could put the variable in cells j, $j+1$, $j+2$, and $j+3$ of the memory in Figure 3.1. The address of this int variable is j, the address of the first cell in the contiguous set of cells where it is stored.

A scalar variable is defined by two components: its address and its *type*. From a variable's type we can tell how many contiguous memory cells it occupies and how to interpret the contents of those cells (as character, integer, or floating-point data, for example).

Our simple model of memory accommodates array variables quite naturally, because it construes memory itself as a very large array. The declaration

  element-type x[*n*];

creates an array x[] that contains n variables of type *element-type*. These variables reside contiguously in memory. If n were 4 and *element-type* were char, we could put x[] into locations j through $j+3$ of Figure 3.1. But if n were 4 and *element-type* were int, we would need 16 contiguous memory cells to store x[], grouped into four ints as shown in Figure 3.2. The address of the array is the address of x[0], sometimes called the *base address* of the array. In Figure 3.2, the

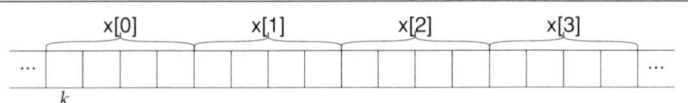

FIGURE 3.2

Space for an array of four integers.

base address of array x[] is k. We shall see some applications of base addresses in succeeding sections.

To find the address of element x[i], we add to the base address of x[] the product of i and the number of cells occupied by a variable of type *element-type*. For example, in Figure 3.2 the address of x[2] is $k+2\times4 = k+8$.

If you are already acquainted with computer memory, you may have noticed that this model does not tell the whole story about such important topics as *bytes* and *alignment requirements*. We shall see a more faithful model of memory in Chapter 6, but the simple model of this section will suffice to describe what happens in memory for the rest of this chapter.

Pointers

A *pointer* variable contains the address of a memory cell. Pointer variables also have types that tell how to interpret the contents of memory starting at the address they contain. The declaration

element-type *p;

means that p is a variable of type "pointer to *element-type*." For example, the declaration

    int *p;

makes p a "pointer to int." The value of p is the address of a location in memory; the contents stored at that address are of type int. Figure 3.3 shows how we often draw pointers.

We can read the declaration

    int *p;

in two ways. One possibility is to group the "*" with "p" and read it like the declaration of a variable with an unusual name: "*p is an

FIGURE 3.3

Illustration of a variable p that points to an int. The single box labelled "int" stands for as many memory cells as are necessary to hold an int.

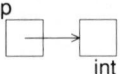

p

int

FIGURE 3.4

A more careful version of Figure 3.3. Each box in the picture actually
represents a set of contiguous cells in the memory array.

int." Thus, the contents of the memory location referred to by the
expression "*p" is an int, so when we follow—or *dereference*—the
pointer p by examining the cell whose address it contains, we will find
an int. The operation of following a pointer is also known as an
indirect reference through the pointer.

The other way to read the declaration is to group "int" and "*"
together, and say that the type of p is int *; in other words, "p
points to an int." This interpretation emphasizes that p is itself a
variable, and suggests that to be strictly accurate we ought to depict
the situation as in Figure 3.4. However, we usually shall not bother to
be this careful.

It makes no sense to dereference a pointer unless we have some
reason to believe that the contents of the addressed memory location
are of the appropriate type. One way to be sure that an indirect reference is sensible is to use the address-of operator, "&", as illustrated in
Program 3.1. The statement

```
p = &x;
```

```
main()
{
    int x;
    int *p;
    p = &x;
    x = 1;
    *p = 2;
    printf("%d\n", x);
    exit(0);
}
```

PROGRAM 3.1

An illustration of pointer variables and the address-of operator. This program
prints 2.

makes p point to x, so the expressions x and *p are equivalent until p changes. After the two assignment statements

```
x = 1;
*p = 2;
```

the value of x is two, a fact we can confirm by running Program 3.1. Let us consider two applications that use pointers and the address-of operator.

Exchanging Values Using Pointers

Now we shall write a function that swaps the values of two integer variables. Our first try might look like function intswap() in Program 3.2. But if we use the test function shown in Program 3.2, we see the following output, which shows that the values of x and y are not properly interchanged:

```
before swap: x=1 y=2
after swap: x=1 y=2
```

```
void intswap(int a, int b)   /* does not work */
{
    int t;
    t = a;
    a = b;
    b = t;
}

void test(void)
{
    int x, y;
    x = 1;
    y = 2;
    printf("before swap: x=%d y=%d\n", x, y);
    intswap(x, y);
    printf("after swap: x=%d y=%d\n", x, y);
}
```

PROGRAM 3.2

A faulty function to interchange the values of its integer arguments, and a test function that reveals the error.

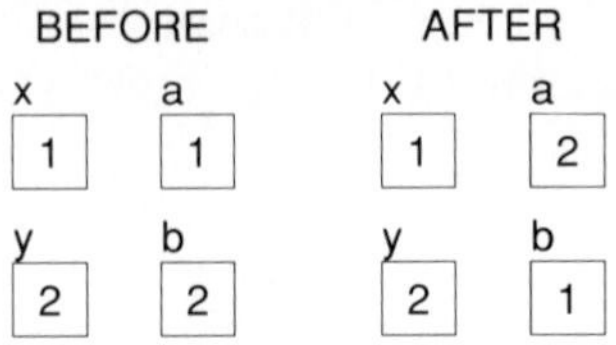

	BEFORE		AFTER	
	x	a	x	a
	1	1	1	2
	y	b	y	b
	2	2	2	1

FIGURE 3.5

In Program 3.2, variables a and b (in intswap()) contain copies of the arguments x and y (in test()).

The values of x and y are not interchanged because when C passes arguments to functions, it always passes *copies* of the arguments, and not the arguments themselves; a common name for this arrangement is *call by value*. Figure 3.5 depicts what happens in intswap(). Function intswap() interchanges the values of the copies a and b, which does not affect the values of the original variables x and y.

With pointers, we can write a function that correctly interchanges the values of two variables. Rather than pass the variables themselves to intswap(), and have only copies switched, Program 3.3 passes pointers to the variables that are to be swapped; it interchanges the contents of the locations they address through pointer dereferencing operations. The output from testing Program 3.3 with the test function in Program 3.2 is

```
before swap: x=1 y=2
after swap: x=2 y=1
```

```
void intswap(int *pa, int *pb)
{
    int t;
    t = *pa;
    *pa = *pb;
    *pb = t;
}
```

PROGRAM 3.3

A function that can be used to interchange the values of two integer variables. The names of the arguments begin with the letter "p" to suggest that they are pointers.

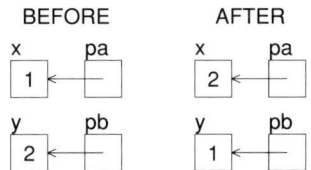

FIGURE 3.6

The operation of int swap () in Program 3.3.

which suggests that Program 3.3 does the job right. Figure 3.6 depicts the operation of the correct version of int swap ().

Pointers for Input

One library function that relies heavily on pointers is scanf(), which is commonly used to read data in various formats into variables. The first argument to scanf() is a format string, which tells how to interpret the input; the remaining arguments are pointers to variables that have room for the input values. For example, function demo() in Program 3.4 reads a floating-point number and an integer into x and n respectively, and prints the value of x^n using function power() from Program 2.4.

Many of the errors that occur when using scanf() are caused by incorrect argument lists that lead scanf() to use an inappropriate value as a pointer. If we forget the address-of operator:

```
scanf("%d", n); /* WRONG */
```

```
void demo(void)
{
    double x;
    int n;
    scanf("%lf %d", &x, &n);
    printf("%g ** %d = %g\n", x, n, power(x,n));
}
```

PROGRAM 3.4

Function demo() uses scanf() to read two numbers from its input. Notice the address-of operator in the list of arguments to scanf().

then `scanf()` interprets n as a pointer to an integer, rather than an integer, and tries to write into the memory location whose address is the value of n; this is a prescription for disaster. If the type indicated by the conversion specification (in the first argument to `scanf()`) and the type of the corresponding variable disagree, then `scanf()` may try to write something that is too big to fit into the variable. If the argument list contains fewer addresses than conversion specifications, then `scanf()` uses undefined values as pointers to places into which to store the values read by the unmatched conversion specifications, which is also likely to yield strange results.

3.2
CHARACTER STRINGS AND ARRAYS

In many applications we need to store names, words, sentences, and other alphabetic (character) data that goes under the general name of *strings*. In C a string is an array of characters. To declare a string s that can contain at most 80 characters, we would write

```
char s[80];
```

Since C arrays all begin at index zero, the first character of the string `s[]` is `s[0]`, and its last character is `s[79]`.

Even if all of the strings that arise in some problem are guaranteed to be at most 80 characters long, they probably will not all be exactly 80 characters long: what we think of as the last character of a string stored in `s[]` probably lies somewhere in the middle of array `s[]`. For example, if we wanted `s[]` to contain the string "`Hi!`", we would store characters in the first three positions in array `s[]`, and we would need to indicate that these are the only relevant positions.

Most C programs rely on the convention that the last interesting character of a string is followed by the *null character*. The value of the null character is zero, but we sometimes write it as '`\0`' to emphasize that we mean the character whose *value* is zero rather than the character that *prints* as "0". When we use the convention of null-termination, string `s[]` contains "`Hi!`" whenever the values of the first four elements of `s[]` are set as follows:

```
s[0] = 'H';
s[1] = 'i';
s[2] = '!';
s[3] = '\0';
```

Notice that we say nothing about the contents of s[4] through s[79]: if the first four characters of another array t[] were the same as those of s[], we would say that t[] contains the same string as s[], regardless of what characters were stored after the null character. In fact, we would say that they contain the same string even if their lengths as arrays were different.

Functions on Strings

The C library includes several functions that perform common operations on strings. All of them use the convention that any strings that appear as arguments are terminated by a null character, so they can be used on character arrays of any length. To show how they do this, we shall write versions of a couple of these functions; to emphasize that the code presented here is not the same as the code for the library functions, we prefix the names of our versions of the functions with "our".

Program 3.5 is a function that calculates the length of its string argument, the number of non-null characters that precede the first null character. The empty brackets in the declaration of argument s indicate that it is an array of characters. They also remind us that the length of s[] *as an array* is irrelevant to the computation: ourstrlen() is useful exactly when we need to find out the length of the *string* that is stored in s[]. The invariant assertion uses the notation s[0:i] as an abbreviation for "s[0] through s[i]." The correctness of ourstrlen() follows directly from this assertion. If we write |s| for the length of the string stored in array s[], we can express the running time of ourstrlen() as $\Theta(|s|)$.

```
int ourstrlen(char s[])
{
    int i;
    i = 0;
    while (s[i] != 0)
        /* ASSERT:  s[0:i] contains no nulls */
        i++;
    return i;
}
```

PROGRAM 3.5

A function to compute string length.

```
int ourstrcmp(char s[], char t[])
{
    int i;
    for (i = 0; s[i] != 0 && s[i] == t[i]; i++)
        /* ASSERT:   s[0:i] == t[0:i] */
        /* s[0:i] contains no nulls */
        ;
    return s[i] - t[i];
}
```

PROGRAM 3.6

A function to test the lexicographical ordering of two strings. Note the empty body of the for-loop.

Program 3.6 is a function to compare two strings; it returns zero if the two strings are the same, and a nonzero value if the two strings are different. The value returned is negative if the first string comes before the second string in lexicographic order, and positive if the first string follows the second lexicographically. (Lexicographic order is a generalization of alphabetical order to include digits and other characters. Since there is no universal way to order non-alphabetic characters, Program 3.6 might produce different results on different computers.) The invariant assertions follow immediately from the continuation test on the for-loop, and imply that ourstrcmp() is correct. The running time of ourstrcmp() is $O(\min(|s|,|t|))$; we can only

```
void ourstrcpy(char dest[], char src[])
{
    int i;
    for (i = 0; src[i] != 0; i++)
        dest[i] = src[i];
        /* ASSERT:   dest[0:i] == src[0:i] */
        /* src[0:i] is unchanged */
    dest[i] = 0;
}
```

PROGRAM 3.7

A function to copy the string src[] to the string dest[]. Argument dest appears first as a reminder of the analogy with assigning a value to a variable (dest = src).

```
main ()
{
    char buf[100];
    buf[0] = '\0';
    printf("(1) ourstrlen(buf) == %d\n", ourstrlen(buf));
    ourstrcpy(buf, "Hello");
    printf("(2) buf:  %s\n", buf);
    printf("(3) ourstrlen(buf) == %d\n", ourstrlen(buf));
    printf("(4) ourstrcmp(buf, \"Hi\") == %d\n",
        ourstrcmp(buf, "Hi"));
    printf("(5) ourstrcmp(buf, \"Hello\") == %d\n",
        ourstrcmp(buf, "Hello"));
    exit(0);
}
```

PROGRAM 3.8

A simple program to exercise the functions in Programs 3.5, 3.6, and 3.7.

give an upper bound on running time, since it depends on where the first inequality (if any) between s[] and t[] lies.

Program 3.7 contains the last string function we shall consider for now. It copies the string in src[] to array dest[]. This version of ourstrcpy() leaves several preconditions unstated; for example, src[] must be null-terminated, and dest[] should be long enough to contain the string in src[]. On the other hand, we include the assertion that src[] does not change, because without it all of the other assertions could be satisfied trivially by replacing the for-loop by the single statement *src = *dest = 0;. Even when all of these assertions and preconditions are added to ourstrcpy(), however, they do not suffice to establish its correctness; we return to this point below.

Program 3.8 exercises these three functions. Running it produces the following output:

```
(1) ourstrlen(buf) == 0
(2) buf:  Hello
(3) ourstrlen(buf) == 5
(4) ourstrcmp(buf, "Hi") == -4
(5) ourstrcmp(buf, "Hello") == 0
```

The output shows that (1) the length of the empty string is zero; (2) the function to copy a string worked correctly; (3) the string "Hello" contains five characters (the null character does not count); (4) "Hello" is lexicographically earlier than "Hi" (the first difference between the

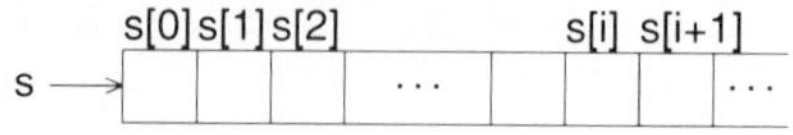

s[0] s[1] s[2]   s[i] s[i+1]

FIGURE 3.7

The relationship between arrays and pointers: s is a pointer to s[0].

two strings is at the second character, and i comes four characters after e); and (5) "Hello" is lexicographically equal to itself.

Although none of this is very surprising, there is one thing worth noting. Function ourstrcpy() changes the string that is stored in one of its arguments. But we saw in Section 1 that functions receive copies of their arguments, and they cannot change the original values of those arguments. Putting these two observations together, we conclude that when function ourstrcpy() is called, it receives a pointer to dest[], and not a copy of dest[]. The next few paragraphs explain how this follows from the relationship between arrays and pointers in C.

Arrays and Pointers

Suppose s[] is an array. The array name s, standing alone without brackets, is a synonym for &s[0]. In other words, the expression s is a pointer to s[0], as illustrated in Figure 3.7. Early in Program 3.8, buf appears as the first argument to ourstrcpy(); since the value of buf is &buf[0], when ourstrcpy() is called its local variable dest also becomes a pointer to buf[0]. Thus, ourstrcpy() can alter the contents of array buf[] by dereferencing through its variable dest (to reach buf[0]) or offsets from it (to reach buf[1], buf[2], buf[3], and so on).

The ellipses in Figure 3.7 illustrate that in general we do not know the length of the array to whose base element s points. For example, when ourstrcpy() is called in Program 3.8, it does not know how long array dest[] is. Indeed, the responsibility for avoiding array references that are out of bounds rests entirely with the programmer. In the examples below, notice the care we take to avoid referring to non-existent array elements.

Just as the name of an array is a pointer to the base element of the array, any pointer can be treated as an array name. If p is a character pointer variable and i is an integer, then the expression p+i is the address of a memory cell i cells in memory away from p; more precisely, p[i] and *(p+i) are synonyms. Since we can treat a pointer

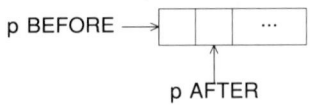

FIGURE 3.8
The situation before and after executing "p++".

as an array name, we could rewrite the headers for the functions in Programs 3.5 through 3.7 as follows:

```
int ourstrlen(char *s)

int ourstrcmp(char *s, char *t)

void ourstrcpy(char *dest, char *src)
```

The resulting functions work exactly as they did before.

Suppose again that p is a character pointer variable. Since p is a variable, we can also add one to it: p++;. After this statement is executed, p points to the character in memory that follows the character to which it pointed before, as depicted in Figure 3.8.

The library versions of many string functions use pointer arithmetic. Program 3.9 shows how we might write Programs 3.5 through 3.7 to use pointers. These functions use the same algorithms as their counterparts that use array operations, but fewer local variables since the arguments themselves (which start out as pointers to the beginnings of strings) change during the execution of the functions. The invariant assertions in these functions use capitalized variable names to represent the original values of the variables. These capitalized names are purely for human consumption; in fact, in functions ourstrcmp() and ourstrcpy(), after we enter the while-loop we have no idea where the beginning of the original string arguments lie.

The pointer-based function ourstrcpy() in Program 3.9 reveals a problem that is not as obvious in Program 3.7. The invariant assertion that string src is not changed by the computation can be violated by the following call to ourstrcpy():

```
char *p;
ourstrcpy(p, p+1);
```

This situation illustrates the difficulty of choosing appropriate invariant assertions. To be complete, we could add the precondition that src

```
int ourstrlen(char *s)
{
    int i;
    i = 0;
    while (*s++)
        i++;
    /* ASSERT: S == s - i */
    return i;
}
int ourstrcmp(char *s, char *t)
{
    while (*s && *s == *t) {
        /* ASSERT: S[0:s-S] == T[0:s-S] contains no nulls */
        s++;
        t++;
    }
    return *s - *t;
}
void ourstrcpy(char *dest, char *src)
{
    while (*dest++ = *src++)
        /* ASSERT: DEST[0:dest-DEST] == SRC[0:dest-DEST] */
        /* SRC[0:src-SRC] is unchanged */
        ;
}
```

PROGRAM 3.9

"Pointerized" versions of Programs 3.5 through 3.7. Capitalized variable names in the assertions refer to the values of those variables when the function was called. Note: for any pointer p, the value of *p++ is the value of *p before the increment operator occurs.

and dest point to null-terminated non-overlapping strings; we might also add explicitly the precondition that dest points to an array long enough to contain the string in src[]. But when a function contains too many assertions and preconditions, it is difficult to determine which are important to its particular job and which are routine. We shall continue to write only those assertions that make it clear why a function works, even though this usually makes our set of assertions formally incomplete.

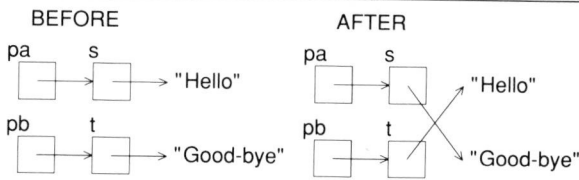

FIGURE 3.9

The operation of `strswap()`. (We use quote marks instead of boxes to depict strings.)

Swapping Strings

Consider the problem of writing a function to swap the strings to which s and t point. Figure 3.9 shows both the initial state of s and t and the state we want to achieve. Notice first that we are not supposed to alter the contents of arrays s[] and t[]; thus, we should not do the job with three calls to `ourstrcpy()`, by a faulty analogy to what Program 3.3 does with integers. Program 3.10 does the right thing, swapping strings by swapping the values of the pointers s and t. It works no matter what the lengths of arrays s[] and t[] are, and it works in constant time. Notice the type of the arguments to `strswap()`: pointer to pointer to char. It often helps to interpret such declarations by trying several divisions into "type" and "variable name." For example, `**pa` is a character, while `*pa` is a character pointer (and hence could point to the first element of a string). A picture like Figure 3.9 can also help.

```
void strswap(char **pa, char **pb)
{
    char *t;
    t = *pa;
    *pa = *pb;
    *pb = t;
}
```

PROGRAM 3.10

A function to interchange the values of two strings. To perform the swap illustrated in Figure 3.9, we would call `strswap(&s, &t)`.

Access to Strings on the Command Line

Sometimes we would like to write programs that accept input directly from the command line that was used to invoke them. As a simple example, we might want to create a program power that can be called with two arguments on the command line to print the value of the first argument raised to the power given by the second argument. Thus the command

```
power 1.12 6
```

should print

```
1.97382
```

Before we write the program, we need to examine the mechanism by which we can gain access to the contents of the command line. The complete prototype for function main() shows that it has two arguments:

```
main(int argc, char **argv)
```

Array argv is an array of argc strings. The long rectangles in Figure 3.10 represent in order the non-blank sequences of characters on the command line; each is terminated by a null character. Thus argv[0] is a string that contains the name of the command itself, argv[1] contains the first argument, and so on. To interpret any of these strings as a number, we need one of the conversion functions like atoi() or atof() that are described in Appendix 2.

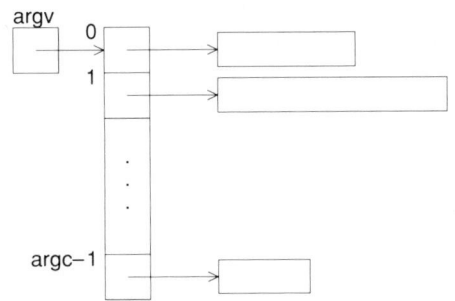

FIGURE 3.10

The arrays with which every C program begins its execution.

```
main(int argc, char **argv)
{
    double x;
    int n;
    demand(argc == 3, usage:   power x n);
    x = atof(argv[1]);
    n = atoi(argv[2]);
    printf("%g\n", power(x, n));
    exit(0);
}
```

PROGRAM 3.11

A program that illustrates access to strings on the command line.

Program 3.11 uses function power() from Program 2.4. The command power 1.12 6 causes argc to have the value 3, and argv to appear as shown in Figure 3.11. Program 3.11 checks for the correct number of arguments, then uses atof() and atoi() to convert from strings the values of x and n for which x^n should be computed. The output from the command

```
power 1.12 6
```

is

```
1.97382
```

as it should be.

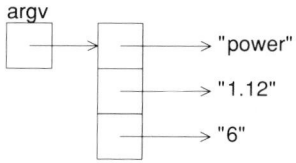

FIGURE 3.11

The appearance of argv when Program 3.11 is called as power 1.12 6. The value of argc is three. All three arguments are null-terminated strings; if we wish to interpret an argument as a number, we must use the appropriate function to make the conversion.

3.3

TYPEDEFS AND STRUCTURES

C's built-in integer and floating-point types are widely applicable and reflect well the characteristics of the computers on which C programs are typically run. However, programmers also find it useful to define their own types, and to create variables of these *user-defined types*.

Typedefs

We often use `typedefs` to make clear the role some variables play. For example, these three lines are from the header file in Appendix C:

```
typedef int boolean;
#define FALSE 0
#define TRUE !FALSE
```

The first line means that we can use `boolean` as the type of a variable, and the other two lines define constant macros for the truth values we shall store in `boolean` variables. These declarations help to make it explicit that an integer variable contains a truth value.

Here is another example of using `typedefs` to help to clarify the interpretation of variables:

```
typedef char *string;
```

When this `typedef` is in force, a variable of type `string` is understood to have type `char *`. Thus the following two declarations are equivalent:

```
char *s, *t;
string s, t;
```

We could also use this `typedef` to declare the type of `argv`, the second argument to `main()`, as

```
string argv[];
```

Some programmers find that this helps to understand the interpretation of `argv` better than the declaration `char **` does, but rest assured that the two declarations are equivalent.

Another worthy use of `typedefs` is to make it easy to change the types of related variables quickly. For example, in a program that deals with money, we might create type `dollar`:

```
typedef int dollar;
```

Later, if the amounts with which the program dealt grew larger than could be contained in an `int`, we could change the `typedef` to `long`, `float`, or `double`.

Although the feature is called `typedef`, it really does not define new types. If the above `typedefs` were in force, we could assign boolean values to `dollar` variables, and vice versa. Thus, `typedefs` are useful to make the purpose of a variable clear and to make it easier to change all variables that are used in a given way, but they add nothing to the type-checking facilities of C.

Structures

A *structure* is a variable that contains several pieces of information. For example, the declaration

```
struct {
    int birth, reign;
} georgeV, edwardVIII, georgeVI, elizabethII;
```

creates variables named after this century's four British monarchs. The *template* between braces declares that each of these variables has two *members*: `birth`, the year in which the monarch was born, and `reign`, the year in which his or her reign began. Figure 3.12 shows how we might draw a variable of type `monarch`. In general we refer to a member of *variable* using the notation *variable.member-name*. For example, we can refer to Elizabeth II's year of accession as `elizabethII.reign`.

When we wish to use structures as arguments to functions, or we want to declare variables of the same structure at several places in a

FIGURE 3.12

A drawing of one of the structures created by the declaration in the text.

program, we separate the definition of a structure template from the declaration of variables of that structure. For example, we might write the above declaration in two pieces:

```
struct monarch {
    int birth, reign;
};
struct monarch georgeV, edwardVIII, georgeVI, elizabethII;
```

The first three lines define a structure template that includes the *tag* monarch; these lines define a new type, struct monarch. The last line declares four variables of this type.

Program 3.12 combines the use of structure tags with typedef in a common way that most of our programs will use. The first line typedefs monarch to be the type struct monarch; this obviates writing struct every time we declare a structure. The next four lines define a structure template for monarch that includes more information than the examples above: a monarch has room for a string, name, in which to store the name of a monarch, and three integers that give elementary facts about the monarch. The declaration of the structure template is followed immediately by the declaration of an array windsor[] of four variables of type monarch.

Function getmonarchs() in Program 3.12 reads a file of lines such as

```
George 5 1865 1910
Edward 8 1894 1936
George 6 1895 1936
Elizabeth 2 1926 1952
```

and stores the information in array windsor[]. Program 3.12 may not work if a monarch's name contains more than 99 characters or if it contains a space character.

Program 3.12 also includes a function that permits us to see the contents of the data structure. Given the sample input shown above, dumpmonarchs() prints the following list:

```
George V, born 1865, rule began in 1910
Edward VIII, born 1894, rule began in 1936
George VI, born 1895, rule began in 1936
Elizabeth II, born 1926, rule began in 1952
```

Writing function roman() is left as an exercise.

```
typedef struct monarch monarch;
struct monarch {
    char name[100];
    int number, birth, reign;
};
monarch windsor[4];

void getmonarchs(void)
{
    int i;
    for(i = 0; i < 4; i++)
        scanf("%s %d %d %d\n",
            windsor[i].name,
            &windsor[i].number,
            &windsor[i].birth,
            &windsor[i].reign
        );
}

void dumpmonarchs(void)
{
    int i;
    for (i = 0; i < 4; i++)
        printf("%s %s, born %d, rule began in %d\n",
            windsor[i].name,
            roman(windsor[i].number),
            windsor[i].birth,
            windsor[i].reign
        );
}
```

PROGRAM 3.12

Declarations and functions for storing and reporting information about the house of Windsor.

3.4
DYNAMIC STORAGE ALLOCATION

In all of the programs we have seen so far, the arrays have been of fixed size, whether they contain integers, floating-point numbers, characters, or monarchs. Such *static arrays* are common, and work fine for applications in which we have a reasonable upper bound on the length of array we need. When we do not know such a maximum, however, we use *dynamic arrays*, whose sizes can be changed.

A program that uses a dynamic array must include a means to find room in memory for the array. This process is called *storage allocation* or *memory allocation*. The C library provides a function malloc() that does this job in a very general way.

Dynamically Allocated Strings

The call malloc() returns a pointer to the base element of an array of n chars, or 0 (the null pointer) if malloc() is unable to allocate an array of the required length. That second clause is important: it is careless to write

```
s = malloc(n);
```

and then refer to s[0], s[1], and so on up through s[n-1] without checking first that s is not 0. We should check for success immediately after calling malloc() and halt the program if malloc() fails:

```
s = (char *) malloc(n);
demand(s, malloc failed);
```

To illustrate the use of dynamically allocated arrays, we shall use them to store the lines typed by a user in an array of strings, with each string corresponding to a single line. Our solution in Program 3.13 uses dynamic arrays to store the input lines, since they are apt to vary widely in length. Program 3.13 also uses a fixed-length array as a buffer into which to read each line; this buffer is longer than any expected line.

Function fill() in Program 3.13 checks whether the memory allocator succeeds, and also avoids running off the end of array line[] when the user types more than MAXLINE lines. When an input line contains more than 999 characters, however, it will be split into several strings and entered into successive positions in array line[]. We leave it as an exercise to fix this behavior so that long input lines are not split.

Dynamic Structures and Arrays

To use malloc() to allocate variables or arrays of variables of some type other than char dynamically, we need to know how many memory cells the variable or array will occupy, since the argument to malloc() is the number of memory cells of storage that are required.

```
#define BUFSIZE 1000
#define MAXLINE 2000

char buffer[BUFSIZE], *line[MAXLINE];

void fill(void)
{
    int i;
    i = 0;
    while (fgets(buffer, BUFSIZE, stdin)) {
        demand(i < MAXLINE, too many lines);
        line[i] = (char *) malloc(strlen(buffer)+1);
        demand(line[i], malloc failed);
        strcpy(line[i], buffer);
        i++;
    }
}
```

PROGRAM 3.13

A program to store up to 2000 input lines, each of fewer than 1000 characters, in an array.

The operator sizeof tells how many memory cells are required to store a single variable of any type.

For example, if variable pd were of type double *, we could make it point to an array of n doubles with the statement:

```
pd = (double *) malloc(n*sizeof(double));
```

After this statement is executed, pd points to the first memory cell of a contiguous array with room for n doubles. As another example, if pm were of type monarch *, we could make it point to a location with enough room to store a variable of type monarch by writing

```
pm = (monarch *) malloc(sizeof(monarch));
```

In all cases we have *cast* the result of malloc() to be a pointer of the appropriate type; this avoids warnings from the compiler about possible differences in type between the value returned by malloc() and the variable in which the value is stored.

Since the type of pm is monarch *, the expression *pm is of type monarch, so *pm has members name, number, and so on. We can use either of two notations to access the name member of *pm:

(*pm).name or pm->name. It is an error to write *pm.name, because the structure member operator ("."). binds more tightly than the pointer dereference operator ("*"), so *pm.name is parsed as *(pm.name), which is incorrect.

Totally Dynamic C

In Program 3.14, we have reworked Program 3.12 to use dynamic arrays so that the resulting structure contains exactly enough room to store the data. Function getmonarchs() returns a pointer to an array of pointers to monarchs, as illustrated in Figure 3.13. (Function makemonarch() is typical in programs that use structures, and is included for completeness.) Since we do not know how many monarchs appear in the input before we start, function getmonarchs() cannot allocate an array of exactly the right size. It can allocate such an array in chunks of reasonable size, however, then trim off the excess after all of the input has been stored, using the library function realloc(); see Appendix B and Chapter 6. Program 3.14 relies on the monarchs' names being of reasonable length.

3.5
SUMMARY AND PERSPECTIVE

We began this chapter with a simple, but moderately detailed, model of computer memory. So long as we use simple scalar variables like chars, ints, and doubles, we can almost ignore this model of memory organization, and just imagine memory as a set of cells of different sizes sprinkled throughout the universe. (Indeed, some theoretical research in data structures and algorithms uses such a model of memory, called a *pointer machine*, that does not permit any array operations.) When we use arrays, however, or arithmetic on pointers, we rely heavily on the properties of the memory model in Section 3.1.

Other Languages

The availability of pointers, structures, and dynamic storage allocation varies widely among imperative programming languages. For example, none of these facilities is available directly in Basic or Fortran, although most versions of Basic support operations on strings. In Fortran, all subroutines and functions receive pointers to their arguments, an arrangement known as *call by reference*; the compiler uses indirec-

```
monarch *makemonarch(char *name, int number,
            int birth, int reign)
{
    monarch *result;
    result = (monarch *) malloc(sizeof(monarch));
    demand(result, malloc failed in makemonarch);
    result->name = strdup(name);
    result->number = number;
    result->birth = birth;
    result->reign = reign;
    return result;
}


#define CHUNK 3

monarch **getmonarchs(void)
{
    int i = 0, maxmon = CHUNK;
    int num, birth, reign;
    char buf[100];
    monarch **house;
    house = (monarch **) malloc(maxmon*sizeof(monarch *));
    demand(house, malloc failed in getmonarchs);
    while (4 == scanf("%s %d %d %d\n",
        buf, &num, &birth, &reign)) {
        /* ASSERT: house[0:maxmon-1] is validly allocated */
        if (i >= maxmon) {
            maxmon += CHUNK;
            house = (monarch **) realloc(house,
                maxmon*sizeof(monarch *));
            demand(house, realloc failed in getmonarchs);
        }
        house[i++] = makemonarch(buf, num, birth, reign);
    }
    /* ASSERT: house[0:i-1] contains all information */
    if (i < maxmon)
        house = (monarch **) realloc(house,
                (i)*sizeof(monarch *));
        demand(house, realloc failed in getmonarchs);
    return house;
}
```

PROGRAM 3.14

A totally dynamic solution to the monarch storage problem.

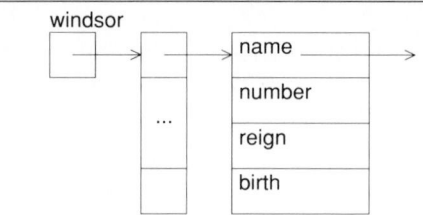

FIGURE 3.13

Data structure for Program 3.14.

tion to interpret references to the arguments of a subroutine or function.

Pascal offers all three facilities: pointers are denoted by ˆ; structures are called *records*, and their members are called *fields*; dynamic storage allocation is accomplished using the function new(). Pointers in Pascal must point to dynamically allocated objects, so one cannot maintain a pointer to an item in a static array. Pascal passes parameters either by value or by reference; the user declares in the function which kind each parameter is, and calls to the function contain no clue that some of the parameters could be changed.

Beyond Strings

Most examples in this chapter use strings, and the relationship between arrays and pointers was explained with particular reference to characters and strings. In fact, all comments in Section 3.2 about arrays, pointers, and arithmetic apply to variables of any type. Thus, if a[] is an array of elements of type *element-type*, then a is a pointer to a[0]. Further, if p is a variable of type pointer to *element-type*, and we assign p = a;, then *p is the same as a[0], and for any integer i, *(p+i) is the same as a[i].

Pointers and dynamic arrays are interchangeable: wherever a C program uses one we could use the other. The relationship between pointers and static arrays is a little bit more restricted. If we declare

```
int vector[10], *pd;
```

then we can change pd but we cannot change vector. Thus, we can set pd to vector and march up the array using pd++;. We cannot, however, write vector++. The sizeof a static array is the product of its dimension and the size of one of its elements; the sizeof a pointer is the same no matter what it points to.

Apart from their use in permitting us to program with strings, pointers might seem to be merely one of the more recondite, and dangerous, features available for programming in C. But pointers lie at the heart of almost every data structure that is more sophisticated than an array, so a solid understanding of how pointers work is important.

There are several ways to increase your facility with programs that use pointers. One is to write a lot of programs that use pointers; the exercises contain several suggestions. Another is to study variable declarations carefully so that the relationships created among variables by pointers are clear. Many programmers find it helpful to draw diagrams like those in this chapter; some advocate using multiple `typedefs` to build complicated types from simple ones. Finally, it is always good practice to write functions that print out some representation of a data structure. Writing such functions can help us to understand pointer relationships, even if we never expect to call them. In practice, we usually have to call such dumping functions when we debug a program.

Pointer Errors

It makes little sense to dereference a pointer unless we know that it points to a value of the appropriate type. Invalid dereferencing is one of the most common errors in programs that use pointers.

A common error of this kind is dereferencing the null pointer. The library of most versions of C defines a value NULL that is guaranteed not to be a valid pointer. The value NULL is often used when we need to indicate that a pointer is invalid; the value returned by an unsuccessful call to `malloc()` is an example. It is bound to be wrong to follow the null pointer expecting to find a variable of any type, so some computer hardware detects an attempt to dereference NULL.

Another example of invalid indirection is referring to a position outside the bounds of an array. This error often goes undetected for a while after it happens, so it can be much later in a program's execution before we realize that something has gone wrong. Careful use of invariant assertions can help to reduce the frequency of errors in array references.

The programs in this chapter are almost free of unsafe array references. However, we noted that some of the functions that read strings rely on a "reasonable" limit on the size of input strings. It is possible to rewrite those functions to be absolutely safe, using a method like the one in Program 3.14 that was used to grow the array of information about the house of Windsor to the right size. Another way to make those functions safer is to have them terminate program execution when they would otherwise exceed array limits.

It is not always easy to determine the appropriate level of safety for a program. In fact, the meaning of "safety" depends on the uses to which the program will be put. In one context it might be safe simply to terminate execution when an invalid pointer dereference is about to happen, whereas in another situation it might be vitally important to keep the program running through such exceptional conditions. The programs in this chapter are safe only in the former circumstances.

EXERCISES

1 Write and execute some calls to `scanf()` and `printf()` in which the types of the arguments do not match the conversion specifications. This will give you some idea of how a program can produce strange results.

2 Another way to store strings is to tote along with each string the number of interesting characters it actually contains. What would be a good data structure for this variety of string?

3 Write a function that reads an arbitrarily long string terminated by a newline into a dynamically allocated array, and returns a pointer to the array.

4 What is the time complexity of function `ourstrcpy()`?

5 It has been observed that `ourstrcpy(p, p+1)` can be interpreted as "shift the string in p one character to the left," and that as long as there is room for a character at p the function works properly. Would it work to use `ourstrcpy(p+1, p)` to shift the string in p one character to the right? Why not?

6 A common operation on strings is *catenation*: appending a second string to the end of a first. The following function uses the algorithms of `strlen()` and `strcpy()` to do the job:

```
void ourstrcat(dest, src)
char *dest, *src;
{
    while (*dest++)
        ;
    dest--;
    while (*dest++ = *src++)
        ;
}
```

Suggest preconditions and invariant assertions for `ourstrcat()`. What is its time complexity?

7 Suppose we need to catenate k strings $s_1, s_2, \ldots, s_k$. What is the time complexity of using the above function $k - 1$ times as in this sequence?

```
ourstrcat(s₁, s₂);
ourstrcat(s₁, s₃);
    . . .
ourstrcat(s₁, sₖ);
```

Suggest a method that has time complexity $O(|s_1| + \cdots + |s_k|)$. Would it be easy to implement by a simple change to ourstrcpy()?

8 Design an algorithm to convert positive integers to Roman numerals. Write a C function that implements your algorithm.

9 Repair Program 3.13 so that it keeps input lines longer than MAXLINE together as a single string.

10 Explain why it is incorrect to write "pm.name" when pm is of type monarch *.

11 Verify the truth of the assertions in Program 3.14.

12 Write a function dumpmonarchs() for the array of pointers to structures in Program 3.14.

13 Assume that the cost of a call to realloc() is proportional to the value of its second argument. Express the asymptotic cost of getmonarchs() in Program 3.14 in terms of CHUNK and the final value of maxmon.

14 Most programming languages permit two-dimensional arrays; for example, in C the definition double matrix[10][10]; declares that matrix is a 10×10 array of variables of type double. Show how to simulate a two-dimensional array of floating-point numbers using a dynamically allocated array of double ** variables. Notice that the contents of array line in Program 3.13 can be interpreted as either a one-dimensional array of lines or a two-dimensional array of characters. What is fundamentally different about the latter interpretation from the two-dimensional array matrix[]?

REFERENCES

The three functions in Program 3.9 are very similar to the versions that are in the C library. They illustrate the conciseness of expression that one can achieve using pointer arithmetic, and it is good to be able to understand programs that are written using lots of pointers. But for many purposes the more familiar array notation is perfectly adequate.

These references offer suggestions about writing reliable C programs:

A. R. Koenig. *C Traps and Pitfalls*. Reading, Mass.: Addison-Wesley, 1989.

T. Plum. *C Programming Guidelines*. Cardiff, N.J.: Plum Hall, 1984.

T. Plum. *Reliable Data Structures in C*. Cardiff, N.J.: Plum Hall, 1985.

Readers who wish to hone their skills at interpreting complicated C expressions might enjoy this book:

A. R. Feuer. *The C Puzzle Book*. Englewood Cliffs, N.J.: Prentice-Hall, 1982.

This article about the syntax used by C to declare types can also help you to understand type declarations more readily:

R. Sethi. "Uniform syntax for type expressions and declarators." *Software—Practice and Experience* 11 (1981): 623–628.

4

Stacks and Queues

In Chapter 2 we saw the abstraction from programs to algorithms. An algorithm expresses the idea of a computation but omits the hardware- and software-specific details that are needed to construct an implementation as a computer program. This chapter introduces another abstraction: from data structures to data types. Data types focus our attention on what we need to do with data, rather than on the details of how the data structure is manipulated by the program. We shall also see some applications of pointers and dynamic storage allocation that are more involved than those in Chapter 3.

4.1
TWO DISCIPLINES FOR PAYING BILLS

Although few enjoy the job, most of us have to pay bills. A common way to deal with the task is to set incoming bills aside as they arrive, then to pay pending bills in marathon check-writing sessions when the mood strikes or creditors insist. We shall assume that such a session of writing checks is run according to Algorithm 4.1. Of the many ways in which one could choose the next bill to pay from the collection of pending bills, we shall discuss two that are simpler (and probably more carefully defined) than most people actually use.

The first rule is called *first-in first-out*, or *FIFO*:

Pay the oldest pending bill.

while bills remain to be paid
  choose a bill
  if there is enough money to cover the necessary check,
    pay the bill
  else
    break

ALGORITHM 4.1

Outline of an algorithm for paying bills.

Whenever this rule is applied in Algorithm 4.1, bills are paid in the order in which they arrive; we continue to pay bills until they run out or the oldest bill is for more money than we have. The FIFO strategy is especially appropriate when money is tight, since creditors usually become more anxious to be paid the longer a bill is outstanding.

The second rule is called *last-in first-out*, or *LIFO*:

Pay the newest pending bill.

When this rule is used in Algorithm 4.1, the bills processed during a session are paid in the reverse of the order in which they arrived. The LIFO method can be used when we always have plenty of money available, since we are unlikely to have to leave bills unpaid because the money runs out before the bills do.

Data Types

To manage the collection of pending bills, we must be able to perform the operations shown in Figure 4.1 on the bills. This set of operations is an example of a *data type*. It describes only what we need to do with the data items in a set, and says nothing about how those items are to be represented or organized. When we select a rule by which to choose bills, we can create a more specific data type, and begin to discuss data structures we might use to implement it.

For example, to use the LIFO rule we would replace the words "a particular" by "the most recent" in Figure 4.1. An appropriate data structure for the LIFO rule is a pile of pending bills. Arriving bills go on top of the pile. During Algorithm 4.1, we examine the top bill on the pile, and remove it if we are able to pay it.

If we wanted to use the FIFO rule, we would replace "a particular" by "the oldest" in Figure 4.1. We could implement FIFO bill-paying in at least two obvious ways using a pile of bills. In one, we add bills at

put a bill into the set

examine a particular bill in the set

remove a particular bill from the set

check whether any bills are in the set

FIGURE 4.1

Primitive operations on a set of bills. The first operation happens when the bills arrive; Algorithm 4.1 uses the other three.

the top of the pile; during bill-paying sessions we always examine (and, if possible, remove) the bottom bill of the pile. In the other, we add bills at the bottom of the pile, and always process the top bill during Algorithm 4.1. Although the two implementations are different, both use the same data type, namely the set of operations in Figure 4.1 with the words "a particular" replaced by "the oldest."

Algorithm 4.1 uses a style of processing that is found in many algorithms: as things come up that need to be processed, store them away some place; now and then, return to the collection and select a new thing to work on. If we express the operations in Figure 4.1 in terms of "things" rather than bills, we have just the operations we need to describe such algorithms. We shall call this data type a *pile*. Piles that use the LIFO and FIFO rules are encountered so often that they have special names, and data structures for implementing them have been studied extensively.

4.2
THE STACK DATA TYPE

A *stack* is a pile that obeys the LIFO rule. Figure 4.2 shows common names for the four operations in the data type stack. Notice that we do not specify the type of the items in the stack: whether it contains integers, floating-point numbers, structures or bills, a data structure that permits the operations in Figure 4.2 can be described as a stack.

The description of *top( )* is deliberately more vague than the descriptions of *push( )*, *pop( )*, and *empty( )*. While it is easy to imagine the effect of the latter three operations on a pile of bills, what it means to "examine" the top stack element depends on how the stack fits into an application. Both *top( )* operations in this section return copies of

push(x) — put x onto the stack

top( ) — examine the top element of the stack

pop( ) — remove the top element from the stack

empty( ) — return true if and only if the stack contains nothing

FIGURE 4.2

The operations associated with the data type *stack*.

the top stack item. In one of the applications in Section 4.4, however, *top*( ) returns a pointer to the top item.

A Sequential Stack Data Structure

Whenever we know a reasonable upper bound on the number of items that a stack will ever contain, we can store it in an array. Algorithm 4.2 contains algorithms to perform the four stack operations on a stack

```
thing stack[N]
int T = −1   /* stack top, starts out empty */

void push(thing x)
      T++
      demand(T < N, stack overflow)
      stack[T] = x

thing top(void)
      demand(!empty( ), top of empty stack)
      return stack[T]

void pop(void)
      demand(!empty( ), pop of empty stack)
      T−−

boolean empty(void)
      return T < 0
```

ALGORITHM 4.2

Algorithms for the four basic operations on a stack stored in an array.

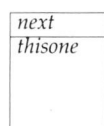

0   *i*   *N* − 1

stack

T : *i*

FIGURE 4.3

Array data structure for a stack.

stored in an array *stack*[ ] with room for *N* things. The value of *T* is
the index of the top of the stack, as depicted in Figure 4.3.

Initially, *T* = −1 and the stack is empty. To push a thing *x* onto
the stack, we increment *T*, check that there is room for *x*, then copy it
into *stack*[*T*]. To pop the top of the stack, we simply decrement *T*; the
popped thing remains in a location in array *stack*[ ], but we should
never see it there because it is at an index larger than *T*. Both *top*( )
and *pop*( ) check that they are not used on an empty stack. To see
whether the stack contains any things, *empty*( ) tests whether *T* is negative.

Each of the operations in Algorithm 4.2 requires $O(1)$ time, which
is the best we can hope to do. Moreover, the algorithms are short,
simple, and robust against errors that involve stack operations. Unfortunately, stacks cannot be stored in arrays when there is no upper
bound on the size of the stack (the *N* in Algorithm 4.2).

A Linked Stack Data Structure

Pointers, structures, and dynamic storage allocation are the tools for a
data structure that imposes no upper bound on the size of a stack. The
first step is to define a structure with room for both a thing and a
pointer, as shown in Figure 4.4.

next
thisone

FIGURE 4.4

An illustration of a structure in which we shall store an item in a linked stack.
The structure is declared in Algorithm 4.3.

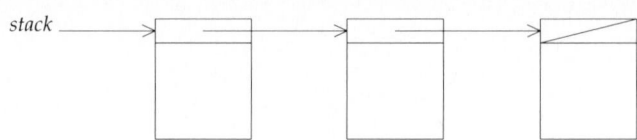

FIGURE 4.5

Picture of a linked stack data structure. The diagonal slash in the last item represents the null pointer.

```
typedef struct item item
struct item {
    item *next
    thing thisone
}

item *stack = NULL   /* pointer to stack top, initially empty */

void push(thing x)
    item *new
    new = malloc(sizeof(item))
    demand(new, memory overflow)
    new→thisone = x
    new→next = stack
    stack = new

thing top(void)
    demand(!empty( ), top of empty stack)
    return stack→thisone

void pop(void)
    demand(!empty( ), pop of empty stack)
    stack = stack→next

boolean empty(void)
    return stack == NULL
```

ALGORITHM 4.3

Algorithms for stack operations in a linked data structure.

Next we create a pointer *stack* that points to the top item, and make each item point to the item below it on the stack, as shown in Figure 4.5. If *stack* is *NULL*, the stack is empty; if an item's *next* member is *NULL*, then it is the bottom item on the stack. Algorithm 4.3 shows how to perform the four stack operations on a linked data structure.

To push a thing *x* onto the stack, we must find room for an *item*; *new* points to the newly allocated space. If the allocation succeeds, we copy *x* into the *thisone* member of *new*, then rearrange pointers to make *new* the top of the stack. The order in which we reset pointers is important: first we make *new→next* point to the old stack top, then we make *stack* point to *new*. If we reversed the order of these assignments, we would lose track of the stack.

To pop the top item from the stack, we simply reset *stack* to point to the item below the top item. If no other variable in the program points to the popped item, its fate is undefined; it may survive for the duration of the program, inaccessibly lost in memory space. We shall return to this point in Section 6.3.

Function *top*( ) returns a copy of the thing in the top stack item, and *empty*( ) tests whether the stack is empty by checking whether *stack* is *NULL*.

To express the running time of operations on piles, we shall add *malloc*( ) to our model of computation as one of the primitive operations; that is, we shall assume that a call to *malloc*( ) takes constant time. In this model, each of the stack operations requires $O(1)$ time.

4.3
THE QUEUE DATA TYPE

A pile that obeys the FIFO rule is called a *queue*. Figure 4.6 shows common names for the operations that define a queue. As we did for

---

enqueue(*x*) — *add item x at the end of the queue*

head( ) — *examine the front item of the queue*

dequeue( ) — *remove the front item from the queue*

empty( ) — *return true if and only if the queue contains nothing*

FIGURE 4.6

Four basic operations for a queue.

```
item *qhead = NULL, *qtail = NULL

void enqueue(thing x)
    item *new
    new = malloc(sizeof(item))
    demand(new, memory overflow)
    new→item = x
    new→next = NULL
    if (empty( ))
        qhead = qtail = new
    else
        qtail→next = new
        qtail = new

thing head( )
    demand(!empty( ), head of empty queue)
    return qhead→thisone

void dequeue( )
    demand(!empty( ), dequeue of empty queue)
    qhead = qhead→next
    if (qhead == NULL)
        qtail = NULL

boolean empty( )
    return qhead == NULL
```

ALGORITHM 4.4

Algorithms for a linked queue data structure.

stacks, we use the word "examine" in the expectation that the application will define *head*( ) exactly.

Broadly speaking, a queue can be stored in either a sequential or a linked data structure by minor modifications to the techniques in Section 4.2. Nevertheless, we shall observe some subtle points in the algorithms for both methods of storing queues.

A Linked Queue Data Structure

We consider a linked data structure for queues first, because it involves only a few changes from the linked stack data structure. Algorithm 4.4 uses the same structure declaration for *item* as Algorithm 4.3. Two

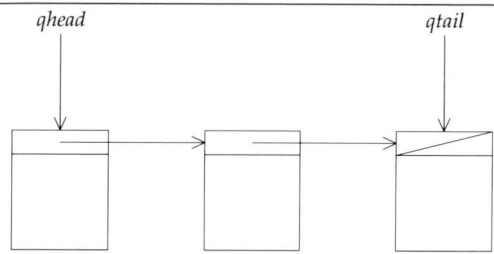

FIGURE 4.7

Picture of a linked queue data structure.

pointers, *qhead* and *qtail*, point to the first and last items on the queue, as shown in Figure 4.7.

Figure 4.7 suggests that *enqueue*( ) affects only *qtail*: *qtail→next* should be set to point to the new item, then *qtail* itself should point to the new item. This is true except when a thing is added to an empty queue, and both *qhead* and *qtail* must point to it.

Similarly, Figure 4.7 suggests that *dequeue*( ) affects only *qhead*: we simply make *qhead* point to the next item on the queue, much as we did to pop an item from a stack. Again, this is true except when removing the front item from a queue leaves it empty, and both *qhead* and *qtail* must be changed.

The algorithms for *head*( ) and *empty*( ) are straightforward modifications of those for stacks. Even though queue operations affect more pointers and must make more tests, all of them run in $O(1)$ time.

A Sequential Queue Data Structure

Some obvious ways to store a queue in an array make for slow queue operations. For example, if we try to mimic the way stacks are stored in an array, always keeping the tail of the queue at *queue*[0], then to enqueue an item we must shift all items in the array by one slot; when the queue is nearly full, this makes *enqueue*( ) run in $\Omega(N)$ time.

To construct a better array data structure for a queue, imagine that the array is circular, as shown in Figure 4.8. We can use the integer mod function to simulate a circular array of N items; to move an array index up one position we add one and take the result modulo N.

Next we must settle what the indexes *head* and *tail* represent. It is natural to let *head* be the index of the head of the queue. We shall let *tail* be the index of the tail of the queue, so that positions *head*, $(head+1)$ mod $N, \ldots,$ *tail* contain queue items. Then when *head* and

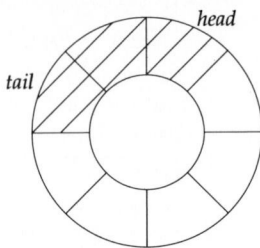

FIGURE 4.8

A circular array in which a queue resides. The cross-hatched area indicates the contents of the queue; this queue grows and shrinks counterclockwise.

tail are the same, the queue contains one item. If we add an item to a one-item queue, then we have $head + 1 \equiv tail \bmod N$. Usually this means $head = tail - 1$; when $tail = 0$, however, we have $head = N - 1$.

```
thing queue[N]
int head = 0, tail = 1

void enqueue(x)
thing x
     tail = (tail − 1) mod N
     demand(!empty( ), queue overflow)
     queue[tail] = x

thing head( )
     demand(!empty( ), head of empty queue)
     return queue[head]

void dequeue( )
     demand(!empty( ), dequeue of empty queue)
     head = (head − 1) mod N

boolean empty( )
     return (head + 1) ≡ tail mod N
```

ALGORITHM 4.5

Algorithms for the four queue operations when the queue is stored in an array. These algorithms assume that the result of a modular computation is always positive.

In general, we can write that when the queue contains k items we have $head + k - 1 \equiv tail$ mod N. The boundary cases for the queue have an important implication for this representation. When the queue is empty, we have $k = 0$ and $head - 1 \equiv tail$ mod N. On the other hand, if we fill all entries in the array, so that $k = N$, we have $head + N - 1 \equiv head - 1 \equiv tail$ mod N. Thus, the values of $head$ and $tail$ cannot tell us whether the queue contains zero or N items. We conclude that we can store only $N - 1$ queue items in an array of N items.

Algorithm 4.5 shows the four queue operations written with this interpretation of the indexes $head$ and $tail$.

4.4
EXAMPLE APPLICATIONS

Stacks and queues are simple data types that figure prominently in many algorithms. In this section we shall see an application of each. Both are simpler than most uses of stacks and queues, because they involve putting all items onto a pile and then taking them all off again; more general algorithms that interleave the operations of adding items to and removing them from a pile appear in Chapters 6, 13, and 14. Notice in the examples that the essence of these data types lies neither in their implementations nor in the names of their operations, but in the operations we need to implement an algorithm.

Storing Long Strings

We saw in Chapter 3 that the C library functions leave it to the user to provide room for any input strings. Although the library provides functions that avoid overrunning the boundaries of an array, it contains no function to read an arbitrarily long string. The function we shall see here fills this gap.

In this problem, the input string is presented from beginning to end and we wish to store the string in the input order; therefore the appropriate rule to obey is FIFO. Our function stores chunks of string on a queue; when it reaches a newline or the end-of-file it makes room for a single contiguous string of the appropriate length and copies the stored chunks into the newly allocated space. Although we could store the string in a queue of characters, in Program 4.1 we have arranged for the queue to hold larger chunks of string; the value of CHUNK should be defined by a macro before the structure template substring is defined.

```
typedef struct substring substring;
struct substring {
    substring *next;
    char text[CHUNK+1]; /* extra room for null character */
};
```

PROGRAM 4.1a

Definitions for a function to read an arbitrarily long string. The macro CHUNK
can be defined to be any positive number, as described in the text.

All of the queue operations in Program 4.1 are implemented by
direct reference to the relevant pointers, rather than as separate functions. This seemed natural since only readstring() is concerned
with the contents of the queue, and the operations are all simple pieces
of code. If several functions in a program needed to use queues of
substrings, however, we would probably write the queue operations as
separate functions, to avoid duplication of both the code itself and the
effort to write that code correctly.

In the first half of readstring(), when it is reading the input
string, the variable len holds the number of valid characters seen so
far on the line. We use this value after the line has been read to allocate space for the whole string. In the second half of readstring(),
the value of len is the number of characters that have been written
into their final destination, the dynamically allocated array result[].
The value of len tells where to begin copying each chunk into
result[], and lets us complete all of the copy operations in
$O(|result|)$ time.

This analysis shows that readstring() runs in linear time. We
can tune its performance by changing the value of CHUNK: chunks that
are too small cause many calls to malloc() and many queue operations; chunks that are too large waste memory space. Ideally, we
would like readstring() to cost little more than the library function
fgets() when a string fits into a single chunk.

Adding Long Integers

Our next example is a program to compute the sum of two positive
integers. The program should impose no upper bound on the size of
the input, as illustrated by the output atop the next page from the
computation of $\lfloor \pi \times 10^{40} \rfloor + \lfloor e \times 10^{40} \rfloor$:

```
   31415926535897932384626433832795028841972
  +27182818284590452353602874713526624977572
  =58598744820488384738229308546321653819544
```

```c
char *readstring(void)  /* read and make room for a line */
/* Stop at either newline or end-of-file. */
{
    int len = 0;
    char buf[CHUNK+1], *result;
    substring *qhead = NULL, *qtail, *new;
    do {
        if (!fgets(buf, CHUNK+1, stdin))
            break;
        /* enqueue chunk most recently read */
        new = (substring *) malloc(sizeof(substring));
        demand(new, memory overflow);
        strcpy(new->text, buf);
        new->next = NULL;
        if (qhead) {
            qtail->next = new;
            qtail = new;
        } else
            qhead = qtail = new;
        len += strlen(buf);
        /* ASSERT:  queue contains len valid characters */
    } while (buf[len%CHUNK-1] != '\n');
    if (!len)
        return NULL; /* reached EOF */
    result = (char *) malloc(len+1);
    len = 0;
    while (qhead) {
        /* ASSERT:  result[0:len-1] is valid */
        /* store and dequeue next chunk on queue */
        strcpy(result+len, qhead->text);
        qhead = qhead->next;
        len += CHUNK;
    }
    return result;
}
```

PROGRAM 4.1b

Function readstring() reads an arbitrarily long string and creates space in
which to store it. Note that the strings stored in the text member of a
substring are null-terminated so that we can use strcpy().

read and store the digits of the first addend
read and store the digits of the second addend
starting with the units digit of each addend,
* and continuing until all digits have been processed*
*   compute the sum digit and carry bit*
*   store the sum digit*
store the carry bit
starting with the high–order digit of the sum,
*   print out the sum*

ALGORITHM 4.6

An algorithm to add two large integers.

Since the numbers with which this program deals can be much larger than the integers handled by any version of C, we shall need to read and process the input numbers, and print the output number, one digit at a time. Algorithm 4.6 is an outline of our solution. It uses the grade-school algorithm for adding two numbers: write the numbers to be added so that their units digits line up; starting from the units column, add the digits in the same column, writing the units digit of the sum and carrying one to the next column when the sum is larger than nine.

Numbers arrive as input with their high-order digits first, but the addition algorithm starts working on the low-order digits of both addends. Therefore we shall process the digits in the input according to a LIFO discipline. On the output side, we compute the sum beginning with its low-order digits, but must print it out starting with its high-order digits, so the sum digits should also be processed in a LIFO fashion. Thus we shall store both addends and the sum in stacks; digits appear in the addend stacks with low-order digits on top, while the top of the sum stack contains high-order digits. Since the program uses three stacks, it is clear that we shall need to write functions that can operate on any of them.

Program 4.2 solves the problem using the data structure scheme just described. Although it retains the traditional names for stack operations, Program 4.2a uses a different kind of pop operation from the one in Section 4.2; this common variant of *pop*( ) both removes the top element and returns it as the value of the function. Function pop() also differs from the version in Algorithms 4.1 and 4.2 because it does not abort execution when the stack is empty. This is convenient because it lets the addition continue as long as digits remain in either addend.

```
typedef struct node node;
struct node {
    node *next;
    int n;
};

#define empty(s)  !(s)

void push(node **s, int n)
{
    node *new;
    new = (node *) malloc(sizeof(node));
    demand(new, memory overflow);
    new->n = n;
    new->next = *s;
    *s = new;
}

int pop(node **s)
{
    int n;
    if (empty(*s))
        return 0;
    n = (*s)->n;
    *s = (*s)->next;
    return n;
}
```

PROGRAM 4.2a

Structure definitions and queue operations for a program to add two large integers. Note that pop() returns the number it pops off the top of the stack, and returns zero when called on an empty stack.

Program 4.2b contains a function to read and print an input number digit by digit, pushing the digits onto a stack. It assumes that the digits 0 through 9 appear contiguously in the computer's character set, and stops processing as soon as it sees a non-digit.

Program 4.2c reads the addends using Program 4.2b; the use of getnum() means that the two addends must be separated in the input by exactly one non-digit character. After reading the two addends, it performs the grade-school addition algorithm, pushing the result digits onto the sum stack. Finally it prints the contents of the sum stack.

```
node *getnum(void)
{
    node *s;
    int n;
    s = NULL;
    while (EOF != (n = getchar())) {
        if (n < '0' || n > '9')
            return s;
        push(&s, n - '0');
        putchar(n);
    }
    return s;
}
```

PROGRAM 4.2b

Function to read an integer and store its digits on a stack. The function also prints the integer as it reads it.

4.5

SUMMARY AND PERSPECTIVE

Two related themes interweave throughout this chapter. The obvious and concrete topic is ways to implement programs that rely on stacks and queues. We have seen how one can use arrays when the size of the stack or queue is bounded in advance, and we have also seen how to use dynamic storage allocation to make data structures that grow as needed.

The other topic is data types. We have seen two important examples, stacks and queues, and we shall see several more in Part II. Whenever we ponder what operations we shall need to perform on the data to solve some problem, we are thinking about data types. Once we understand the necessary operations, we have a choice of data structures and styles in which to implement them, as Sections 4.2 and 4.3, as well as the examples of Programs 4.1 and 4.2, illustrate.

It is surprisingly difficult to give an exact definition of a data type in abstraction from the use we intend to make of it. For example, does the "examine an item" operation for piles return a copy of the item or the item itself (perhaps indirectly through a pointer)? Strictly speaking, Programs 4.1 and 4.2 use different operations when they remove an item from their respective piles: Program 4.1 returns a pointer to the head string on the queue, while Program 4.2 returns a copy of the top integer on a stack. Nevertheless, both programs clearly obey a pile

```
main()
{
    node *a, *b, *sum;
    int carry, sumdig;

    /* read and print addends */
    putchar(' ');
    a = getnum();
    putchar('\n');
    putchar('+');
    b = getnum();
    putchar('\n');

    /* perform addition */
    sum = NULL;
    carry = 0;
    while (!empty(a) || !empty(b)) {
        sumdig = pop(&a) + pop(&b) + carry;
        push(&sum, sumdig%10);
        carry = sumdig/10;
    }
    if (carry != 0)
        push(&sum, carry);

    /* print result */
    putchar('=');
    while(!empty(sum))
        printf("%d", pop(&sum));
    putchar('\n');
    exit(0);
}
```

PROGRAM 4.2c

A program to add two large integers.

discipline. In general, it is more important to offer a cogent explanation for the structure of a program than to provide loophole-free definitions of the data types it uses.

Information Hiding

Thinking about data types can help to promote a style of programming that exhibits *information hiding*. The idea of information hiding is that the portion of program that implements the main algorithm is written in terms of operations on some data type, and functions are used to perform all operations on objects of that type, such as accesses and updates. In the best case, information hiding makes it possible for a different data structure to be installed without requiring any change to the main algorithm and program. Even if such a dramatic change never happens, having all of the code related to a data structure in one place makes it easier to maintain.

For example, suppose we wished to make strings a data type, and we defined a new type `string`. In Representation 1, let a string be a `char *`, as used in Chapter 3. In Representation 2, let a `string` be a `struct` that contains the length of the string, a pointer to the dynamically allocated array where the string is stored, and the length of that array. Obviously, the algorithms to compute string length and to catenate strings are different for the two representations: since we need to know where a string argument ends, in Representation 1 we must traverse the entire length of each string argument; on the other hand, in Representation 2 we can access the end of a string immediately. A program that uses information hiding would simply call a function to catenate two strings, regardless of which string representation was actually used. Information hiding at this level of operation is a good idea, and the string functions in the C library facilitate it.

On the other hand, complete information hiding requires that we write *all* operations on strings in terms of functions. Thus, we would have to refer to the ith character of a string using some sort of function call (perhaps `readstr(s, i)` to read the ith character of s and `writestr(s, i, c)` to make the ith character of s be c). This can become downright tiresome, and might also impose an unacceptable penalty on program performance, as when we wish to move from the ith to the $(i+1)$st character in a string.

The goal of complete information hiding is elusive in practice. Sometimes the only reasonable implementation of an important operation uses information about the internal structure of a data type. More often difficulties arise after a substantial amount of the program has been written, because some operation that was not foreseen to be necessary was omitted from the specification of a data type. In either case, the operation is usually implemented in the best way possible, and a working program is produced. A complete change to the data structure at some later date might require more work than if information had been perfectly hidden; it is entirely possible, however, that such drastic changes will never be contemplated.

Information hiding is meant to help us write programs whose structure makes it clear which parts of the program affect which pieces of data. Just as data types are useful to guide our thinking, but should not be a hindrance because of the difficulty of defining them precisely, information hiding should not be seen as a straitjacket into which we must fit programs.

EXERCISES

1 What rule describes each of the following?
   (a) cars waiting to go through a car wash;
   (b) trays at the entrance to a cafeteria;
   (c) the pages of a desk calendar;
   (d) the order in which jobs are output on a computer printer.

2 Implement a pile whose rule for choosing the "particular" element is to select an element randomly from those in the pile, with each element equally likely to be chosen.

3 Revise Algorithm 4.2 so that T points one after the current stack top, to the next available space.

4 Program 3.14 demonstrates that with suitable use of pointers and `realloc()` we can implement a stack in an array and still permit the stack to grow arbitrarily large. Is there any reason to fault this approach to implementing a stack?

5 If a program uses two stacks whose total size is known, then the stacks can share the same array, both growing toward the middle of the array, each starting from one end. Implement such a scheme.

6 Revise Algorithm 4.3 so that *top( )* returns a pointer to the top element on the stack.

7 Redraw Figure 4.5 to show the state of the pointers after a pop operation.

8 Implement *top( )* when *pop( )* is defined as in Program 4.2.

9 An expression is in *postfix* form if the operators appear after their operands; for example, '1 2 +' means the sum of 1 and 2. More generally, '1 2 + 3 4 + ×' is probably more familiar as $(1+2) \times (3+4)$. Write a program that evaluates a postfix expression composed of single digits and operators.

10 Why does the enqueue operation in Algorithm 4.4 set *new→next* to *NULL*?

11 Redraw Figure 4.7 to show the state of the pointers after an item *new* is enqueued.

12 Revise Algorithm 4.4 to return a pointer to the head element of the queue.

13 The queue in Algorithm 4.4 is referenced by two auxiliary pointers, *head* and *tail*, and any nonempty queue includes a node with a null pointer. It has been suggested that one of the two auxiliary pointers could be stored in place of this null pointer, and then the

queue could be referenced by only one auxiliary pointer. Show how to do this so that the running time of all queue operations remains constant.

14 A textbook author decided to implement queues as shown in Algorithm 4.5. The author first wrote the statements that move the head and tail as follows:

```
head = (head - 1)%N;
tail = (tail - 1)%N;
```

After some puzzled debugging, the now irate author changed these statements to read:

```
head = (head + N - 1)%N;
tail = (tail + N - 1)%N;
```

Why? Would this matter on your computer?

15 Revise Algorithm 4.5 so that *tail* is the index of the next available space in the queue. What is the maximum number of items the queue can hold in this implementation?

16 It is possible to store queue elements in all N slots of an array. We need only maintain a boolean variable that keeps track of whether the queue contains any elements. How much more code does it take to implement such a scheme?

17 A *dequeue* (or *double-ended queue*) is a data type that allows us to add or remove elements at both ends. Explain how to store a dequeue in an array. Describe a linked structure that could hold a dequeue.

18 Revise Program 4.1 to avoid unnecessary copying when the entire input string fits into one chunk.

19 Suppose Program 4.1 used `strcat()` instead of `strcpy()` to create the result string, and also did not keep the current number of valid characters in `len`. What would its running time be?

20 What is the running time of Program 4.2 in terms of the number of digits in both addends?

21 Rewrite Program 4.2 so it uses a function to compute the required sum, rather than including the code in function `main()`.

22 Revise Program 4.2 to accept both positive and negative integers.

23 Revise Program 4.2 to accept numbers that include a decimal point.

24 Revise Program 4.2 to store numbers in chunks of more than a single decimal digit.

25 Revise Program 4.2 so that it always aligns the printed numbers on their units digits.

26 Write a program to simulate a grocery store checkout counter, with customers who arrive at random times and require a random amount of time to check out. There are two ways to approach the problem: construct one long queue from which customers dequeue to the next available counter, or construct as many queues as there are counters open. Which is easier to program? Which do you see more often in real stores? Why?

A permutation can be *realized using one stack* if it can be created from the input 1, 2, ..., n by a sequence of moves of the form either (1) pop the stack (if possible) or (2) push the next input number onto the stack. Thus, on 1, 2, 3, the sequence *push, pop, push, pop, push, pop* realizes the permutation 1, 2, 3, while the sequence *push, push, pop, push, pop, pop* realizes the permutation 2, 3, 1.

27 Which permutation of 1, 2, 3 cannot be realized using one stack?
28 What permutations of 1, 2, ..., n cannot be realized using one stack?
29 What permutations of 1, 2, ..., n can be realized using *two* stacks?

REFERENCES

To stress the difference between data structures and data types, some authors call the latter "abstract data types." An early description of data types appears in

C. A. R. Hoare. "Notes on data structuring." In *Structured Programming*. London and New York: Academic Press, 1972.

In C, when we write the functions that compose a data type we must specify the types of the items that belong to it: we cannot define just a "stack"; we must specify that it contains integers, floating-point numbers, or some structure. Some programming languages, including a descendant of C, offer more general facilities with which to define data types.

B. Stroustrup. *The C++ Programming Language*. Reading, Mass.: Addison-Wesley, 1986.

5

Linked
Lists

In Chapter 4 we used linked structures to maintain stacks and queues. The principal advantage they enjoy over arrays for implementing those data types is that they require no *a priori* estimate of the maximum size to which the data structure will grow. In this chapter we shall use pointers to link together dynamically allocated structures in more flexible ways than we saw in Chapter 4. The first two sections present the ideas for several important operations on linked list data structures and an application of linked lists to store sets. Later sections describe some tricks of the linked-list trade and some more tangled list structures.

5.1
LISTS

Suppose we had some items stored in structures whose *info* member contained data and whose *next* member contained a pointer to another such structure of the same type. Figure 5.1 shows how we could hook

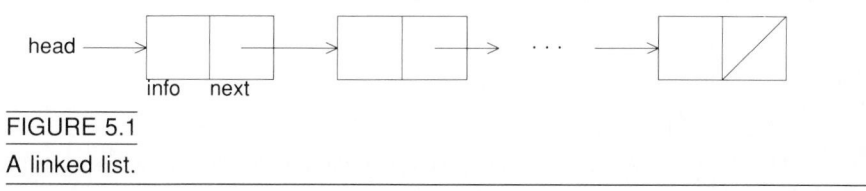

FIGURE 5.1
A linked list.

them together using their next members; *head* points to a structure variable (or *node*) from which all other nodes can be reached by following *next* pointer members. This data structure is called a *linked list*. (Although Figures 4.5 and 5.1 are very similar, a linked list should not be confused with a stack. A linked list is a data structure, but a stack is a data type. We could say, however, that a stack can be stored in a linked list.)

A linked list like Figure 5.1 represents a *sequence:* every item but one has a predecessor, and every item but one has a successor. Depending on the application, we might want to perform any of a number of operations on a sequence. Therefore, we shall not canonize a particular set of operations as the data type "sequence." Instead, we shall consider some of the operations that we might want to perform on a sequence, and see a few of the subtleties involved in implementing those operations when a sequence is stored in a linked list. Then, in Section 5.2, we shall make some more detailed decisions about both the operations we need for a data type and how we want to perform them on linked lists.

Finding a Matching Item

Given a pointer *head* to the first node in a linked list, and a description *d*, Algorithm 5.1 returns a pointer to the earliest item in the list that matches *d*, or *NULL* if the list contains no such item. It uses the same sequential search algorithm as Program 1.2.

The time Algorithm 5.1 takes to find the earliest matching item depends on the distance of that item from the head of the list. If the list contains n items and no item matches *d*, then Algorithm 5.1 takes $\Theta(n)$ time. If the earliest item that matches *d* is i items from *head*, Algorithm 5.1 takes $\Theta(i)$ time. To keep the expression for time complexity simple, we would like to state a time bound for *find( )* that is independent of i. The most conservative and cautious way to do this

---

item * *find*(*item* * *head*, *description d*)
    item * *p* = *head*
    while (*p* && *p*→*info does not match d*)
        p = *p*→*next*
    return p

ALGORITHM 5.1

Find the first item that matches description d in the linked list that starts at *head*.

item ∗*pos find*(*item* ∗*head*, *i*)
   demand(*i* > 0, *index to posfind must be positive*)
   while (*head* && −−*i*)
      head = *head* →*next*
   demand(*head*, *list has no ith element*)
   return head

ALGORITHM 5.2

Return a pointer to the ith item in the linked list to which *head* points.

---

is to state the time bound for the *worst case*. Since in the worst case for *find*( ), $i = n$, we say that its worst-case time complexity is $O(n)$.

Finding the ith Item

Given *head* and an integer i, to retrieve the ith item on the list, counting *head* as the first item, we traverse the list as shown in Algorithm 5.2. Because we must step over $i-1$ items on the way to the ith item from *head*, it takes $\Theta(i)$ time to reach the ith item from the head of a linked list. Compare this to the corresponding operation on arrays, where we can reach the ith item in $O(1)$ time.

Arrays perform at least as well as linked lists for these two operations. This could tempt us to think that the main advantage of linked lists over arrays is that they do not impose an upper bound on the length of a sequence. When we consider operations that rearrange a sequence, however, we shall see clear advantages that linked structures offer over arrays.

Inserting an Element

Given a sequence and an item we wish to add to it, it usually takes two steps to insert the item: find the place where the item should be inserted, then add it to the sequence. We have already discussed the cost of finding a place in a linked list. To focus our attention on the cost of the actual insertion, we shall assume that we already have a pointer p to the item after which we wish to insert item *new*, as shown in Figure 5.2. We can perform the insertion by changing two pointers: *new*→*next* and *p*→*next*, as illustrated in Figure 5.3 and stated in Algorithm 5.3.

We can insert an item after a given item in a linked list in $O(1)$ time. By contrast, when we insert an item into the middle of an array,

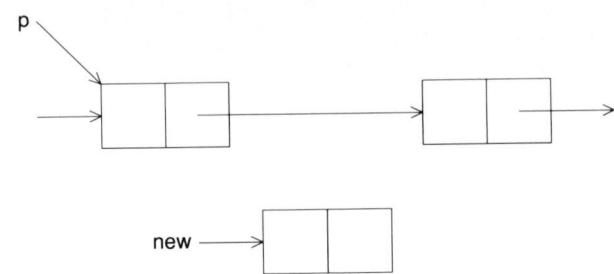

FIGURE 5.2

The situation before *new* is inserted after *p*. The unlabelled arrow that points at *p* and the arrow that points at *p→next→next* indicate the pointers that hook *p* and *p→next* into the data structure.

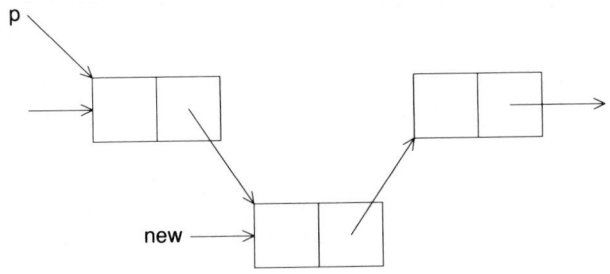

FIGURE 5.3

The situation after *new* has been inserted after *p*. The rest of the data structure has not changed.

void insert_after(item *p, *new)
    new→next = p→next
    p→next = new

ALGORITHM 5.3

Inserting the item to which *new* points after the item to which *p* points. The order in which we change the pointers is important: reversing the order of these statements would cause us to lose track of the portion of the list that starts at *p→next*.

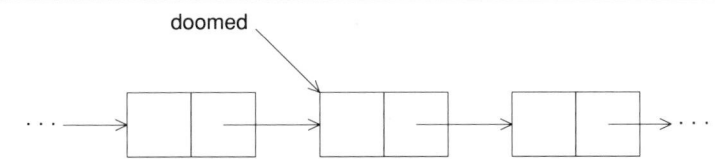

FIGURE 5.4

Local situation before deletion of item *doomed*.

we must shift some of the remaining items by one place; in the worst case this takes time linear in the length of the list.

Deleting an Element

Since we can insert an item after a given item in a linked list in constant time, we might hope to perform a similar feat when deleting an element. Let *doomed* point to the item that we wish to remove from the list, as shown in Figure 5.4. At first, it looks as if the job should be as simple as it was when we composed Algorithm 5.3: all we need to do is make the node that precedes *doomed* point to *doomed*→*next*. Unfortunately, there is no quick way to find the node that precedes *doomed*; there is no way to "back up" along pointers. So, the best we can do is traverse the list from its head to find the predecessor of *doomed*, then adjust pointers. Since it takes time linear in the length of the list to search for the predecessor of *doomed*, this solution takes $O(n)$ time when the list contains *n* items.

If, however, we were given a pointer to the predecessor of *doomed* then we could delete the node in constant time, as shown by Algorithm 5.4 and Figure 5.5. Thus we see that linked lists have the same advantage over arrays for deletion as they have for insertion.

*void delete_after(item *p, item *doomed)*
   demand(p→next == doomed, p does not precede doomed)
   p→next = p→next→next

ALGORITHM 5.4

Item deletion given a pointer to the preceding item. The argument *doomed* appears so that *delete_after( )* can *demand* that *p* is its true predecessor.

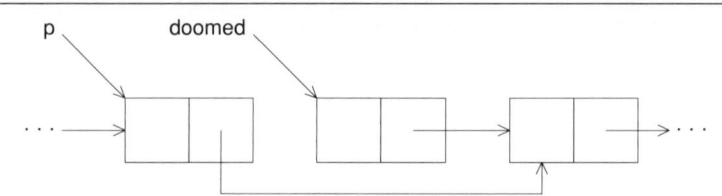

FIGURE 5.5

Local situation after item *doomed* has been deleted.

Comparison of Linked Lists with Arrays

Given pointers to the appropriate places in a linked list, we can insert or delete an item in constant time. This compares quite favorably with representing a sequence in a contiguous array, when adding or removing an item takes linear time. To exploit the possibility of fast sequence rearrangement using linked lists, however, we must have exactly the right pointers available: if we have a pointer to a node just one too late in the list, we must traverse the entire list again to find the pointer we really need.

The full name of the linked data structure in Figure 5.1 is *singly linked list*. Such lists exhibit a kind of one-sidedness, in that operations that involve a node and its successor can be performed in constant time, but operations that involve a node and its predecessor require a linear-time traversal of the list.

Finding a matching item in a linked list, and adding or deleting an item in a list, are typical operations on linked lists. The algorithms we have seen so far for these operations are incomplete for practical use. Algorithm 5.3, for example, does not apply to an empty list whose *head* is *NULL*. In other words, with what we have seen so far we could never insert an item into a linked list; it may be small comfort to realize that this means we would never need to use Algorithm 5.4 to delete an item either. The general lesson is that when programs use linked lists, we must take special care that they treat the null pointer correctly.

5.2
APPLICATION: SETS

To illustrate programming with linked lists, we shall use them to store finite sets of elements from an ordered universe. These "sets" are the garden-variety sets of elementary mathematics: they contain elements

empty(*set s*) — *is set s empty?*

member(*set s*, *item n*) — *is n in set s?*

insert(*set s*, *item n*) — *add n to set s*, if it is not already present

unite(*set* s_1, *set* s_2) — *form the union of sets* s_1 *and* s_2.

FIGURE 5.6

The illustrative data type *set*.

from a universe, and no element appears more than once. Of the many possible primitive operations on sets, we shall provide those shown in Figure 5.6. These operations were chosen because they illustrate some important points about programming with linked lists; an application might well require different set operations.

We shall store each set in a linked list. Since no element appears more than once in a set, its linked list will contain no duplicate elements. We shall also require that the elements in a set appear on its linked list in the same order as their ordering in the universe: if the ordering is alphabetical, the lists are in alphabetical order; if the ordering is numerical, the list elements appear in ascending order. These two requirements—non-duplication of elements and ordering of the list—are invariant properties of the data structure we shall build; any function that operates on sets can assume that they hold when it first sees them, and should ensure that they hold when it is finished with them. The purpose of the ordering property will become clear when we implement *unite*( ).

To keep the illustration simple, Program 5.1 implements sets of integers; the same principles apply to sets drawn from some other ordered universe. Program 5.1a shows the relevant structure definitions: an `element` is a node in the linked-list representation, and a `set` points to an `element` that is the first node of a linked list that stores a set.

Printing Set Contents

We begin with Program 5.1b, a diagnostic function that prints the contents of any set by walking down its list. This operation is not mentioned in Figure 5.6: apparently the application does not require it. It is, however, a good example of the *scaffolding* that often proves helpful during the construction of a program. We can use `dumpset ()` to take

```
typedef struct element element;
struct element {
    element *next;
    int value;
};
typedef element *set;
```

PROGRAM 5.1a

Structure definitions for sets stored as ordered linked lists.

```
void dumpset(set s)
{
    while (s) {
        printf("%d ", s->value);
        s = s->next;
    }
    printf("\n");
}
```

PROGRAM 5.1b

A function to print out the contents of a set.

snapshots of the data structure as we build and debug the program. The act of writing the scaffolding reassures us that we understand how the data structure will look, and it is sure to prove useful as we continue our work.

Testing for the Empty Set

In this representation, a set is empty if and only if its pointer is null. The *empty( )* operation is so simple we can write it as a macro:

```
#define empty(s) (s == NULL)
```

Although it is common to write a one-line function as a macro, as shown here, you certainly may write *empty( )* as a function if you prefer.

Searching

When we begin to write member(s, n), it is tempting to draft a simple loop that walks down the list starting at s looking for n:

> *while (s→value < n)*
>   *s = s→next*

(We can use the inequality shown in the *while*-test because of the invariant ordering property of the data structure.) This might be acceptable as an informal expression of a member-finding algorithm, whose execution assumes some intelligence on the part of the human reader. But it will fail badly if translated directly into C. First, if *s* is empty, the test in the loop immediately dereferences the null pointer. Second, even if *s* is not empty, when *n* is larger than any element in the set, this loop blithely walks off the end of the list, again dereferencing the null pointer. The loop test must check that *s* is not null before dereferencing it to find *s→value*. In Program 5.1c, notice the care we take not to dereference the null pointer in either the while-condition or the computation of the return value.

Inserting a New Element

When we write insert(s, n), we must decide first what the type of its arguments will be. While it is natural to make the list head of type set, there are two obvious possibilities for the type of the thing to be inserted: element * and int. If we choose element *, then insert() can simply find the proper place at which to link the new node into the list. This is a good choice when the elements of sets are already stored in structures that have room for the necessary pointers, but it would be inconvenient for our problem. Every call to insert()

```
boolean member(set s, int n)
{
    while (s && s->value < n)
        /* ASSERT:  n has not been seen yet */
        s = s->next;
    return s && s->value == n;
}
```

PROGRAM 5.1c

A function to test whether an item belongs to a set.

```
element *makeelement(int n)
{
    element *p;
    p = (element *) malloc(sizeof(element));
    demand(p, malloc failed in makeelement);
    p->value = n;
    return p;
}
```

PROGRAM 5.1d

A function to create space for an item of a set.

would have to be preceded by some code to create a node containing the new integer; this would be inconvenient, and the effort would be wasted if the new element were already present in the set. On the other hand, if we let the new thing be of type int, we impose upon insert() the job of allocating a node for it. In either case, we shall need the auxiliary function shown in Program 5.1d to create an element that contains a particular integer.

We shall write insert(s, n) to accept a pointer to the list head, s, and an integer n. We know from Section 5.1 that once we have the appropriate pointer we can link the new node containing n into the list headed by s in constant time. So let us consider how we might find where n belongs. We could try to use the same loop for this job as member(s, n) does to find n:

$$while\ (s\ \&\&\ s{\rightarrow}value\ <\ n)$$
$$s\ =\ s{\rightarrow}next$$

But this loop leaves s pointing to the element before which n should be inserted (or NULL if n is larger than any element of the list); it moves one node too far.

The following loop leaves s pointing at the element after which we should insert n:

$$while\ (s\ \&\&\ s{\rightarrow}next\ \&\&\ s{\rightarrow}next{\rightarrow}value\ <\ n)$$
$$s\ =\ s{\rightarrow}next$$

It works unless n belongs before the first element in the set, which we could handle as a special case. Algorithm 5.5 shows a common insertion method that uses a second pointer following behind the first. If the trailing pointer is null after the while-loop, then the new element

```
s = listhead
sp = NULL
while (s && s→value < n)
        sp = s
        s = s→next
if sp ≠ NULL/* insert new after s */
        new→next = s
        sp→next = new
else /* new becomes first element */
        new→next = s
        listhead = new
```

ALGORITHM 5.5

An element insertion algorithm that uses a trailing pointer *sp* that follows along the list one item behind *s*.

---

becomes the new head of the list; otherwise, the new element is inserted immediately after the node to which the trailing pointer points.

If we could be sure that there was always a node in the list that should precede any possible element of the set, we could avoid writing special code to handle the insertion of elements at the beginning of a set. Figure 5.7 illustrates a special element, *dummy*, that precedes the actual list head of the set. Once we make *p* point to *dummy*, we can walk down the list with the following loop:

```
while (p→next && p→next→value < n)
        p = p→next
```

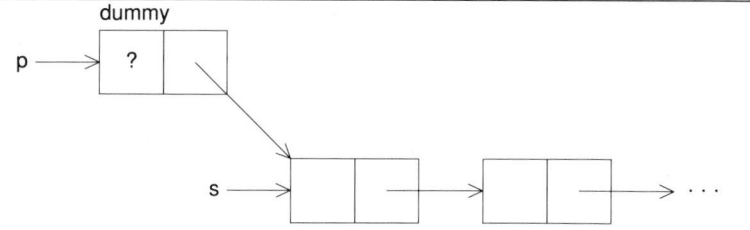

FIGURE 5.7

Illustration of another approach to element insertion. The '?' in the `info` member of `dummy` means that the contents of that member are garbage.

```
set insert(set s, int n)
{
    element dummy, *p, *new;
    p = &dummy;
    p->next = s;
    while (p->next && p->next->value < n)
        p = p->next;
    demand(p, impossible p);
    if (!(p->next && p->next->value == n)) {
        /* n is not present, so insert it */
        new = makeelement(n);
        new->next = p->next;
        p->next = new;
    }
    return dummy.next;
}
```

PROGRAM 5.1e

A function to insert an element into an ordered linked list.

Let us see how this solution fares in the face of the troublesome boundary cases above.

- If s points to an empty list, then $p \rightarrow next$ is null, so p points to the dummy element after the *while*-loop finishes executing.

- If the new element belongs before the first element in the list, then at the end of the loop, p points to the dummy element.

- If the new element belongs after the last element of the list, p is left pointing at that last element.

In all cases, p points to the node after which *new* should be inserted, and the correct head of the list after insertion is $dummy \rightarrow next$.

Program 5.1e shows function insert(), which is written to preserve the data structure invariant that forbids duplicate elements in sets. The correct way to call insert() is:

```
s = insert(s, n);
```

because the function can change the value of the list head.

```
set unite(set s₁, set s₂)
    set s₃ = NULL
    while (s₁ ≠ NULL)
        s₃ = insert(s₃,s₁→value)
        s₁ = s₁→next
    while (s₂ ≠ NULL)
        s₃ = insert(s₃,s₂→value)
        s₂ = s₂→next
    return s₃
```

ALGORITHM 5.6

Naive algorithm to form set union.

Forming the Union of Two Sets

Finally we come to `unite()`, which should exploit the ordering of the lists. A naive way to form the union would be to use `insert()` repeatedly on elements of both sets, as shown in Algorithm 5.6. This algorithm seems terrible because it takes no advantage of the data structure invariants. In fact, even if s_2 is empty, so that computing the union amounts to copying s_1 into s_3, Algorithm 5.6 uses $\Theta(n^2)$ time to do the job.

We can do much better than Algorithm 5.6 by using the ordering property of the linked lists. Program 5.1f shows how to create the union in a single pass down the two lists for the arguments and the list that represents the result; it traverses simultaneously the lists to which s_1 and s_2 point, copying the smaller of the values pointed to, and advancing the pointer that points to the smaller value. If we use $|s|$ to denote the number of elements in set s, we can say that Program 5.1f runs in $O(|s_1|+|s_2|)$ time.

Program 5.1f uses the same technique of creating a dummy element as Program 5.1e; this avoids making a special case of adding the first element to the list that represents the result. Program 5.1f also takes care to advance both pointers when both sets contain the same value, to avoid duplicating that element in the resulting set. Finally, Program 5.1f shows one way to make the code that finishes up the union operation apply no matter which set first runs out of elements. If you find it too confusing to have `s1` pointing to elements of the second set, you can declare another `set` variable that will point to the remainder of either set; it is well worth saving the effort of programming and debugging two `while`-loops that do the same job.

```
set unite(set s1, set s2)
{
    element dummy, *p;
    p = &dummy;
    while (s1 && s2) {
        if (s1->value < s2->value) {
            p->next = makeelement(s1->value);
            s1 = s1->next;
        } else if (s2->value < s1->value) {
            p->next = makeelement(s2->value);
            s2 = s2->next;
        } else { /* handle duplicate elements */
            p->next = makeelement(s1->value);
            s1 = s1->next;
            s2 = s2->next;
        }
        p = p->next;
    }
    /* copy remainder of one set */
    if (!s1)
        s1 = s2;
    while (s1) {
        p->next = makeelement(s1->value);
        p = p->next;
        s1 = s1->next;
    }
    return dummy.next;
}
```

PROGRAM 5.1f

Linear-time algorithm to form the union of two sets stored as ordered linked lists.

Testing

Now that we have implemented the basic functions on our data structure for sets, we shall build some more scaffolding to make sure that they work correctly. (An even better idea would be to test each function after writing it and before going on to the next.) Function test() in Program 5.1g lets us issue commands that test the functions in a variety of situations. Input to the function is a sequence of lines that contain a character that tells which function to test and any operands that function requires; an unrecognized character is a signal to stop testing. Program 5.1g echoes the input lines to make it easy to

```
void test(void)
{
    element *s[10];
    char cmd;
    long i, n, op[3];
    while (EOF != (n = scanf("%c %d %d %d\n",
            &cmd, &op[0], &op[1], &op[2])))  {
        printf("   command: %c ", cmd);   /* echo command */
        for (i = 1; i < n; i++)
            printf("%d ", op[i-1]);
        printf("\n");
        switch(cmd) {
        default:
            return;
        case 'e':
            printf("set %d is%s empty\n",
                op[0], empty(s[op[0]])?" ":" not");
            break;
        case 'm':
            printf("%d is%s in set %d\n",
                op[1], member(s[op[0]],op[1])?
                    " ":" not", op[0]);
            break;
        case 'i':
            s[op[0]] = insert(s[op[0]], op[1]);
            break;
        case 'u':
            s[op[2]] = unite(s[op[0]], s[op[1]]);
            break;
        case 'd':
            printf("set %d: "); dumpset(s[op[0]]);
            break;
        }
    }
}
```

PROGRAM 5.1g

A function that permits user-directed testing of the functions in Programs 5.1a through 5.1f.

interpret the output; we might want to disable this if we used test()
interactively. Since test() is designed purely for our testing purposes, it does not check that the required operands are present and
have reasonable values.

```
   command: e 1
set 1 is   empty
   command: d 1
set 1:
   command: i 1 2
   command: i 1 8
   command: i 1 4
   command: d 1
set 1: 2 4 8
   command: e 1
set 1 is not empty
   command: m 1 6
6 is not in set 1
   command: m 1 4
4 is   in set 1
   command: i 1 6
   command: i 1 8
   command: d 1
set 1: 2 4 6 8
   command: i 2 3
   command: i 2 9
   command: i 2 1
   command: i 2 7
   command: i 2 5
   command: u 1 2 3
   command: d 3
set 3: 1 2 3 4 5 6 7 8 9
   command: u 1 3 4
   command: d 4
set 4: 1 2 3 4 5 6 7 8 9
   command: q
```

FIGURE 5.8

Output from one run of the testing function in Program 5.1g.

Figure 5.8 contains some output from a small set of test commands. The commands shown exercise the difficult cases for insert(). Thus, we make sure that elements are inserted correctly at the head, middle, and tail of a list, and that duplicate elements are not inserted into a list. We check union() by forming the union of sets 1 and 2 in set 3, then verify that it works even when one set is a subset of the other by forming the union of sets 1 and 3 in set 4. Of course, we also check that empty() and member() work correctly.

5.3
MISCELLANEOUS TOOLS FOR LINKED STRUCTURES

In this section we shall see several techniques that can be useful in programs that use linked lists. Each of them is a simple idea, and each can be applied separately or in conjunction with the others.

Header Nodes

When our access to a linked list is through a pointer to its first node, an insertion can force us to change this access pointer. We can avoid the need for this change if we set up the list with a distinguished first node that never changes, which is often called a *header*.

A simple kind of header node has the same structure as other nodes on the list. Usually, we treat the data in the header node (other than the *next* pointer, which points to the first "real" node on the list) as garbage. In effect, the first node on such a list is like a permanent node *dummy* in Figure 5.7. Of course, functions that operate on the list must not treat the garbage in the header as valid data.

Occasionally there is a natural interpretation for data members in a header node. For example, suppose we use linked lists to store polynomials $\sum_{i=0}^{n} c_i x^i$, where each node contains a nonzero coefficient c_i, and the nodes appear in increasing order of exponent, as shown in Figure 5.9. If we wanted the representation of a polynomial to contain a header node, we could insist that the first node in the list contain the constant term, c_0, whether or not it is zero. If we add a term to a polynomial represented this way, we can be sure that the pointer to the header will not need to change, although the data in the header might be altered.

A header can also have a structure different from that of the nodes in the list. Such a header is a convenient place to store auxiliary information about the list, such as the number of items it contains, and can also be useful to store several pointers to different parts of a list. For

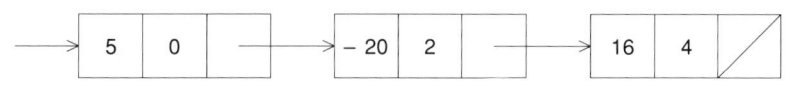

FIGURE 5.9

Representation of the polynomial expression $16x^4 - 20x^2 + 5$ as an ordered linked list whose header contains the constant coefficient.

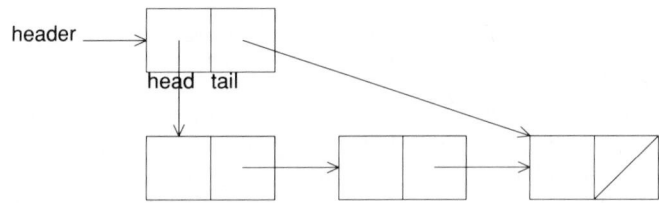

FIGURE 5.10

Use of a header node to store the *head* and *tail* pointers of a queue stored as a singly linked list.

---

example, when a queue is represented in a singly linked list as in Figure 4.7, functions that operate on the queue must have access to both pointers. Rather than pass both queue pointers explicitly to such functions, we can store them in a header node, and pass queue functions a pointer to the header node. (See Figure 5.10.)

Sentinels

Sentinels are like header nodes that sit at the end of a linked list. A sentinel contains some data that will cause us to stop as soon as we see it during a walk down the list. Two examples of sentinels should make the idea clear.

Suppose that we were storing numbers in increasing order in a linked list. In Section 5.2, as we walked down a list searching for the place at which to insert an element, we had to be sure not to go off the end:

> *while* ($p{\rightarrow}next$ && $p{\rightarrow}next{\rightarrow}value$ < n)
> p = $p{\rightarrow}next$

But if we knew that the last node in the list contained the value $+\infty$, as in Figure 5.11, then we could dispense with the first test in the *while*-condition:

> /* *assuming end sentinel containing* $+\infty$ */
> *while* ($p{\rightarrow}next{\rightarrow}value$ < n)
> p = $p{\rightarrow}next$

If there is an obvious value that can be used to simulate $+\infty$, sentinels like this can be very useful. If a list contains alphabetic strings, for example, a string of non-alphabetic characters that is lexicographi-

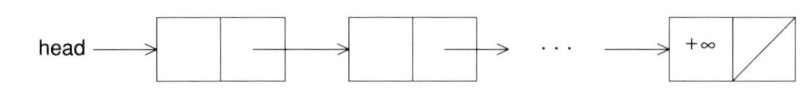

FIGURE 5.11

This ordered linked list contains a sentinel value in its last node.

cally larger than any possible alphabetic string could serve as $+\infty$. On the other hand, if a list contains numbers and we pick a large number *BIG* to serve as a sentinel value, it may be hard later to find an error caused by trying to find or store a number greater than *BIG* in the list.

Our second example of sentinels can be used even on an *unordered* linked list if we have ready access to the end of the list (perhaps by maintaining a pointer to the last node). The standard algorithm to insert an element must check to avoid running off the end of the list:

> *while* ($p{\rightarrow}next$ && $p{\rightarrow}next{\rightarrow}value \neq n$)
> $p = p{\rightarrow}next$

But if we place the element to be inserted in a sentinel node at the end of the list, we can guarantee that the second test in the *while*-condition will fail before $p{\rightarrow}next$ becomes *NULL*, so we can omit the first test altogether:

> /* *assuming last element in list is n* */
> *while* ($p{\rightarrow}next{\rightarrow}value \neq n$)
> $p = p{\rightarrow}next$

If n is already present in the list, notice that after this operation the list will contain two copies of it, as illustrated in Figure 5.12. Other code that deals with this list must be careful not to treat the value in the sentinel node as part of the list.

Circular Lists

Singly linked lists whose tail nodes point to their heads, as in Figure 5.13, are said to be *circularly linked*. Circularly linked lists, or *circular lists*, are useful in many applications, and programming with them shares most features of working with regular singly linked lists.

One major difference in programming with circular lists, however, arises in connection with their traversal. The algorithm for walking down a singly linked list

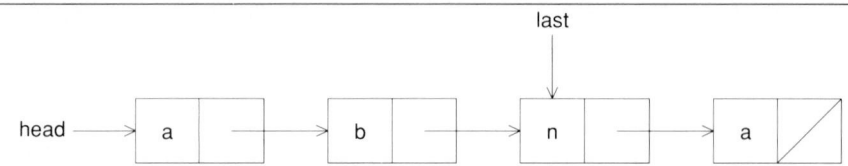

FIGURE 5.12

A linked list with a final sentinel node. Note that the sentinel could contain a value that duplicates an element in the list. The contents of the sentinel should be depicted as garbage except during a search.

$p\ =\ head$
$while\ p\ \neq\ NULL$
$\quad process\ p$
$\quad\quad p\ =\ p{\rightarrow}next$

will loop forever on a circular list.

If we know that the list is not empty, then the following algorithm correctly traverses the circular list to which p points:

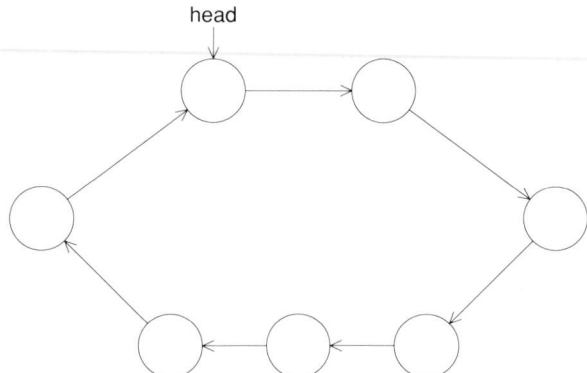

FIGURE 5.13

A circularly linked list. The drawing omits the explicit "box" that contains the pointer in each node; of course, the actual node template must still have room for that pointer.

```
op = p = head    /* op is original p */
do {
      process p
      p = p→next
} while (p ≠ op)
```

Coping with an empty circular list requires more work. Sometimes the nature of the application guarantees that empty circular lists never occur. We can also avoid the problem by using header nodes.

Some applications naturally call for a circular list. For example, the boundary of a polygon is a closed loop: it has no obvious starting point. Thus, a circular list of the vertices of a polygon is a natural way to store its boundary.

If we have a pointer to any node in a circular list, then we can reach all other elements on the list. This stands in contrast to regular linked lists: if we want to pass to a function both a particular node and the list on which it resides, we must pass two pointers as parameters to the function.

Doubly Linked Lists

Each node in a *doubly linked list* points to both its successor and its predecessor, as shown in Figure 5.14. Because both of a node's neighbors can be reached in constant time from the node, it is possible to insert a new node before or after a given node in a doubly linked list in constant time; it is also possible to delete a node from a doubly linked list in constant time given a pointer to the doomed node itself.

These appealing properties of doubly linked lists are balanced by two drawbacks. Obviously, they use twice as many pointers as singly linked lists. Another difficulty is less obvious until one programs doubly linked lists: each node contains two pointers that need to be maintained consistently, so there are twice as many chances to set pointers incorrectly. To alleviate this second problem, it is a good idea for some function to check that the pointers of adjacent nodes are consistent.

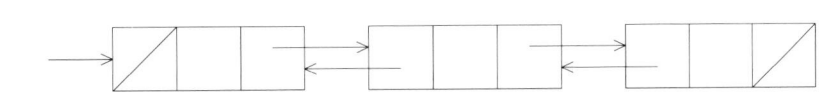

FIGURE 5.14

Doubly linked list.

To construct a doubly linked list we need to add space for another pointer to the definitions of the node structures. It is common to call this member *prev*, so that for a node *p*, $p \rightarrow next$ points to *p*'s successor and $p \rightarrow prev$ points to *p*'s predecessor. This is fine so long as the list has a "preferred direction" in which it will be traversed. If we need to traverse a doubly linked list in both directions, however, the *prev/next* scheme forces us to write two versions of traversal code, one for following *next* pointers, and one for following *prev* pointers.

Although this duplication of code might not seem onerous, especially for simple tasks like inserting elements, it soon becomes tedious to write (and debug!) twice what is essentially the same code. We can avoid this code duplication by changing the `struct` declaration to use an array `link` of two pointers, as illustrated in Program 5.2. Function `traverse()` in Program 5.2 can be used to visit the list contents in either direction from p. It accepts a parameter `process`, which points to a function that performs the appropriate action at each node during the traversal. On the way it uses a `demand()` to check that the double links are consistent.

```
typedef struct node node;
struct node {
    node *link[2];
    int value;
};

void traverse(node *p, int dir, int (*process)(node *))
{
    demand(dir == 0 || dir == 1, bad direction in traverse);
    while (p) {
        (*process)(p);
        demand(!p->link[dir] ||
            p->link[dir]->link[1-dir] == p, \
            inconsistent links);
        p = p->link[dir];
    }
}
```

PROGRAM 5.2

Portions of a program to dump a doubly linked list of integers in either direction from the given pointer.

Summary

Adding headers, sentinels, and circular linking to regular linked lists can help to make programs shorter and to reduce the need to cope with special cases. None of these three techniques changes the asymptotic running time of any list operations we have considered. On the other hand, making a list doubly linked makes it possible to perform many more rearrangement operations in constant time, an improvement over singly linked lists, at the price of somewhat more complicated code to handle the increased number of pointers.

There is a variety of techniques for programming with linked lists. Each method is useful in its own right, and they can be combined in many ways. A circularly doubly linked list with sentinel values in the header node might be considered to be the top of the line. But if we need only a few of the available features, we can often make do with a less ornate data structure that is easier to program and debug.

5.4
MULTIPLY LINKED STRUCTURES

Linked lists appear in many guises besides those of the preceding sections. They are useful whenever we know no reasonable upper bound on the size of something we shall need to store, and also when we might need to make frequent changes to the order in which things are stored.

In many applications, nodes have several pointers that link them into different list structures. The resulting structures are often called *multiply linked lists*, *multilinked lists*, or *multilists*. Figure 5.15 depicts two linked lists, one of students and one of classes. It also shows a list for one student that represents the classes in which that student is enrolled. Each student could have such a list, and indeed each class could have a similar list of students. Evidently, it quickly becomes difficult to draw a complete pointer diagram for such multiply linked structures.

One useful variant of multilists appears frequently in operations on matrices. Suppose we needed to store a matrix with 10,000 rows and 10,000 columns. Since such a matrix has 10^{10} elements, it would be impractical on almost any computer to try to represent the matrix as a familiar two-dimensional array. Suppose, however, that we also know that the matrix only has around 30,000 non-zero elements. Then we can represent the matrix using 20,000 linked lists, half of which represent the rows, while the other half represents the columns. This method saves more than space: it also saves the time a program would

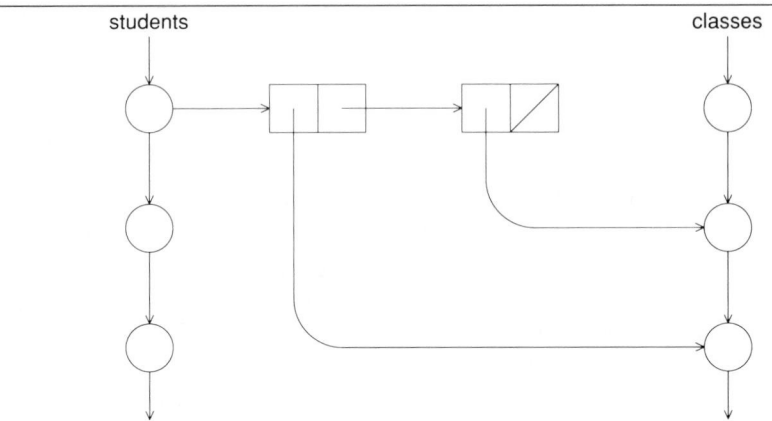

FIGURE 5.15

A simple multilinked structure.

otherwise have to spend skipping over long stretches of zero entries. The illustration of a 4×3 matrix in Figure 5.16 suggests how we might set up pointers for its linked representation. For such a small example, of course, the savings in space over a two-dimensional array is unimpressive.

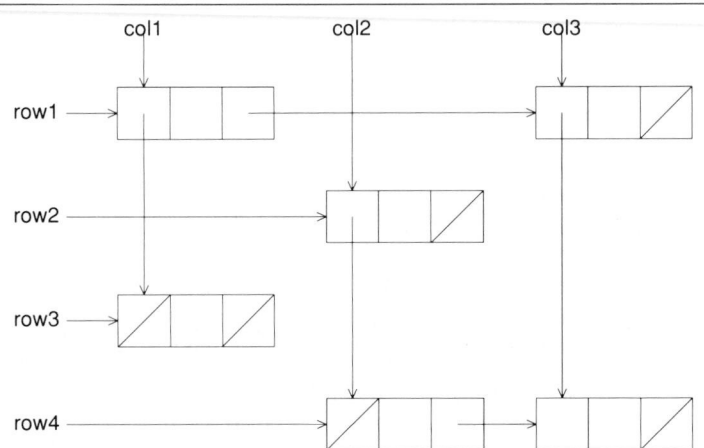

FIGURE 5.16

A pointer-based representation of a two-dimensional matrix.

5.5

SUMMARY AND PERSPECTIVE

The simple idea of structures that contain pointers to other structures has profound implications for the ways we can structure data in programs. Once this idea becomes familiar, it is almost second nature to draw diagrams to illustrate the pointer relationships that hold a data structure together. In fact, drawing the pictures often proves to be easy compared to the effort of correct implementation that copes correctly with all boundary cases.

"Linked list" includes a variety of both straightforward and elaborate data structures. The basic ideas for searching and rearranging lists are simple, but we often commit subtle errors when we turn them into programs, especially when the null pointer is a possible but forgotten value. Careful thought about processing the boundary elements—usually the first and last elements—of a list can lead to much simpler programs with many fewer cases to consider.

It is usually wise in the early stages of writing programs to write scaffolding functions, such as those that print the contents of a data structure. Such functions are invaluable aids to debugging; programmers who do not write such functions early in program development often find later that they wish they had done so. Sometimes we can even discover inconsistencies in our idea for the data structure (like using one pointer for two different things) when we try to implement the scaffolding.

Assertions about the expected state of the data structures at various points in programs can also help in avoiding errors. It should come as no surprise that finding the correct assertion is often more than half the battle: it is easy to choose an incorrect assertion that fails even though the program is correct, or one that is true even though the program is doomed.

In the end, there is no single right way to build pointer-based programs. Practice can give us greater confidence and familiarity with writing programs that use pointers. It is a good idea to reflect now and then on what techniques or idioms recur in programs; these are likely to be useful in the quest for consistent, correct pointers.

EXERCISES

1 Suppose you had a list stored in an array, and you were implementing a search function that would return the index of the sought item in the array. What should your function return if the search were unsuccessful?

2 What is the complexity of the functions in Program 5.1?

3 Revise member () to return a pointer to the sought item if it is found.

4 Implement a version of insert () that expects the new item to be packaged in a structure of the appropriate type.

5 Implement function insert () of Program 5.1e so that the following function header is valid:

```
void insert(set *s, int n)
```

What difference does this make in how one calls insert ()?

6 Express the complexity of the version of *unite*( ) given in Algorithm 5.6 in terms of $|s_1|$ and $|s_2|$ for any s_1 and s_2.

7 The version of unite () in Program 5.1f leaves its two argument sets intact. Write a version of unite () under the assumption that it may destroy either or both argument sets.

8 Define the set operations *delete*( ) and *intersect*( ) and implement corresponding C functions that fit into Program 5.1.

9 Discuss the merits of and problems with implementing a C function find_before(s, n) that returns a pointer to the element in s that precedes the smallest element greater than or equal to n.

10 Complete this table of the worst-case time complexity of various operations on various data structures for sequences, assuming that n items are in the sequence:

Operation	Array	Singly Linked List	Doubly Linked List
Empty?			
Find	$O(n)$		
Insert after		$O(1)$	
Insert before			$O(1)$
Delete		$O(n)$	

11 Write a function that reverses the order in which the nodes appear on a singly linked list.

12 Write a function to insert a node into a linked list that contains a sentinel node.

13 Write a function that can traverse a circularly doubly linked list in either direction.

14 Write a function that could serve as the argument process to Program 5.2. (A simple possibility is a function to print the contents of the node.)

15 An application uses ordered linked lists to represent the contents of a coin drawer. Each node in a list represents a certain number of coins of some denomination, and the nodes are ordered by increas-

ing value of denomination. Write a function that coalesces together all of the "penny" nodes, all of the "nickel" nodes, and so on.

16 The following problem arises in the implementation of an algorithm. (K. Hoffman, K. Mehlhorn, P. Rosenstiehl, and R. E. Tarjan, "Sorting Jordan sequences in linear time using level-linked search trees," *Information and Control* 68 (1986), 170–184.) Real numbers are stored in increasing order on a doubly linked list. Whenever we need to insert a number, we are also given a pointer to a node. Usually, that node should be one of the neighbors of the new item; occasionally, however, the pointer is off by one node, so that one of *its* neighbors should be neighbor to the new item. Write a three-statement algorithm to insert the new item into its correct place.

17 Using the ordered list representation to represent polynomials as suggested in Section 5.3, write functions to add, multiply, and evaluate polynomials.

18 Write a package of string functions in which strings are represented as linked lists.

19 What information must be stored in the nodes of Figure 5.16?

REFERENCES

Linked lists are treated in Chapter 2 of
D. E. Knuth. *Fundamental Algorithms*. Vol. 1, *The Art of Computer Programming*. 2d ed. Reading, Mass.: Addison-Wesley, 1973.

6

Memory Organization

Pointers and dynamic storage allocation unsettle many people who are comfortable with elementary programming. When they write programs that use linked data structures, they worry uneasily, wondering "what's *really* going on?" To answer this question completely, we would need to know the language in which the program was written, which compiler and operating system were being used, and what hardware the program was running on. We can, however, give an incomplete answer whose outlines apply to most programming environments.

We shall use C programs to illustrate various aspects of memory organization during our discussion. The same principles that govern how a program's storage is organized hold for other languages, although the flexibility with which programmers can manipulate memory varies considerably.

6.1
MORE ABOUT MEMORY

Chapter 3 described memory as an array of character-sized cells. Most computers organize memory further into an array of *words*, each of which contains the same number of cells, or *bytes*. In our examples we shall assume that each word contains four bytes, as depicted by Figure 6.1. The memory in Figure 6.1 is also an array of bytes, and we can continue to think of it this way. However, its structure as an array of words affects how pointers and variables are stored.

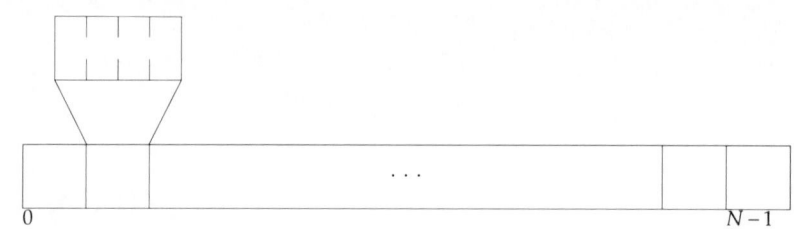

FIGURE 6.1

Memory as an array of words, with one word expanded to show the individual bytes. The number of words (*N*) is typically a power of two.

Addresses

Every byte in memory has an address. The form of this address depends on the particular computer. On a *byte-addressable* computer, each byte has an address, and the address of a word is the address of one of the bytes in the word. Whichever byte gives its address to the word that contains it (highest or lowest address are two popular choices), all word addresses on a byte-addressable computer are congruent modulo the number of bytes in a word.

On a *word-addressable* machine, the words are numbered from zero, as shown in Figure 6.2. Thus, each word has an address. To give the address of a byte, however, we must give both the address of the word to which it belongs and an *offset* that tells which byte of the word we mean. In contrast to byte-addressable computers, pointers on word-addressable computers are of different sizes. If an int fits into a word, for example, than a pointer to an int is a word address, but a pointer to a char must be a byte address.

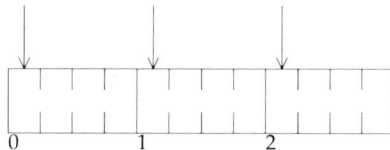

FIGURE 6.2

The arrows depict the natural pointers on a word-addressable machine. A pointer to an individual byte must be expressed as the address of the word to which it belongs, together with an offset.

Alignment Requirements

With the word structure of memory may come restrictions on how values are stored. A typical example of such a condition, which we shall adopt as part of our examples, is that an integer must reside within a word. Thus, we cannot store an int in just any four contiguous bytes: the four bytes must lie in a single word. This is an example of an *alignment requirement*, which tells how values of various types must be aligned with respect to word boundaries in memory.

Alignment requirements imply that the address of any piece of dynamically allocated memory space must be able to serve as the address of any kind of variable. For example, since every int must lie in a word, the address of every dynamically allocated piece of memory will be the address of a word. Alignment requirements are particularly important to structures: a structure must start at a properly aligned address, and every member of a structure must be correctly aligned in memory as well. When this requirement meets the C rule that structure members are stored in memory in the order in which they are declared in the structure template, the result can be a structure with a lot of unused space.

For example, the following two structures occupy different amounts of space, even though they contain the same information:

```
struct {
    char c1, c2;
    int n;
} s;
struct {
    char c1;
    int n;
    char c2;
} t;
```

Structure s fits into two words; the first word contains c1 and c2 (and two unused bytes), and the second contains n. On the other hand, structure t must occupy three words; the first word contains c1 and three unused bytes, the second contains n, and the third contains c2 and three unused bytes.

The memory of every C program obeys the rule that if the first items in two structures are of the same number and type, then the items will reside in memory in the same format in both structures. This rule can be useful when we need to construct linked lists of different kinds of nodes. For example, the structures shown in Figure 6.3 could be used to create a linked list of circles and rectangles. Given a pointer to a node, its next member points to the next figure on the

```
typedef void figure;

typedef struct circle {
    figure *next;
    int kind;
    point center;
    double radius;
} circle;

typedef struct rectangle {
    figure *next;
    int kind;
    point sw, ne;
} rectangle;
```

FIGURE 6.3

Both structure templates in these declarations begin with the same types of members in the same order: `figure *`, `int`, and one `point`. Structures of these types could be linked through their `next` members into a single linked list of `figure`s.

list, and its kind member tells which kind of figure it represents. Thus, we can traverse the list by following next pointers, and use kind members to find out when we reach each node what kind of figure it contains.

Unions

All of the variables we have seen so far, including those of user-defined types, can store only one kind of value. When we need to store different types of values in a single variable, C's *union* data type can be useful.

The declaration

```
union u {
    char c[4];
    int n;
    float x;
} uvar;
```

defines a variable uvar that can contain either an array of four chars, or a single int, or a single float. Access to the members of a union uses the same notation as access to the members of a structure:

```
struct circdata {
    point center;
    double radius;
};

struct rectdata {
    point sw, ne;
};

typedef struct figure figure;
struct figure {
    figure *next;
    int kind;
    union fig {
        struct circdata circle;
        struct rectdata rectangle;
    } fig;
};
```

FIGURE 6.4

Declaration of a structure in which we can store either a circle or a rectangle.

uval.n is an int, while uval.x is a float. Since uvar is a single variable, however, only one of its members can contain its value at any single time. If we store an int in uval.n and then refer to uval.x or uval.c[2], the result is undefined. A union occupies as much memory as is needed to store a value of the largest possible type that it could contain.

Figure 6.4 shows how we could use unions to build a linked list of circles and rectangles. Unfortunately, using unions introduces an additional level of hierarchy into our data structure: given a pointer p to a figure whose kind was circle, we would have to write p->fig.circle.radius to access its radius.

6.2
VARIABLES AND THE RUNTIME STACK

Figure 6.5 shows a common way to organize a program's memory or *address space*. Static and external variables, which exist for the entire lifetime of the program, reside in a region of high addresses. Each time a function is called, a *frame* or *activation record* is created that con-

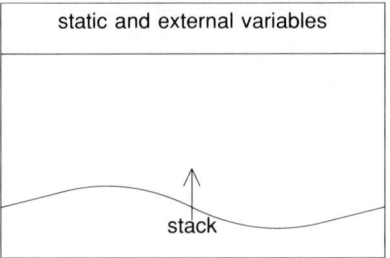

FIGURE 6.5

A common memory organization: static and external variables are stored in a region with high addresses, while stack frames grow from low addresses. Since functions have different numbers and types of arguments, the frames on the stack are likely to be of different lengths.

tains room for the function's automatic variables. The frames form a *runtime stack* that grows from the low addresses in memory.

To illustrate the operation of the runtime stack, consider the operation of Program 2.1 when it computes 1.1^5. Each invocation of power2() creates a fresh frame on the stack, complete with its own set of automatic variables (n, x, and y) local to power2(). Figure 6.6 shows the state of the stack at the beginning of the third recursive call to power2().

Memory that is dynamically allocated comes from the empty space between the static and external variables and the runtime stack. It is usually organized in a *heap* that starts somewhere outside the clump of global variables and grows toward the stack, as shown in Figure 6.7.

```
power2():   x = 1.1; n = 1; y = ?
power2():   x = 1.1; n = 2; y = ?
power2():   x = 1.1; n = 5; y = ?
main():     i = 5; constant = 1.1; result = 1.4641
```

FIGURE 6.6

Partial contents of the stack of Program 2.1 at the beginning of the third recursive call to power2() during the computation of 1.1^5. The question marks indicate undefined values. The value of result in main() is 1.1^4. The stack also contains information about where in each function the frame above it was called; we need this information to know where to resume execution when that frame is popped from the stack.

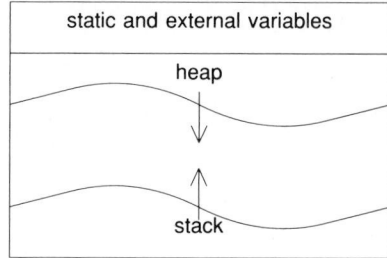

FIGURE 6.7

The memory organization of Figure 6.5, updated to show the heap of dynamically allocated nodes growing down toward the runtime stack.

A program can run correctly as long as the top of its stack lies below the bottom of its heap. When the top of the stack and the bottom of the heap threaten to cross, however, either because the runtime stack is growing or more dynamically allocated storage has been requested, the program has exceeded its memory requirements, and execution must stop immediately.

Initialization of Memory in C

The declaration of any variable can include a value to which it should be set at the start of its existence. For example, getmonarchs() in Program 3.14 declares and sets i and maxmon. Default rules apply to variables that are not initialized explicitly. At the beginning of program execution, static and external variables are assigned the value zero; for example, Program 1.4 assumes that numfind and numseen start with the value zero. On the other hand, the starting value of automatic variables is undefined. Figure 6.7 suggests the reason for this rule. The part of memory that contains static and external variables can be cleared once before the program executes, and need never be initialized again. But an automatic variable resides on the stack; before it receives a value explicitly, it contains garbage—pieces of some variable from a now-defunct stack frame.

Dynamically allocated storage can contain old values stored when they were allocated previously, or pointers used to maintain the heap of space that is available for dynamic allocation. Thus, the library function malloc() makes no guarantees about the contents of the space it returns. The alternative function calloc() is available if it is important that dynamically allocated space contain all zeros.

6.3

A SIMPLE HEAP MANAGEMENT SCHEME

The C library provides several functions to manage the heap. We saw malloc() used several times in Chapters 3 through 5 to allocate space from the heap. Its companion function free() *de-allocates*, or returns to the heap, space allocated by malloc(); this space is then available for future allocations. Our programs have never used free(). As we noted in Chapter 4, they can leave dynamically allocated nodes inaccessibly lost in space. If memory space were scarce, however, we could revise them to free space explicitly when appropriate.

In this section we shall see a simple scheme to implement malloc() and free(). Despite its limitations, many systems use a scheme much like this one.

When a program starts executing, its static and external variables occupy a fixed amount of space. Room for its runtime stack and any dynamically allocated storage must be obtained from the operating system. While the system takes care of growing the runtime stack, the program must manage its dynamically allocated storage, taking care to grow the heap space when necessary. We shall suppose that a system function *expand*( ) is available to grow the heap space; its argument tells how much more room we want, and it returns a pointer to a contiguous amount of memory of the requested size if possible, or a null pointer if the requested expansion is impossible.

In our data structure for the heap, all dynamically allocated nodes, whether occupied or vacant, are linked together on a circular list that is ordered by their memory address. Figure 6.8 shows a typical node. When the program calls malloc() to allocate space dynamically, malloc() returns a pointer to the first word of the *info* member; the program can store whatever it wants in that space. The first part of the node tells whether the node is occupied or vacant, and contains the pointer that links it into the circular list of nodes.

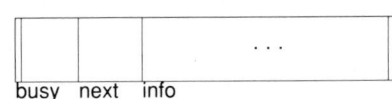

busy next info

FIGURE 6.8

A typical node in a simple heap management scheme. The busy member contains a boolean value that tells whether the node is occupied. Since the length of the info member is variable, we use double lines to indicate the node boundaries.

FIGURE 6.9

Dynamic memory arranged as a circular list of busy and free nodes. The slashed region represents a part of memory that the program may not use.

Figure 6.9 suggests some useful properties of this data structure. First, although the size of a node is not stored explicitly, it can be derived as the difference between the node's address and the address of the next node on the list. Second, if the pieces of memory returned by *expand( )* do not have contiguous addresses, then addresses not available to the program can be excluded from the heap by treating them as an occupied node. Finally, if two adjacent nodes on the list become vacant, the ordering of addresses makes it possible to *coalesce* them into a single larger node.

When we no longer need the space in some node, *free( )* can de-allocate it simply by setting its *busy* member to zero.

Access to the heap is through a single pointer, *rover*, which always points to the last node allocated or de-allocated. When space is requested, *rover* chases down the list in search of a sufficiently large vacant node, coalescing as it goes. As soon as *rover* points to a node with enough room, *malloc( )* chops off a piece of the appropriate size and marks it occupied, adds the remainder of the node to the heap as a free node, and finally returns *rover* as a pointer to the newly allocated space. If *rover* returns to where it started, then no node in the heap is big enough, so *malloc( )* calls *expand( )* with an appropriate argument, hooks the space returned into the heap, and returns *rover* pointing to an appropriate chunk of the new space.

Other Library Functions

The C library also provides functions `calloc()` and `realloc()` to manage the heap. Function `calloc()` is a variant of `malloc()` that returns space cleared to zero, as mentioned in Section 6.2.

Function `realloc()` accepts a pointer p to space allocated from the heap and a size n in bytes. Let *np* be the number of bytes in the node to which p points. As we saw in Program 3.14, the call `realloc(p, n)` returns a pointer to space on the heap whose first min(np, n) bytes are the same as the min(np, n) bytes starting at p; it may also de-allocate the node to which p points. A simple way to implement `realloc()` is to call `malloc(n)`, then copy $\min(np, n)$ bytes starting at p into the space returned by `malloc()`. If we know the details of the heap management scheme, however, we can implement a version of `realloc()` that is faster than this general scheme. If n < np, then `realloc()` can simply chop the appropriate amount off the end of the node to which p points, link it into the heap, and return the original value of p. If np < n, but enough unallocated space follows the node to which p points in the heap so that we can grow it in place to contain at least n bytes, then `realloc()` can do this and avoid copying any data.

Performance

The good news about this scheme for heap management is that a node can be de-allocated in constant time. The bad news is that the worst-case time required for allocation is dreadful. If every allocation requires a complete traversal of the list, followed by a call to *expand( )*, then it takes $\Theta(n^2)$ time to perform n allocations. If this happened in the programs of Chapter 4, for example, the time for memory management would swamp the time the programs spend manipulating stacks and queues. We would have to ask how appropriate it is that our model of computation counts a call to `malloc()` as a primitive step.

Obviously, we hope that our scheme will not often exhibit its worst-case behavior. Indeed, some of its features are intended to improve the algorithm's behavior over that of the obvious implementation. For example, *rover* is left pointing at the last node where something happened, while the obvious thing to do is to start searching from the highest node address each time. To see why *rover* roves like this, consider what would happen if we first allocated many tiny nodes, then began a spate of allocating and de-allocating larger nodes. If each search for space began at the same place in the list, then each allocation would have to traverse all of the tiny nodes before it reached the region where a larger node might be found; by leaving *rover* at the site of the last action, however, we hope to avoid examining any tiny nodes most of the time.

The above description is also vague about the "appropriate argument" to *expand( )* when the available dynamic memory must grow. The vagueness hints at the possibility of tuning the algorithm's performance. Instead of requesting just enough extra space to accommodate the user's request, the algorithm can obtain a larger chunk, most of which becomes part of the circular list available for future allocations. We can use statistics accumulated by the allocator to adjust the size of this chunk and so improve the performance of the algorithm.

Specialized Allocation

Any general heap management scheme can impose severe penalties on
the unwary user. When a profile of program execution reveals that
memory management takes more program time than any other computation, and the program's performance must be improved, we can take
some of the load from the general functions by writing our own functions to manage nodes that are allocated frequently. An easy way to
do this is to maintain a pile of free nodes; the function to allocate a
node calls malloc() only when the pile is empty; the function to free
a node adds the node to the pile.

Program 6.1 shows a way to reduce the number of calls to
malloc() much further than we can by using piles of malloc()ed
nodes. It stores free nodes on a stack whose top is *freelist. When
it needs more nodes, it calls malloc() to allocate an array of CHUNK
nodes, and carves the array into free nodes that it pushes onto the

```
node *freelist;

node *nodealloc(void)
{
    node *p;
    if (!freelist) {
        printf("calling malloc()\n");
        freelist = (node *) malloc(CHUNK*sizeof(node));
        demand(freelist, out of memory);
        for (p = freelist; p < freelist + CHUNK - 1; p++)
            p->next = p+1;
        p->next = NULL;
    }
    demand(freelist, empty free list);
    p = freelist;
    freelist = freelist->next;
    return p;
}

void nodefree(node *p)
{
    p->next = freelist;
    freelist = p;
}
```

PROGRAM 6.1

Functions to do private allocation for a popular kind of node.

stack. Using these functions, we can allocate a total of n nodes in only $\lceil n/\text{CHUNK} \rceil$ calls to malloc(); we save not only time but also some of the space malloc() uses to maintain its heap. Of course, it is very important that we use nodefree() to free nodes allocated by nodealloc(). The technique in Program 6.1 works for any value of CHUNK and any type of structure that has a member by which it can be hooked into a free list.

Programs 3.14 and 5.1d contain functions makemonarch() and makeelement(), whose only job is to allocate memory for structures and fill their members with information. Now we can see that these structure-building functions do more than keep our programs tidy. We write them first using malloc() as if it were an efficient general-purpose storage allocator. Later, if we discover that we need to use specialized algorithms to allocate some kinds of nodes, we can confine the details to the structure-building functions.

6.4
PHYSICAL MEMORY ORGANIZATION

A typical computer has two kinds of memory: *primary* and *secondary* storage. Primary storage can be read and written much faster than secondary storage, so the two kinds of memory are also called *fast* and *slow*. When a computer system is designed, and one must decide how much fast and how much slow memory to provide, the speed advantage of fast memory has to be balanced against its higher cost and the fact that it is usually *volatile*: when the power is turned off, its contents disappear, while the contents of slow memory will survive indefinitely.

Virtual Memory and Paging

A program's *working set* is the actual amount of memory it uses; think of it as the part of Figure 6.7 in which the program can store data. When a program's working set fits into fast storage, the nature of slow storage is largely irrelevant to the program's performance. If a program's working set is larger than available fast storage, however, then, while the operating system continues to support the illusion that memory is arranged in a single big array as shown in Figure 6.7, some of the working set is actually stored in slow memory. The program is said to use *virtual* memory, since its *physical* memory layout is quite different from a single homogeneous array of storage locations.

To manage virtual memory, the address space in Figure 6.7 is divided into *pages*, each of which contains a modest fraction of the whole space—typically between 512 bytes and 4 kilobytes. The program need store in physical memory only those pages that it actually uses. The aim of virtual memory management is to keep frequently referenced pages in fast memory, so that most memory references can be performed quickly. Since the popularity of any particular page can increase or decrease during the execution of a program, algorithms that manage virtual memory must move pages between primary and secondary storage. The terminology reflects the desirability of being in fast memory: a page in primary storage is said to be *paged in*, while a page in secondary storage is *paged out*; moving pages between the two states is called *paging*.

Several different paging rules are used to decide when to move a page between the two kinds of storage. These rules are based on predictions about which pages the program will need next. For example, one popular rule says that whenever a location on a page is referenced, the page should be paged in, and whenever a page must be paged out, the *least recently used (LRU)* of all pages should be banished to secondary storage. The idea that motivates the LRU paging rule is that a program can be expected to refer to several variables on a single page, which makes it worth bringing the entire page into fast memory, and that a page that has not been referenced in a while probably will not be referenced for a while longer.

Of course, any paging rule embodies only a guess about the actual sequence of memory references that the program will perform, and it is easy to imagine ways to make this guess fail miserably. For example, suppose we use the LRU paging rule, fast memory has room for 1024 pages, and the working set contains 1025 pages. A program that cycles through the pages and examines one variable on each page will cause one page-in operation and one page-out operation for each variable reference. Such a failure of any paging rule leads to *thrashing*, in which the program spends most of its time swapping pages between fast and slow memory, and gets little real work done.

In Chapter 2 we adopted a model of computation in which access to any variable takes constant time. The uncertainty introduced by paging suggests that this model may be unrealistic for a program that uses virtual memory. This oversimplification notwithstanding, we shall stick with the simple model, always remaining mindful of its limitations.

External Data Structures

If we suspect that a program's working set will be larger than available fast memory, and that we know enough about the application to do a

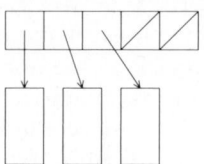

FIGURE 6.10

One possible organization for a file system. The top rectangle is a header node that points to pieces of the file.

better job of paging than the operating system, then we can use an *external data structure* that takes the physical organization of memory into account. Such data structures usually store in fast memory enough data to permit us to go directly to the relevant part of slow memory whenever necessary. To evaluate these data structures, we can revise our model of computation to reflect a large cost whenever a pointer to slow memory must be dereferenced.

File systems are a familiar example of an external data structure. A common arrangement divides all of secondary memory into pieces of modest size, some of which serve as header nodes from which pieces of the file can be reached, as shown in Figure 6.10. If the header nodes can be linked together, then no arbitrary limit on file size need be imposed.

6.5

SUMMARY AND PERSPECTIVE

Even the simplified picture of computer memory in this chapter is complicated. It seems to have layers built on layers, what with a storage allocator that carves memory into chunks of variable size, built on top of an operating system that makes different kinds of memory look like a long array of uniform cells. The reality for most computers is several times more complicated. A single computer may have several kinds of primary memory. In order from fast to slow, these are registers, caches, and core.

C programmers can prefix the declaration of a variable by the word `register` to indicate that the variable will be accessed so often that it should be stored in the fastest possible memory. This should be understood as a hint to the compiler; if a register is available, the compiler may store the variable in the register, but it may also ignore the hint entirely.

As simple as it is, our model of memory explains the serious consequences of such common programming errors as references to locations outside the bounds of any array and invalid operations indirect through pointers. A particularly insidious error is to dereference a *dangling pointer*, which points to a node that has been freed. After we call `free(p)`, p still points to a node on the free list. We may be able to read or write *p for a while, but we are almost sure to have trouble when the node is re-allocated. Because the effects of the error may not appear for some time after it occurs, such errors can be very hard to find.

A good algorithm for heap management would be very fast all the time and would use little memory space for its own bookkeeping. Unfortunately no such algorithm is known for the general problem of dynamic memory allocation, so we compromise and use simple algorithms, hoping that they will be fast enough. The general problem of heap management includes two more issues that were not mentioned in Section 6.3.

Garbage Collection

The heap allocation scheme in Section 6.3 assumes that memory that is no longer needed will be freed explicitly. This approach places the burden of using memory efficiently squarely on the programmer. In some systems, the heap management scheme includes facilities to reclaim storage for future allocation once it is no longer being used by the program. This operation is usually called *garbage collection*. There is no question that automatic garbage collection is convenient; unfortunately, it is hard to implement for C because there is no way to tell in general which memory words contain pointer values.

Compaction

Heap management schemes also face the problem of *fragmentation*. A sequence of allocations and de-allocations of nodes can leave the available space divided up into tiny regions, so that a request for a large region cannot be met even though there is enough unused space overall. For example, in Figure 6.11 no request for a node larger than two words can be honored, even though a total of six words is available.

The *compaction* operation is designed to alleviate the problem of fragmentation. The idea is to shove all nodes as far to one end of

FIGURE 6.11

In this picture of memory fragmentation, occupied nodes are marked with diagonal strokes.

memory as possible, leaving a large hunk of free space at the other end. Although the idea is simple, its execution is complicated by the fact that all pointers to nodes that move must be changed to reflect the compaction.

EXERCISES

1 Examine the values returned by sizeof on arguments of various types. Deduce what you can about the alignment requirements that cause this behavior.

2 Design an appropriate structure point for the declarations in Figures 6.3 and 6.4.

3 Figure 6.5 depicts only one possible arrangement of memory; a simple alternative would be to put the global variables under the stack. Write a program to determine what memory organization the program itself uses.

4 Functions scanf() and printf() accept a variable number of arguments. How can they do this?

5 Revise Programs 4.1 and 4.2 to free space when it is no longer needed.

6 Describe a situation in which it is impossible to re-allocate space using malloc() and free(), but realloc() can do the job.

7 We would like to store an $n \times n$ matrix that contains only $O(n)$ non-zero entries. If we allocate the matrix using calloc(), the allocation will take $\Theta(n^2)$ time just to clear the matrix entries. Show how to store the matrix without clearing the $n \times n$ space. (*Hint*: Use auxiliary pointer-based structures to indicate which matrix entries are valid and which contain garbage.)

8 Suggest some reasons why we might not want to use *expand*( ) in Section 6.3 as an allocator.

9 Modify Program 6.1 to store the arrays returned by malloc() in a linked list. If a program allocates n nodes, and then has no more need of nodes, show how to free all n nodes in $\lceil n/CHUNK \rceil$ calls to free(), rather than n calls to nodefree().

10 What are the time and space complexity of the following iterative algorithm to search a list?

void find(node *head, description d)
    while (head && head→item does not match d)
        head = head→next
    return head

11 What are the time and space complexity of the following recursive algorithm to search a list?

void traverse(node *head, description d)
    if (head && head→item does not match d)
        return traverse(head→next, d)
    return head

12 Invent a dynamic storage allocation scheme when all nodes are the same size. Is garbage collection any simpler for this case?

The memory allocator described in Section 6.3 uses the *first-fit* rule: it satisfies the request with the first space it finds. In the *best-fit* rule, the smallest node that accommodates the request is returned; the idea is to avoid chopping up a large space if a smaller space is available to be chopped instead.

13 How could we use the best-fit rule with the memory allocator discussed in Section 6.3? What effect would it have on the algorithm's time and space complexity?

In the *reference count* scheme for garbage collection, each node contains a value that tells how many pointers point to it. When a node's reference count becomes zero, the node is garbage and can be collected.

14 What kinds of data structure can escape being collected as garbage under a reference count scheme even though no node in the structure is reachable from a static, external, or automatic variable?

15 Implement a garbage collection scheme that uses reference counts. Does your solution require explicit statements to increment and decrement reference counts at every pointer change, or can you find a way that is easier on the programmer?

16 The *lazy* approach to garbage collection is to collect only in emergencies. Thus, when an allocation fails, we sweep through memory hoping to pick up and de-allocate enough garbage to permit the program to continue. This common approach has the serious practical flaw that it permits erroneous programs to consume vast amounts of memory before they are discovered. Suggest some

other times when it might be reasonable to perform garbage collection.

17 Is there any way to implement memory compaction if the types of variables and structure members are not available?

REFERENCES

The C standard contains several dicta about memory management in C programs. In "old C" programs, a pointer that can point to a variable of any type (such as the value returned by `malloc()`) is given the type `char *`. ANSI C uses `void *` for the type of such a generic pointer, whence the declaration of `figure` in Figure 6.3.

The LRU rule for paging is analyzed in

D. D. Sleator and R. E. Tarjan. "Amortized efficiency of list update and paging rules." *Communications of the ACM* 28 (1985): 202–208.

The following reference contains a hierarchical memory model that is intended to reflect the structure of memory more closely:

A. Aggarwal, B. Alpern, A. K. Chandra, and M. Snir. "A model for hierarchical memory." In *Proc. 19th Ann. Symposium on Theory of Computing.* (1987) 305–314.

Exercise 7 is from Chapter 2 of

A. V. Aho, J. E. Hopcroft, and J. D. Ullman. *The Design and Analysis of Computer Algorithms.* Reading, Mass.: Addison-Wesley, 1974.

Part II

Efficient Algorithms

7

Searching

One of the most common jobs we face in programming is to search a collection of information to find items that match a description. Indeed, in Sections 1.3 and 5.2 we solved two kinds of searching problem using a brute-force approach: examine the items one by one until we either find a matching item or determine that no such item is present. In this and the next two chapters we shall see several searching methods that can offer much better performance than this naive algorithm.

Section 7.1 is a general orientation to the variety of problems subsumed under the topic of *searching*. The remaining sections introduce some important ideas that appear in many solutions to searching problems. Even though some of the methods offer no better performance in the worst case than naive sequential search, they are interesting because they illustrate several different aspects of searching problems and their solution.

7.1
ASPECTS OF SEARCHING

In our previous discussions of searching, the goal has been to find items that "match some description." Now that searching is the focus of our interest, we shall adopt a more formal setting. The items are stored in a *dictionary* (sometimes called a *symbol table*). Each item in the dictionary has a *key*. The goal of searching is to retrieve items in the dictionary that have a particular key. Usually we think of the items as structures with a member that contains the search key, but our searching methods apply equally well when the items are simple scalars, or when the value of an item's key is a function of one or more structure members.

Henceforth we shall assume that search keys are *unique*, so that no two items in the dictionary have the same key. Thus a search operation can return either zero or one item. In fact most searching algorithms can be modified readily to cope with dictionaries that contain multiple items with the same key, and we adopt this restriction for the following technical reasons. When keys are not unique, the search operation must be able to return an arbitrary number of items, so the type of the result cannot be *item* or *item**, but must be *set of items* or *list of items*; moreover, any bound on the time complexity of such a search operation must include the number of items returned. In brief, permitting non-unique keys in the dictionary would introduce complications without adding much to our understanding of searching.

Static and Dynamic Dictionaries

Two common frameworks for discussing searching are the abstract data types in Figures 7.1 and 7.2. The static dictionary of Figure 7.1 is constructed by some unspecified algorithm, and is available to us for searching, but we cannot change the set of items it contains. The

---

search(k) — *return the item whose key is k,*
   or NOTFOUND if no such item is present

FIGURE 7.1

Operation available given a *static dictionary*. The appropriate way to return *NOTFOUND* depends on the application.

---

insert(k) — *insert an item whose key is k*

delete(k) — *delete the item whose key is k*

search(k) — *return the item whose key is k,*
   or NOTFOUND if no such item is present

FIGURE 7.2

Operations available in a *dynamic dictionary*.

dynamic dictionary of Figure 7.2 can be searched like its static relative, but we can also add or remove items. In common with many other searching applications, those in Sections 1.3 and 5.2 both require a data type intermediate in power between static and dynamic dictionaries: we need to add items, but never need to delete them; such a dictionary might be called *semi-dynamic*.

Measures of Performance

The search algorithms in this chapter use *binary key comparisons* that tell for two keys whether one is less than, equal to, or greater than, the other. We call a comparison *successful* if the items compared are equal, and *unsuccessful* otherwise. Since the goal of a search operation is to find an item whose key is equal to a given key, search algorithms make at most one successful comparison. On the other hand, they may make many comparisons that are unsuccessful. Thus, we measure the time complexity of a search algorithm by counting the number of unsuccessful comparisons it makes.

A search operation is *successful* if it finds an item in the dictionary with the given key; otherwise it is *unsuccessful*. A successful search is usually faster than an unsuccessful search, which must verify the absence of the sought item by looking everywhere it might be stored. Thus, we often state the time complexity of search algorithms as the time to execute an unsuccessful search operation.

There are several ways to analyze and compare the performance of searching algorithms. The familiar worst-case running time is always a possibility, and is usually easy to compute.

The *expected* cost of each operation is another useful measure of performance. To calculate it, we need to make assumptions about the distribution of requests and keys. The validity of expected cost measurements depends strongly on how well the distribution assumption corresponds to reality.

The *amortized* cost of an operation is a third kind of performance measure. To compute it, we calculate the total cost of a sequence of operations, then assign costs to each individual operation so that the total of all operation costs adds up to at least the cost of the sequence. If we must be able to bound the running time of each operation, then amortized cost is too weak to be of much use. On the other hand, when we care only about the total cost of a sequence of dictionary operations, the amortized cost can reveal that performance is better than is suggested by the worst-case cost of each operation, since a large number of cheap operations can offset the cost of a single expensive operation.

On-line and Off-line Problems

If we must fulfill search requests immediately, as in most applications, the search problem is said to be *on-line*. If the algorithm can examine the entire sequence of search requests before it fulfills any of them, the problem is *off-line*. Although most practical applications involve on-line problems, a good solution to a related off-line problem can be useful as a base of comparison, since it gives an informal lower bound on the performance of any on-line algorithm.

As we study searching methods, it is useful to examine them to see what kind of dictionary they support, how their operation cost is measured, and how suitable they are for on-line applications. Some algorithms apply to all kinds of problems; others exhibit superior performance under one cost measure for a particular problem. Even when a searching technique applies only to a restricted problem, however, it may suggest ways to solve more general problems.

7.2
SELF-ORGANIZING LINKED LISTS

Linked lists are a natural choice of data structure for the dictionary problem. They are simple to implement, yet versatile enough to support many forms of access, from purely static to fully dynamic. It is obvious that the linked list in which a dictionary is stored must change whenever an item is inserted or deleted. The clever idea behind self-organizing linked lists is to modify the list during search operations as well; the self-organizing lists we shall see in this section change whenever a sought item is found.

The following rule defines the *move-to-front* strategy for maintaining a self-organizing linked list: when an item is found, move it to the head of the list. (We also insert items at the front of the list.) This rule is meant to keep frequently referenced items close to the front of the list, letting items that are needed less often drift toward the rear of the list. An advantage of move-to-front is that it can be implemented using $O(1)$ operations to move found items, and no additional space in the list nodes; it requires little time, space, or programming effort beyond the comparisons and pointer-chasing already needed to perform simple sequential search.

In the worst case, sequential search in a linked list of n items must examine all of them, so it requires $\Omega(n)$ time. Furthermore, even if we use the move-to-front rule, a crafty adversary who knows the state of our data structure can always request that we search for the last item in the list, so a search can require $\Omega(n)$ time. Obviously, such straightforward worst-case analysis will not indicate any advantage of the move-to-front rule over simple sequential search, in which the sequence of items is fixed.

But there are reasons to expect better performance from the move-to-front rule than worst-case analysis suggests. You may be wondering already how often you will meet crafty adversaries in practice. The intuition behind the move-to-front rule also offers grounds for hope. In most applications, it is reasonable to expect that some items will be referenced more frequently than others. For example, in the problem we considered in Section 1.1, we probably buy food more often than we pay the rent; in turn, the rent is due more often than bills like automobile insurance and magazine subscriptions. We can formalize our inchoate hope by studying a related off-line problem.

Imagine that you were required to solve an off-line problem using simple sequential search on a static dictionary. That is, before you answer any search requests you can examine the entire sequence, and order the items in the dictionary any way you wish; after you answer one search request, however, you may not rearrange the dictionary any further. Your best strategy would be to examine the search sequence, arrange the items in decreasing order by search frequency, and finally answer the search requests. Thus, the most popular item would appear first on the list, then the next most popular item, and so on, with the least frequently sought item last on the list. Let us call this the *optimal fixed order*.

Given a sequence of search requests, which we understand to insert items that are not found, we shall count the number of unsuccessful comparisons made to satisfy them when we use simple sequential search on the list in optimal fixed order, and when we use the move-to-front rule in self-organizing search on an initially empty list. This reflects the overall time complexity of both algorithms well, because each search operation performs only a constant amount of other work—one successful comparison, and a list rearrangement in the case of the move-to-front rule. The following result summarizes the analysis:

(∗) A sequence σ of searches on a list using the move-to-front rule makes at most twice as many unsuccessful comparisons as simple sequential search makes on the optimal fixed order for σ.

To see how remarkable (∗) is, consider that move-to-front uses no information about the distribution of search frequencies, while the optimal fixed order uses complete information about that distribution; even with this handicap, move-to-front performs within a factor of two of the best we can do on a fixed list.

First we prove (∗) when the sequence contains two items, A and B. Suppose that of the m searches in sequence σ, k are for A, $m-k$ are for B, and $k \geq m/2$. We shall count the number of unsuccessful comparisons each algorithm makes while it performs the searches in σ. Since the sequence contains at least as many searches for A as for B, "$A\ B$" is an optimal fixed order for σ. Simple sequential search makes $m-k$ unsuccessful comparisons during searches for B, and no unsuccessful comparisons during searches for A, for a total of $m-k$ unsuccessful comparisons.

On the other hand, when we use the move-to-front rule, we make one unsuccessful comparison whenever the wrong item is at the front of the list. We can use this observation to prove that move-to-front makes at most two unsuccessful comparisons for each search in σ for B. Let $\beta_1, \ldots, \beta_{m-k}$ be the search requests for B in σ. If β_1 is preceded by a search that inserts A into the list, then move-to-front makes one unsuccessful comparison when it performs β_1. For $1 \leq i < m-k$, if a search for A appears between β_i and β_{i+1}, the search for A causes one unsuccessful comparison, and β_{i+1} itself causes one unsuccessful comparison; for the analysis we shall attribute the first unsuccessful comparison to β_i. Finally, if β_{m-k} is followed by a search for A, that search causes one unsuccessful comparison; again, charge it to β_{m-k}. Since each β_i causes at most two unsuccessful comparisons, move-to-front makes at most $2(m-k)$ unsuccessful comparisons, and we have proved (∗) for a dictionary of two items.

To prove (∗) when the dictionary contains n items, we note that move-to-front enjoys the *pairwise independence property*: if A and B are any two items in the list, then their relative order in the list at any time depends only on which was last sought; in other words, searches in σ for an item other than A and B do not change whether A appears before or after B. Therefore, the number of times A is encountered during searches for B (and hence causes an unsuccessful comparison), or vice versa, is independent of the searches for other items.

In a dictionary of n items, each pair of items has the pairwise independence property. We can add the unsuccessful comparisons attributable to each pair to find the total number of unsuccessful comparisons used by either algorithm. Since (∗) is true for each pair of items in σ, when we sum over all of the pairs we find that the number of unsuccessful comparisons made by move-to-front is at most twice the number of unsuccessful comparisons made by simple sequential search on the optimal fixed order, and we have proved (∗) for a dictionary that contains any number of items.

Fact (∗) suggests that move-to-front is not bad as a practical algorithm. It can be used for static, semi-dynamic, and fully dynamic dictionaries, and it adds no asymptotic cost and little programming effort to simple sequential search. Moreover, it offers some promise of considerably better performance than simple sequential search, because we rarely have the opportunity in practice to work off-line and create the optimal fixed order.

Fact (∗) tells us only how much *worse* move-to-front can perform than simple sequential search on the optimal fixed order. In many cases, move-to-front performs better. For instance, if the dictionary contains two items, and if all k search requests for one item precede all $m-k$ of those for the other, then move-to-front makes at most two unsuccessful comparisons, while simple sequential search still makes $m-k$. This observation illustrates that move-to-front is particularly well suited when a pattern of references exhibits *locality*: roughly, items tend to wax and wane in popularity. The move-to-front rule moves popular items to the front, lets them drift back as they drop in popularity, then pulls them to the front again when they are needed.

7.3
BINARY SEARCH

Suppose we were given a fixed array of items in increasing order by search key. We shall see algorithms in Chapter 11 with which to create such an array; the important points to notice are that we can access any item in the array in $O(1)$ operations, and we are not permitted to rearrange the array. We can solve the static dictionary problem on the items in the array using the powerful yet simple *binary search* algorithm.

A search operation consists of a sequence of comparisons. The idea of binary search is to choose this sequence carefully, so that each comparison eliminates from consideration roughly half of the remaining items. Program 7.1a contains a small example array on which we shall perform binary search for Vesuvius. At the first step, binary search determines where Vesuvius should lie with respect to the middle element, hill[3], or Esquiline. The string comparison reveals that the sought item comes after the middle element. Therefore, we need never examine hill[0:3] in our search for Vesuvius: since hill[] is in alphabetical order and Esquiline is in hill[3], Vesuvius cannot lie in hill[0:3].

Thus, we must search for Vesuvius among hill[4:6]. Proceeding recursively, we compare Vesuvius to the middle element, hill[5], or Quirinal. Since Quirinal comes before Vesuvius, we can eliminate hill[4:5] as possibly containing Vesuvius. The

```
char *hill[] = {
    "Aventine",
    "Caelian",
    "Capitoline",
    "Esquiline",
    "Palatine",
    "Quirinal",
    "Viminal"
};
```

PROGRAM 7.1a

An array that contains the names of the seven hills of Rome.

final step of binary search is to see whether `hill[6]` contains `Vesuvius`. It doesn't (since Vesuvius is a mountain near Naples, not a hill of Rome), so binary search terminates unsuccessfully.

One way to depict binary search is to draw line segments that connect the array elements against which successive iterations compare the sought item. Such a picture for the above example is extremely brief, but the larger example in Figure 7.3 illustrates how the sequence of comparisons used by binary search homes in on the sought item.

Another way to understand binary search is to observe that it reduces the interval of the array that can possibly contain the sought item, as suggested by Figure 7.4. Binary search terminates either when the sought item is found or when this interval becomes empty. This interpretation suggests an invariant assertion with which to verify the correctness of Program 7.1b, an implementation of binary search.

To analyze the worst-case time complexity of binary search, we count the number of comparisons made during an unsuccessful search on an array of size $2^k - 1$. (Note that a successful binary search can cost much less than an unsuccessful binary search.) After the unsuc-

0 1 2 3 4 5 6 7 8 9 10 11 12 13 14 15 16 17 18 19 20 21 22 23 24 25 26 27 28 29 30

FIGURE 7.3

Illustration of binary search: the line segments connect successive array elements examined in the search for 20.

```
     0  1  2  3  4  5  6  7  8  9 10 11 12 13 14 15 16 17 18 19 20 21 22 23 24 25 26 27 28 29 30
     [                                     >                                                   ]
                                           [                              <                    ]
                                           [          >          ]
                                                [  <  ]
                                                []
```

FIGURE 7.4

Illustration of the same binary search as Figure 7.3: the interval in which 20 could possibly lie shrinks steadily. The inequality signs show the array elements with which the sought item is compared at each step, and the result of the comparison.

cessful comparison with the middle element of an interval of size $2^j - 1$, we recur on an interval of size $2^{j-1} - 1$. Therefore the time complexity $T(n)$ of unsuccessful binary search on an array of length $2^k - 1$ obeys this recurrence relation:

```
find(char *s)
{
    int lo, mid, hi;
    lo = 0;
    hi = sizeof(hill)/sizeof(char *) - 1;
    while (lo <= hi) {
        /* ASSERT:  if present, s must lie in hill[lo:hi] */
        int cmpresult;
        mid = (lo + hi)/2;
        cmpresult = strcmp(hill[mid], s);
        if (cmpresult < 0)
            lo = mid + 1;
        else if (cmpresult > 0)
            hi = mid - 1;
        else
            return mid;
    }
    return NOTFOUND;
}
```

PROGRAM 7.1b

Binary search program for the array declared in Program 7.1a. The value assigned to hi is the number of elements in hill[].

$$T(2^k - 1) = T(2^{k-1} - 1) + 1, \ k > 1;$$
$$T(1) \quad = 1.$$

(7.1)

Equation (7.1) is similar to Equation (2.2); its solution is

$$T(n) = \log_2(n + 1).$$

(7.2)

Binary search uses $O(\log n)$ comparisons to search in a sorted array of n items, when $n = 2^k - 1$ for some integer $k > 0$.

In fact, even if n is not one less than a power of two, the number of comparisons used by binary search remains $O(\log n)$. To see this, we write the following recurrence relation, in which the expression for even n reflects the fact that the "middle" or $(n/2)$th element of an array of even length n splits it into two arrays of lengths $n/2 - 1$ and $n/2$:

$$T(n) = T\left\lceil \frac{n-1}{2} \right\rceil + 1, \text{ odd } n > 1;$$

$$T(n) \leq \max\left\{ T\left\lceil \frac{n}{2} - 1 \right\rceil, T\left\lceil \frac{n}{2} \right\rceil \right\} + 1, \text{ even } n > 0; \quad (7.3)$$

$$T(1) = 1;$$

$$T(0) = 0.$$

We can verify by induction that Equation (7.3) admits the solution

$$T(n) = \lceil \log_2(n + 1) \rceil.$$

(7.4)

This analysis shows that the worst-case performance of binary search is much better than that of sequential search. Program 7.1 also shows that binary search is simple enough to be practically useful. Binary search illustrates a simple but essential idea of algorithm design, often called *divide and conquer*. Each comparison divides the array into two pieces. One of these pieces can be ignored in subsequent steps; the other piece is further processed ("conquered") by the algorithm. Since each step cuts the size of the remaining problem approximately in half, binary search is bound to arrive at a trivial problem after roughly $\log_2 n$ comparisons.

Thus, binary search is a very appealing algorithm. Unfortunately, in the form seen here it is practical only for static dictionaries. In the next section we shall see a data structure with which to apply the idea of binary search to dynamic problems.

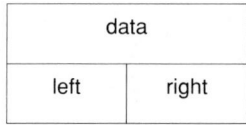

FIGURE 7.5

A typical node in a binary tree. In a program, `left` and `right` are apt to be pointers to the roots of the left and right subtrees.

7.4
BINARY TREES

Binary trees are an important and fundamental data structure. We shall see in Section 7.5 and Chapter 9 how to use them to solve searching problems. First, however, we shall define them and see some of their properties.

Figure 7.5 shows a typical node in a binary tree. It has room for data, and for edges that connect it to two children—*left* and *right*. A *binary tree* is defined to be either

(a) empty, or

(b) a node whose left and right children are binary trees.

Figure 7.6 illustrates this recursive definition of binary tree.

The *root* of a binary tree is the unique node that is not the child of any other node. Because the definition of binary tree is recursive, each

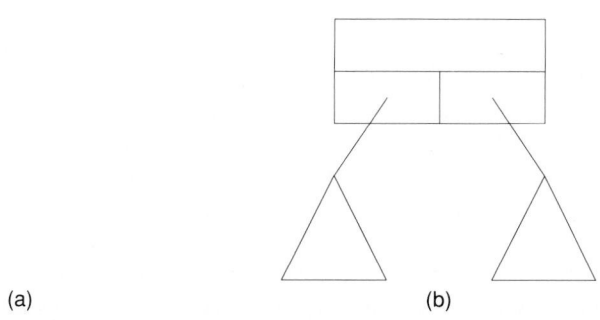

(a)   (b)

FIGURE 7.6

Definition of a binary tree: (a) the empty tree; (b) the recursive picture.

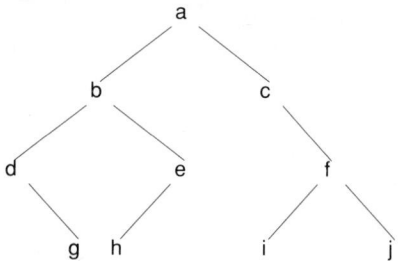

FIGURE 7.7

Example binary tree. We shall often omit the boxes around tree nodes, as we have done here.

node in a binary tree is the root of a binary tree, which is called the *subtree* rooted at that node. A node that has no children is called a *leaf* or an *external node*. Nodes with children are called *internal nodes*. In the binary tree in Figure 7.7, the root contains a, and the leaves contain g, h, i, and j; the internal node that contains f is the root of a binary tree with three nodes. We usually draw binary trees growing down the page from their roots; this turns out to be convenient for most purposes.

Applications of Binary Trees

Binary trees are ideal for representing many relationships that hold among data elements. A familiar example that arises in family histories is the *ancestor tree*, in which a node's left child contains its father and a node's right child contains its mother. (An ancestor tree represents only the relationships of parent and great^k-grandparent for $k \geq 0$ (and the obvious inverses: child and great^k-grandchild). The more general term *family tree* includes diagrams in which people's spouses and siblings are represented, so that relationships such as wife, husband, brother, sister, and ith cousin j times removed can be deduced from the diagram.) When a node's child is empty, the identity of that ancestor is unknown (or at least unstated). Figure 7.8 shows an ancestor tree.

Binary arithmetic expressions have a natural representation as binary trees. Each internal node contains an operator, and each external node contains a value. Figure 7.9 shows the binary tree that corresponds to a moderately complicated arithmetic expression. Such binary trees may be used in compilers for high-level languages, which

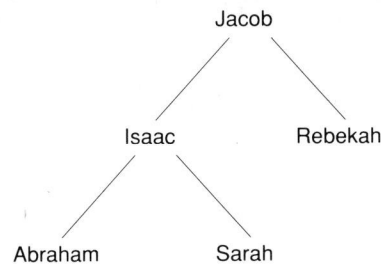

FIGURE 7.8

Ancestor tree for Jacob. (Source: the book of Genesis in the Hebrew Scriptures; in early *sūrahs* of the Qu'rān, Jacob and Isaac are reported to be brothers, which would lead to a different tree.)

must represent the arithmetic expressions in programs in a form suitable for translation into a lower-level language.

Traversal Orders

For most data structures we need a systematic way to visit every item they contain. Perhaps the most common use of such a *traversal* is to dump the contents of a data structure. Arrays and linked lists usually have obvious traversal orders. In binary trees, however, several traversal orders can be defined. We shall use the binary tree shown in Figure 7.7 to illustrate the various orders.

The recursive definition of a binary tree suggests that we formulate traversal algorithms recursively. In general, when a traversal algorithm is applied to a binary tree, either the tree is empty (case (a) in

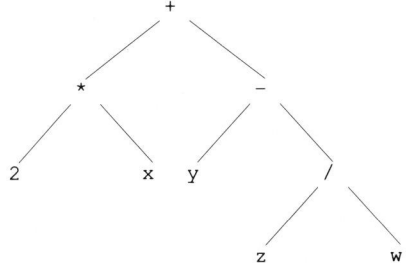

FIGURE 7.9

Binary tree that represents the arithmetic expression $2x + (y - z/w)$.

```
preorder(r)
    if (!r)
        return
    visit(r)
    preorder(r→left)
    preorder(r→right)
```

ALGORITHM 7.1

Algorithm to traverse a binary tree rooted at r in *preorder*.

---

the definition) and traversal is trivial, or the traversal algorithm is applied to both children of the tree's root. The three traversal orders in Algorithms 7.1, 7.2, and 7.3 differ in when the root is visited compared to when its children are processed. Figure 7.10 shows the results of applying these three traversal algorithms to the tree in Figure 7.7.

```
inorder(r)
    if (!r)
        return
    inorder(r→left)
    visit(r)
    inorder(r→right)
```

ALGORITHM 7.2

Algorithm to traverse a binary tree rooted at r in *inorder*, which is also called *symmetric order*.

```
postorder(r)
    if (!r)
        return
    postorder(r→left)
    postorder(r→right)
    visit(r)
```

ALGORITHM 7.3

Algorithm to traverse a binary tree rooted at r in *postorder*.

```
preorder:     a  b  d  g  e  h  c  f  i  j
inorder:      d  g  b  h  e  a  c  i  f  j
postorder:    g  d  h  e  b  i  j  f  c  a
```

FIGURE 7.10

The order in which the nodes of the binary tree in Figure 7.7 are visited in each of three traversal orders.

The appropriate traversal order depends on the job to be done. For example, given an expression tree, an inorder traversal will print the expression it represents in its familiar form. If we wish to evaluate the expression, however, postorder is more appropriate: the subtree rooted at each node defines a value, which cannot be calculated for a particular node until the values of both of its subtrees are known.

Path Length

Given any two nodes in a tree, say x and y, the *path* between them is the unique sequence of edges one follows to go from x to y. The *length* of a path is the number of edges it contains. For example, in Figure 7.7, the path from the node that contains e to the node that contains f passes in sequence through nodes containing b, a, and c, and has length 4.

Let T be a binary tree rooted at r, and let x be any node in T. The *depth* of x in T is the length of the path from r to x. In Figure 7.7, the depth of the root (which contains a) is zero; the depth of all leaves is 3. The *internal path length* of T, $IPL(T)$, is the sum of the depths of all of its nodes. The internal path length of the tree in Figure 7.7 is 20.

7.5

BINARY SEARCH TREES

To apply the binary trees of Section 7.4 to the dynamic dictionary problem of Section 7.1, we shall store items in the nodes of a binary tree. To take advantage of the binary search idea in Section 7.3, we add the following data structure invariant: the keys of the items stored at nodes are encountered in increasing order during an inorder traversal of the tree. The result is a *binary search tree*, depicted abstractly in Figure 7.11. The invariant property implies that both subtrees of the

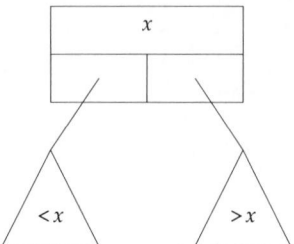

FIGURE 7.11

Abstract view of a binary search tree: all elements in the left subtree of the root have keys that are less than the key at the root; similarly, the keys of all elements in the right subtree of the root are greater than the key at the root.

root are also binary search trees; this is important to the design and verification of binary search algorithms.

Binary Search Trees as Dictionaries

Algorithm 7.4 follows a path from the root of a binary search tree, using the same divide-and-conquer strategy as Program 7.1.

The algorithm for inserting an item into a binary search tree is similar to the search algorithm. In fact, one way to express it is: pretend that you are searching for the new item; when you reach a leaf and discover that the item is not present, insert it as the appropriate child of the leaf you reached.

The algorithm to delete a node from a binary search tree is somewhat more complicated than the algorithms for search and insertion. Let d be the doomed node. If d is a leaf, then deletion is straightfor-

```
search(r,key)
    if (r→data == key)
        return r
    else if (r→data < key)
        return search(r→left,key)
    else
        return search(r→right,key)
```

ALGORITHM 7.4

Search algorithm for a binary search tree rooted at r.

ward. If d has one child, we make it a child of d's parent. But if d has two children, we must rearrange the tree more drastically after deleting it. To preserve the data structure invariant, we replace d by either its inorder predecessor or its inorder successor. The node that replaces d can have at most one child, so moving it causes at most a constant amount of further rearrangement of the tree. For example, to delete the root of the tree in Figure 7.7, we would move either the inorder predecessor, e, or the inorder successor, c, to the root; either move leaves a single subtree that replaces the moved node.

Application: Counting Word Frequencies

To illustrate binary search trees, we shall write a program that uses them to count how many times each word appears in a sequence of words. To simplify the program, assume that each line of the input contains a single word. Program 7.2 reads such input and prints the binary search tree it constructed from the sequence; the count member of each node in the tree tells how many times its word was encountered.

Since any newly encountered word must be added to the dictionary, while a word that has already been seen must have its count incremented, it is natural in Program 7.2a to have update() perform both search and insertion on the binary search tree; update() uses pointer arguments so that it need not return a value. In Program 7.2b, dump() prints the tree of words during an inorder traversal; its argument indent is used to print tree nodes at the right level.

As an example, Figure 7.12 contains the result of processing the beginning of a familiar children's story.

Performance of Binary Search Trees

Binary search trees rely on the principle of divide and conquer. To analyze their performance, let $T(n)$ be the number of comparisons made during an unsuccessful search in a binary search tree. The following recurrence relation governs $T(n)$:

$$T(n) \leq \max_{0 \leq k < n} \{ T(n-k-1), T(k) \} + 1, \ n > 1;$$

$$T(1) = 1; \qquad\qquad (7.5)$$

$$T(0) = 0.$$

Equation (7.5) is very different from Equation (7.3): there is no guarantee that the two subtrees of a node will be approximately the same size. Because of this difference, Equation (7.5) admits the unfavorable solution $T(n) = n$.

```
typedef struct _node node;
struct _node {
    char *word;
    int count;
    node *left, *right;
};

node *tree;

void update(char *s, node **root)
{
    int cmpresult;
    if (!*root) {
        *root = (node *) calloc(1, sizeof(node));
        (*root)->word = strdup(s);
        (*root)->count++;
        return;
    }
    cmpresult = strcmp(s, (*root)->word);
    if (cmpresult < 0)
        update(s, &((*root)->left));
    else if (cmpresult > 0)
        update(s, &((*root)->right));
    else
        (*root)->count++;
}
```

PROGRAM 7.2a

Structure definitions and a function to insert words into a binary search tree.

It is possible to construct a binary search tree that achieves this worst-case time complexity. If a binary search tree has only one leaf, then we use n comparisons to search for an item that belongs in order between the leaf and its parent. We can generate such a long, skinny tree by inserting items into a binary search tree in order or in reverse order by key. An example of data that yields a tree with a strong tendency to favor scrawny growth appears in Figure 7.13, which shows the binary search tree produced by Program 7.2 on the beginning words of the Preamble to the Constitution of the United States; the arrival of the first four words in reverse alphabetical order gets the whole tree off to an unbalanced start.

Thus, the worst-case time complexity for searching in a binary search tree is no better than that for sequential search in an array or

```
void dump(node *root, int indent)
{
    int i;
    if (!root)
        return;
    dump(root->left, indent+1);
    for (i = 0 ; i < indent; i++)
        printf("    ");
    printf("%d:%s\n", root->count, root->word);
    dump(root->right, indent+1);
}

main()
{
    char buf[100];
    while (fgets(buf, 100, stdin)) {
        buf[strlen(buf)-1] = '\0';
        update(buf, &tree);
    }
    dump(tree, 0);
    exit(0);
}
```

PROGRAM 7.2b

The remaining functions for Program 7.2, which prints a binary search tree showing word frequencies.

linked list. We know, however, that not all insertion sequences give rise to long, skinny trees: Figure 7.12 shows a relatively short, bushy tree. This suggests that we might want to analyze the expected performance of searching in a binary search tree.

We use the internal path length to measure the performance of searching in a binary search tree. It tells how many unsuccessful comparisons would be made if each of the tree nodes were sought once. For a given tree T on n nodes, if each node is equally likely to be the one sought, $IPL(T)/n$ is the expected number of unsuccessful comparisons performed during a single search. In the worst case, where the binary search tree is as long and skinny as possible, $IPL = \sum_{i=1}^{n} (i-1) = \Theta(n^2)$, and the average search requires $\Theta(n)$ unsuccessful comparisons.

The shape of the binary search tree produced by a sequence of n insertions is determined by which permutation of sorted order the input sequence represents. Assuming that each of the $n!$ permutations

```
    2:a
            1:girl
                1:hood
        2:little
            1:named
1:once
                1:red
                    1:riding
            1:there
        1:time
    1:upon
        1:was
```

FIGURE 7.12

Output of Program 7.2 when the sequence of input words is "once upon a time there was a little girl named little red riding hood".

is equally likely to be the input sequence, we can build a representative binary search tree by inserting random numbers into it one at a time. Program 7.3 does this; it works with a modified version of update() that sets global variable p1 to the length of the path it traversed during an insertion, or −1 if the item was already in the tree;

```
                    1:a
                1:form
            1:in
                1:more
        1:of
            1:order
    1:people
            1:perfect
        1:states
    2:the
        1:to
            1:union
    1:united
1:we
```

FIGURE 7.13

Output of Program 7.2 when the sequence of input words is "we the people of the united states in order to form a more perfect union".

```
void buildtree(int n)
/* build a binary search tree by n random insertions,
/* report internal path length whenever tree has 2**k nodes */
{
    int d = 1, i, ipl = 0;
    for (i = 0; i < n; i++) {
        /* ASSERT: tree now contains i nodes */
        if (i == d) {
            printf("%d %d\n", i, ipl);
            d *= 2;
        }
        do {
            pl = 0;
            update(frand(), &tree);
        } while (pl < 0);
        ipl += pl;
    }
}
```

PROGRAM 7.3

A function to construct a binary search tree on n nodes using random insertion. It calls a slightly different version of update() from the one in Program 7.2.

it keeps a running total of the internal path length, and reports it every time the tree doubles in size.

Figure 7.14 shows a plot of the output produced by Program 7.3. The plot appears on a log-linear scale; since the data lie almost on a straight line of modest slope, it is natural to guess that the expected search time in a binary search tree constructed by n random insertions is $\Theta(\log n)$. In fact, it is possible to prove that the expected length of a search in such a tree is a little less than $2 \log_e n \approx 1.4 \log_2 n$. This result applies only to binary search trees when they are used to implement a semi-dynamic dictionary.

The analysis of a binary search tree used as a fully dynamic dictionary is an open problem. If we use *asymmetric deletion*, always replacing a node by its inorder predecessor, then n random insertions followed by an alternating sequence of random deletions and insertions generates a tree whose expected internal path length is $\Theta(n^{3/2})$, which leads to an expected search time of $\Theta(\sqrt{n})$; it takes a long sequence of deletions and insertions before this behavior becomes apparent, however.

It is conjectured that if deletion is performed *symmetrically*, so that deletions alternate between replacing the doomed node by its inorder

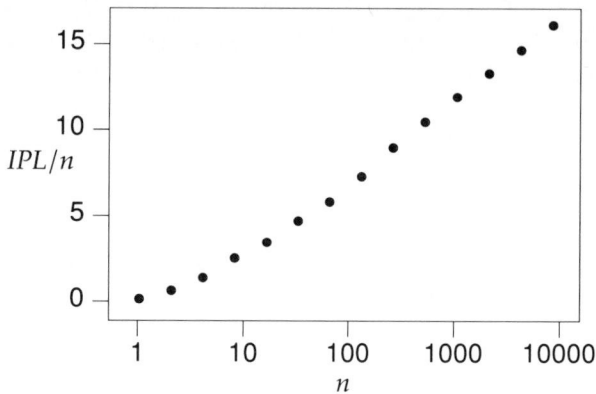

FIGURE 7.14

The increase in internal path length as the binary search tree constructed by Program 7.3 grows.

predecessor or replacing it by by its inorder successor, then the expected search time remains $\Theta(\log n)$.

7.6
SUMMARY AND PERSPECTIVE

We have seen a variety of searching problems, but we have seen no algorithms for the dynamic dictionary problem that exhibit good worst case behavior: they all degenerate to sequential search. Nevertheless, this chapter contains the roots of some important ideas for the design of good searching methods.

The self-organizing linked lists of Section 7.2 exhibit *adaptive* behavior: the dictionary changes according to a rule that is intended to make future searches less costly. Adaptive algorithms are difficult to analyze, but they can be excellent practical solutions.

The idea of divide and conquer in Sections 7.3 and 7.5 appears throughout the study of algorithms and data structures. Since we can use it to achieve $O(\log n)$ search time in the worst case for static dictionaries, it is natural to hope for the same kind of time bound in the dynamic case. Unfortunately, binary search trees make their worst showing when the input is neat and orderly, but can be expected to do quite well on randomly ordered input. We shall see this kind of counterintuitive behavior again in Chapter 11. Chapter 9 shows how to create a dynamic dictionary with good worst-case search behavior, but with a considerably more complicated program. We shall see in Chapter 8 that much simpler methods offer better expected performance on any input, even though their worst-case complexity is the same as that of sequential search.

It is tricky to evaluate algorithms by comparing their expected performance. Often it is easiest to analyze an algorithm when its input is uniformly distributed. When this models the input data well, the analysis is helpful. But if the input data has some other distribution, then the result of an expected-case analysis under the assumption of a uniform distribution may be misleadingly optimistic.

Importance of Information Hiding

This chapter holds an important lesson in the use of data types during program construction. When we first write a program, it is usually good practice to use the simplest possible data structures and algorithms that do the job. For example, to solve many searching problems we begin with a brute-force sequential approach. Should we discover later that this simple technique makes the program too slow or costly, we shall want to replace it by a better algorithm or data structure.

If the dictionary is a global variable whose contents are accessed and modified by explicit manipulation throughout the program, then changing to a different searching method will be difficult and prone to error. On the other hand, if we use the dictionary through a collection of well-chosen functions, and only those functions examine or alter the contents of the dictionary directly, then the job of improving the search method used by the program will be much easier.

EXERCISES

1 Implement a semi-dynamic dictionary as a self-organizing linked list whose search operation uses the move-to-front rule; use it in Program 1.2.

2 Consider the set S composed of all sequences of m searches that reference each of n items the same number of times.

(a) Show that for any element of S, any permutation of the n items is an optimal fixed ordering.

(b) What is the performance of simple sequential search on any sequence in S?

(c) What sequence in S gives the best possible performance of the move-to-front rule?

(d) What sequence in S gives the worst possible performance of the move-to-front rule? Can you find an answer that proves that (*) in Section 7.2 is not valid if two is replaced by any smaller number?

3 Prove that the optimal fixed order for simple sequential search is defined by arranging the items in order by decreasing frequency of request.

4 In the *count* rule for self-organizing linked lists, each item is augmented to include space for a counter that is incremented whenever the item is found, and the list is maintained in non-decreasing order by count from head to tail.

(a) Implement a self-organizing linked list that uses the count rule.

(b) Show that a sequence of searches using the count rule makes at most twice as many unsuccessful comparisons as simple sequential search on the optimal fixed ordering.

5 Move-to-front costs too much when lists are stored in arrays. An alternative rule for self-organizing lists that is suitable for lists stored in arrays is called *transpose*: whenever an item is found, it is swapped with the item that precedes it on the list (unless it is already at the head of the list).

(a) Implement a self-organizing list using transpose.

(b) Show that m searches on an n-element list using the transpose rule can require $\Omega(mn)$ comparisons even when the optimal fixed ordering uses only $O(m+n)$ comparisons.

6 One rule of thumb used to quantify the notion that some items in a dictionary are more popular, and hence more often sought, is the *80-20 rule*. It says that 80% of the searches are for 20% of the items. In turn, of the remaining 20% of the searches, 80% of them are for 20% of the less popular items, and so on.

(a) Define a probability distribution $\{ p_i \mid 1 \le i \le n \}$ such that p_i is the probability of searching for item i, and the distribution obeys the 80-20 rule.

(b) What is the performance of simple sequential search on the optimal fixed ordering for a sequence that obeys the distribution defined in (a)?

7 Let $H_n = \sum_{i=1}^{n} 1/i$, the nth *harmonic number*.

(a) Show that $\lim_{n \to \infty} H_n = \infty$.

(b) Show that $H_n - \log_e n = O(1)$.

8 *Zipf's law* gives another probability distribution for searches. It says that of m searches among n items, $m/(iH_n)$ searches will be for the ith most popular item. What is the performance of simple sequential search on the optimal fixed ordering for Zipf's law?

9 In a long array, binary search can use more comparisons to find an item near the beginning of the array than sequential search would use. Can you devise a strategy that avoids this penalty?

10 What does binary search do if it is applied to an array that is not ordered by search key?

11 Write binary search as a recursive function. Compare the space complexities of the iterative and recursive versions.

12 Here is an informal reason to believe that $T(n) = O(\log n)$ in Section 7.3, based on its value when $n = 2^k - 1$. Suppose we knew that we could search faster in an array of size m than in an array of size n, with $m > n$. Then we could write a binary search procedure that pretends that the array of length n is actually of size m, and search it within the smaller time bound. Since we live in an orderly universe, this cannot happen, so $T(n)$ must be monotone— that is, $T(n) \le T(n+1)$ for $n \ge 0$.

(a) Write a binary search procedure that pretends that an array of length n is actually $2^{\lceil \log_2 n + 1 \rceil} - 1$ long.

(b) Why doesn't this argument apply to Algorithm 2.2 (exponentiation by repeated squaring)?

13 Verify that Equation (7.2) solves Equation (7.1).

14 Verify that Equation (7.4) solves Equation (7.3).

15 Notice that $T(n) = \min\{n, 1\}$ also solves recurrence (7.5). What does this tell you about solving recurrence inequalities?

16 Show that any recurrence relation of the form

$$T(n) = T(n/k) + 1, \ n > 1;$$

$$T(1) = 1.$$

has the solution $T(n) = O(\log n)$. What is the base of the logarithm in the exact solution?

17 Show how to add parent pointers to the nodes of a binary tree. That is, show how they can be kept current through the operations of deletion and insertion.

18 Show that the preorder traversal of a binary expression tree yields the prefix form of the expression.

19 Show that the postorder traversal of a binary expression tree yields the postfix form of the expression.

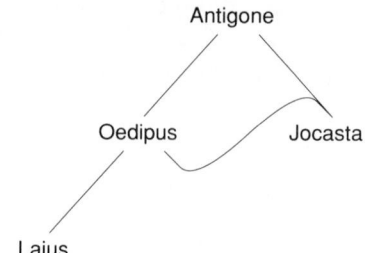

Oedipus   Jocasta

Laius

FIGURE 7.15

Ancestor "tree" for Antigone. (Source: *Oedipus Rex*, Sophocles).

20 Show how to label any binary tree on n nodes with integers from 1 to n so that its preorder traversal is in sorted order.

21 The preorder traversal of a binary tree is 'a b c d e f g h i', while its inorder traversal is 'c d e b f a i h g'.

(a) What is the tree?

(b) Show that inorder and preorder traversal together determine the tree uniquely.

22 Show that inorder and postorder determine a unique binary tree.

23 Draw a tree that has the same preorder and postorder traversal.

24 Draw two different trees that have the same preorder and postorder traversals.

25 Is the ancestor diagram shown in Figure 7.15 a binary tree?

26 The tree in Figure 7.7 is labelled in *level-order*. Give an algorithm to label an arbitrary binary tree in level order.

27 Why is the path between any two nodes in a binary tree unique?

28 Explain why the inorder successor of a node with two children can have at most one child.

29 Describe a sequence of insertions that gives rise to a long, skinny binary search tree in which the items are not inserted either in order or in reverse order by key.

30 What is the smallest possible value of the internal path length in a tree of n nodes?

31 Show that the average value of the internal path length of a binary tree on n nodes is $\Theta(n^{3/2})$. Section 7.5 suggests that a binary tree created by random insertion has expected internal path length $\Theta(n \log n)$. Reconcile the two statements.

32 How many of the child pointers in a binary tree with n nodes are null?

33 A binary tree is *threaded* by making all right child pointers that would normally be null point to the inorder successor of the node, and all left child pointers that would normally be null point to the inorder predecessor of the node. Write an algorithm to thread a binary tree.

34 Let B_n be the number of binary trees on n nodes. Explain the recurrence relation

$$B_n = \sum_{i=0}^{n-1} B_i B_{n-i-1}, \; n > 1;$$

$$B_0 = B_1 = 1.$$

Show that

$$B_n = \frac{(2n)!}{n!(n+1)!}.$$

35 Replace the array of Program 1.2 by a binary search tree, and the sequential search by binary search. Run the program on randomly generated data to see how performance is affected.

REFERENCES

An introduction to self-organizing sequential search appears in

J. L. Bentley and C. C. McGeogh. "Amortized analyses of self-organizing sequential search heuristics." *Communications of the ACM* 28 (1985): 404–411.

The move-to-front rule is also within a constant factor of the best possible self-organizing rule; this result is presented in

D. D. Sleator and R. E. Tarjan. "Amortized efficiency of list update and paging rules." *Communications of the ACM* 28 (1985): 202–208.

The following reference surveys amortized analysis:

R. E. Tarjan. "Amortized computational complexity." *SIAM Journal of Algebraic and Discrete Methods* 6 (1985): 306–318.

Column 4 of the following reference contains a careful construction of a binary search program:

J. Bentley. *Programming Pearls*. Reading, Mass.: Addison-Wesley, 1986.

A variety of binary tree traversals are described in

A. Berztiss. "A taxonomy of binary tree traversals." *BIT* 26 (1986): 266–276.

It is hard to analyze the behavior of binary search trees under random insertions and deletions, even in the case of trees with three nodes:

A. T. Jonassen and D. E. Knuth. "A trivial algorithm whose analysis isn't." *Journal of Computer and Systems Sciences* 16 (1978): 301–322.

Of course, it is possible to study binary search trees by simulation:

J. L. Eppinger. "An empirical study of insertion and deletion in binary search trees." *Communications of the ACM* 26 (1983): 663–669.

Eppinger's paper inspired others to prove some results about binary search trees:

J. Culberson. "The effect of updates in binary search trees." In *Proc. 17th Ann. Symp. on Theory of Computing*. (1985): 205–212.

8

Hashing

The searching algorithms in Chapter 7 use only binary key comparisons as they traverse a dictionary in search of an item with a given key. We could implement those algorithms even if we were not allowed to see keys at all, so long as we could call a function to tell us the result of comparing the keys of two items. When we can see the keys, however, we can use other searching algorithms that take advantage of this additional capacity. The *address calculation techniques* in this chapter can offer excellent ways to maintain a static or dynamic dictionary.

8.1
PERFECT HASHING

Suppose an application needs to search by name for one of the planets in our solar system. We could store the names in alphabetical order in an array and use binary search to find any planet name with at most $\lceil \log_2(9+1) \rceil = 4$ string comparisons. Program 8.1 uses a very different strategy to store planet names so that any name can be found by computing a single function.

Program 8.1 stores planet names in a *hash table*. Macro h(s) in Program 8.1 computes a *hash function* that uses arithmetic operations to scatter key values through the *slots* in the hash table. In Figure 8.1, the debugging output from Program 8.1, we see that each key hashes to a different slot; we say that h(s) computes a *perfect* hash function on the names of the planets.

```
#define MAGICNUMBER 15
#define h(s) ((s[0] + s[1])%MAGICNUMBER)

typedef struct planet {
    char *name;
    int nummoons;   /* number of moons */
    double sundist; /* distance to sun, in megamiles */
} planet;

planet solarsys[MAGICNUMBER];

void install(char *name, int nummoons, double sundist)
{
    planet *p = &solarsys[h(name)];
    fprintf(stderr, "%2d %s\n", h(name), name);
    demand(p->name == 0, planet collision);
    p->name = name;
    p->nummoons = nummoons;
    p->sundist = sundist;
}

void init(void)
{
    /* source:  Information Please Almanac 1983, p. 369 */
    install("Mercury", 0, 36.00);
    install("Venus", 0, 67.27);
    install("Earth", 1, 93.00);
    install("Mars", 2, 141.71);
    install("Jupiter", 16, 483.88);
    install("Saturn", 12, 887.14);
    install("Uranus", 5, 1783.98);
    install("Neptune", 2, 2795.46);
    install("Pluto", 1, 3675.27);
}

main()
{
    init();
    exit(0);
}
```

PROGRAM 8.1

A program that uses perfect hashing on the names of the nine planets in our solar system.

```
13 Mercury
 7 Venus
 1 Earth
 9 Mars
11 Jupiter
 0 Saturn
 4 Uranus
14 Neptune
 8 Pluto
```

FIGURE 8.1

Debugging output from Program 8.1.

Program 8.1 probably seems unfairly miraculous. It gives no clue about how to devise a perfect hash function for another set of keys. (It's not easy.) And if we needed to store a dynamic dictionary, when we would not know in advance which keys would be stored in the dictionary, it would be impossible to devise a practical perfect hash function. For general use, hashing algorithms must cope with *collisions* that happen when the keys of two items in the dictionary hash to the same value. Sections 8.2 and 8.3 present two basic approaches to resolving collisions.

8.2
COLLISION RESOLUTION USING A PROBE STRATEGY

We can handle collisions with a *probe strategy* when the slots in the hash table have room for a single item and all items in the dictionary must be stored in one of these slots. For a given item, the strategy defines a sequence of probes to make into the table when we search for an item. We look in the first slot in the sequence; if the item is there, we are done. If not, we examine the second slot in the sequence; again, if the item is there, we are done. Otherwise, we continue through the probe strategy, examining the slots until we find the item, reach an empty slot, or return to the first slot we examined. Both of the latter two conditions mean that the item is not in the table.

Incremental probe strategies are common and easy to implement. They use two functions on keys, $hash()$ and $incr()$. The probe sequence for key is $hash(key)$, $hash(key)+incr(key)$, $hash(key)+2\times incr(key),\ldots,$ $hash(key)+i\times incr(key),\ldots,$ where all elements of the sequence are taken modulo the size of the hash table. Algorithm

```
find(key) /* in an M-position hash table */
    try = h = hash(key)
    i = incr(key)
    do
        if (table[try] == 0)
            report "not found"
        else if (table[try] == key)
            report "found"
        /* increment to next probe position */
        try = ((try + i) mod M + M) mod M
    while try ≠ h
    report "not found and table full"
```

ALGORITHM 8.1

Algorithm to search in a hash table using an incremental probe strategy. The statement that increments *try* ensures that it does not become negative.

8.1 shows how to search using an incremental probe strategy. When we need to insert an element, we follow the insertion algorithm until we reach an empty slot, then put the new element into that slot.

Linear Probing

A probe strategy that uses a constant increment function, say, $incr() = -1$, is called *linear probing*. To illustrate linear probing, we shall build a hash table in a 26-position array with the hash function that maps a string to the first letter it contains. We begin by inserting Bach and Dvorak, which yields the following hash table (showing only non-empty slots):

```
B:   Bach
D:   Dvorak
```

In a hash table that is maintained with a probe strategy, a *chain* is the sequence of occupied slots that are examined by the probe strategy during a search for an item that is not in the table. For linear probing, the chains are contiguous occupied slots in the hash table. In this table, the chains that start at slots B and D are both of length one.

Next we insert Beethoven. Since it hashes to the slot occupied by Bach, we invoke the linear probing strategy and Beethoven drops into slot A. Now the table looks like this:

```
A:   Beethoven
B:   Bach
D:   Dvorak
```

This hash table contains three non-empty chains, two of length one (starting at A and D) and one of length two (starting at B).

When we insert Debussy, slot D is already occupied, so linear probing takes over again to yield this table:

```
A:   Beethoven
B:   Bach
C:   Debussy
D:   Dvorak
```

This table contains four chains of positive length, one each of lengths 1, 2, 3, and 4. How did we get from a table whose longest chain contains two items to a table that includes a chain of length four? When Debussy was inserted, it caused the chain that started at B to be tacked onto the end of the chain that starts at D; we say that the two chains *coalesced*.

Finally, we shall insert Chopin. The linear probing strategy takes it past Debussy, Bach, and Beethoven before it settles into slot Z.

```
Z:   Chopin
A:   Beethoven
B:   Bach
C:   Debussy
D:   Dvorak
```

Note that on its way from slot C to slot Z, Chopin encountered no other items that hash to C. The coalescing of neighboring hash chains lengthened the search time for items with with hash value C even though none had yet been entered into the table.

This illustration suggests that hashing with linear probing might not be much better than sequential search. Part of the reason for the dismal performance of our example is that the hash function does not spread out the composers' names through the table; its chief virtue, in fact, is that it is easy for people to compute at a glance. On the other hand, no matter what hash function and probe strategy one uses, there is always a danger that chains will coalesce to create long search paths. Indeed, in the worst case all elements hash to the same key, linear probing degenerates to sequential search, and it takes $\Theta(n^2)$ time to insert n items.

Simulation of Linear Probing

To gain some insight into the expected performance of linear probing on random input, we shall gather some statistics. We use the random name generator in Program 1.3 to generate input consisting of four-letter strings. The insertion function in Program 8.2 calculates two statistics about the number of probes required to insert each item into the hash table: `succlen` accumulates the total length of the probe sequences that ended with a new item being inserted into the table, and `num` tells how many items there are in the table. Since the number of probes used to insert an item is the same as the number of probes that we would need to find the item during a subsequent search, `succlen/num` is the average number of probes that a successful search in the table would use.

The performance of hashing with linear probing depends on the hash function. Figure 8.2 shows the results obtained with three simple hash functions. If σ is a string, let σ_i be the ith character of σ, for $0 \le i < |\sigma|$. Function $h_0(\sigma) = \sum_{i \ge 0} \sigma_i$ simply adds the characters in σ; this is not likely to be a good hash function, since a four-letter string can hash to only 104 (= 4×26) different values, and since any permutation of the same four letters receives the same hash value. Function $h_1(\sigma) = \sum_{i \ge 0} (i+1)\sigma_i$ multiplies or *weights* each character by its position in σ; thus, two words that are permutations of the same set of letters can get different hash values under $h_1()$. Function $h_2(\sigma) = \sum_{i \ge 0} (i+1)^2 \sigma_i$ weights each character by the square of its position in σ. We can see from Figure 8.2 that the performance of these functions is directly related to the weight they give to character position—the more, the better.

As the number of occupied slots in a hash table increases, it becomes more likely that long chains will coalesce. We can express the expected length of search paths in an M-slot hash table that contains N items in terms of the *load factor*, $\alpha = N/M$. If every possible sequence of insertions is equally likely, and the hash function randomly distributes keys through the table, then the expected length of a successful search path in a hash table loaded to α of its capacity is approximately

$$\frac{1}{2}\left[1 + \frac{1}{1-\alpha}\right]. \tag{8.1}$$

In Figure 8.3, function (8.1) is plotted along with the data obtained when hash function h_2 was used in Program 8.2; evidently h_2 distributes its input very well.

```c
#define TABSIZE 199
char *table[TABSIZE];

int num; /* number of occupied slots in table */
int succlen; /* total length of all successful searches */

int insert(char *s)
{
    int h, try, len = 1;
    try = h = hash(s)%TABSIZE;
    do {
        if (table[try] == NULL) {
            table[try] = strdup(s);
            succlen += len;
            num++;
            return NOTFOUND;
        } else if (!strcmp(table[try], s))
            return FOUND;
        try = (try - 1 + TABSIZE)%TABSIZE;
        len++;
    } while (try != h);
    /* table full:  no room for new item */
    return FULL;
}

main()
{
    char buf[6];
    while (fgets(buf, 6, stdin))
        switch (insert(buf)) {
        case NOTFOUND:
            printf("%d %g\n", num, (double) succlen/num);
            break;
        case FULL:
            exit(0);
        }
    exit(0);
}
```

PROGRAM 8.2

Part of a program to test hashing with linear probing, accumulating statistics about the number of probes used when a new item is inserted. The three identifiers FOUND, NOTFOUND, and FULL are used to return the result of the insertion operation to the calling function.

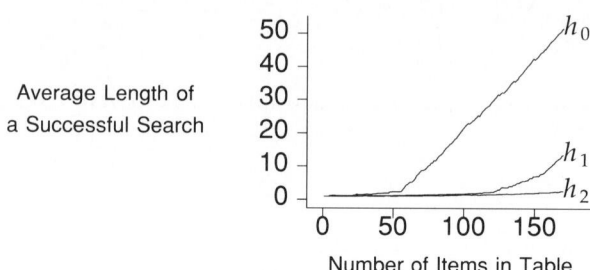

FIGURE 8.2

Statistics gathered from Program 8.2. Three different hash functions were used: $h_k(\sigma) = \sum_{i \geq 0}(i+1)^k \sigma_i$.

The expected length of an unsuccessful search path when we use hashing with linear probing tells the expected amount of work to insert a new item or to determine that an item is not present. This can be quite different from the expected length of a successful search path: if every slot in the hash table contains an item that hashes to that slot, then a successful search takes one probe, but an unsuccessful search must examine every slot in the table. The expected length of an unsuccessful search in a hash table filled to α of its capacity is approximately

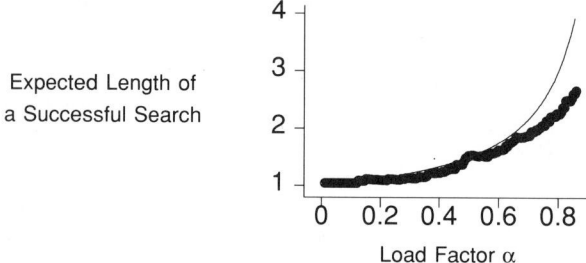

FIGURE 8.3

The narrow line shows the graph of function (8.1). The dark line shows the data gathered from Program 8.2 using hash function $h_2(\ )$.

$$\frac{1}{2}\left[1+\frac{1}{(1-\alpha)^2}\right]. \qquad (8.2)$$

Expressions (8.1) and (8.2) are both approximations. Indeed, they are undefined when $\alpha = 1$, that is, when the table is full. However, both expressions are good approximations to the expected lengths of successful and unsuccessful searches as long as α is not too close to 1. Their asymptotic behavior reinforces our intuition that we never want α to get close to 1, because when hash tables are nearly full, they exhibit terrible performance.

General Problems with Probe Strategies

Any collision resolution strategy that uses probe sequences faces two problems: the size of the table must be fixed in advance, and search times increase dramatically as the table becomes nearly full. We can address both of these problems by choosing a maximum acceptable load factor $\hat{\alpha}$, so that when the load factor exceeds $\hat{\alpha}$, we allocate a larger table and re-hash all items into it.

Collision resolution strategies that use probe sequences have a third problem that cannot be solved so easily. If we use a hash table to store a fully dynamic dictionary, how can we delete items? We cannot just mark as empty the slot in which the deleted item resides: that slot might also be keeping two coalesced chains together, so that marking it empty would cause searches for some items in one of the chains to fail. We could mark the slot as deleted, so that searches proceed over it, and a new item can be stored into it. Eventually this leaves all slots either occupied or marked "deleted," however, so every unsuccessful search must examine all slots in the table. Algorithms that actually delete items but preserve all chains can be devised, but they are complicated and tricky to get exactly right.

8.3
COLLISION RESOLUTION USING LINKED LISTS

Rather than store the items themselves in the slots of a hash table, we can make the slots contain pointers to linked lists of items. Under this scheme, the composers in Section 8.2 would appear in three lists:

```
B:   Bach, Beethoven
C:   Chopin
D:   Dvorak, Debussy
```

This arrangement has several nice properties. Since a linked list is composed of items whose keys hash to the same value, chains never coalesce. No matter how small we make the hash table, the number of items that can be stored in it is limited only by the amount of memory that can be allocated dynamically. Finally, we can delete an item from the dictionary using the straightforward algorithm to remove a node from a linked list.

Function `insert()` in Program 8.3 inserts an item into a hash table of linked lists. Figure 8.4 shows the result of using Program 8.3 with the same input and hash functions as were used to generate Figure 8.2. Even when we use the poor hash function $h_0()$, which does not generate a good spread of hash values, the average successful search examines only 2.5 items.

If we assume that all input sequences are equally likely, and that the hash function randomly distributes keys over the table, then the analysis of hashing using linked lists is straightforward: when N items are inserted into an M-slot table, the average length of a linked list is N/M. When N/M becomes large, the average search time will also be large; it can be reduced by increasing M and re-hashing. In contrast to collision resolution that uses a probe strategy, however, this re-allocation improves the search time, but is not absolutely necessary for the program to continue operating.

8.4
SUMMARY AND PERSPECTIVE

The two main ingredients of hashing algorithms are a hash function to spread key values through the table slots and a strategy to cope with keys that hash to the same value. Perfect hash functions obviate strategies for collision resolution, but they are difficult to compute, especially when they must be *minimal*, so that the hash table contains no more slots than items.

Hashing with a probe strategy to resolve collisions generates many interesting problems for theoretical analysis. It is an extremely simple algorithm, and is the only feasible solution when a language does not support pointers and dynamic storage allocation. It is limited by the fixed size of the table and the difficulty of deletion.

```
typedef struct item item;
struct item {
    item *next;
    char *s;
};

#define TABSIZE 199
item *table[TABSIZE];
int num; /* number of items in table */
int succlen; /* total length of all successful searches */

int insert(char *s)
{
    int h, len = 1;
    item **try;
    h = hash(s)%TABSIZE;
    try = &table[h];
    while (*try) {
        if (!strcmp(s, (*try)->s))
            return FOUND;
        len++;
        try = &((*try)->next);
    }
    *try = (item *) calloc(1, sizeof(item));
    demand(*try, calloc failed);
    (*try)->s = strdup(s);
    demand((*try)->s, strdup failed);
    num++;
    succlen += len;
    return NOTFOUND;
}
```

PROGRAM 8.3

Function to insert an element into a hash table of linked lists, accumulating statistics about the number of items seen during insertion.

Hashing with linked lists is an excellent solution to many searching problems. At the price of some space for pointers, we obtain a table of potentially unlimited size that readily supports insertions and deletions.

Many other hashing schemes are hybrids of the ideas presented in this chapter. One idea is to store all items in the table, but also to store pointers in the table that link together items whose keys have identical hash values. Thus, a successful search will examine only slots

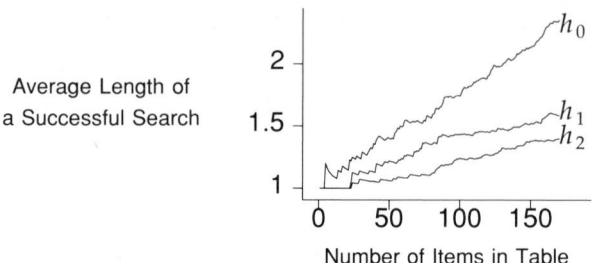

FIGURE 8.4

Statistics gathered using Program 8.3. As in Figure 8.3, hash function
$h_k(\sigma) = \sum_{i \geq 0} (i+1)^k \sigma_i$.

that contain items with the same hash value as that of the sought item;
we need only examine other items when we seek space in which to
store a new item.

In another variation of hashing, each slot can contain several items;
the slots are usually called *buckets*. An important application of this
variation is to have the table contain pointers to pages of virtual
memory, then to store many items on each page; each page serves as
the bucket for a given hash value. This makes it possible to search in a
large dictionary using only a couple of paging operations.

Good Hash Functions

Hashing schemes are called address calculation techniques because
they use the computer representation of the keys to calculate addresses
at which to search, and do not rely only on key comparisons. When
we design hash functions to perform address calculation we must balance carefully between two desirable properties: a hash function
should spread keys over the table well, and should also be inexpensive
to compute.

The worst case of hashing is easily realized by the constant hash
function: $hash(\sigma) = 0$; any hashing algorithm degenerates to sequential
search with this terrible hash function. On the other hand, if we have
a good hash function that spreads keys out evenly over the table, then
under appropriate circumstances the expected time for either kind of
hashing algorithm to perform searching and modification operations is
bounded by a constant.

To bound the expected time for hash table operations when we resolve collisions with a probe strategy, we need to bound $N/M = \alpha$ by a constant less than one. Of course, from expressions (8.1) and (8.2) we know that the constant expected time for the hash table operations will depend on the value of α. To obtain constant expected time when we use linked lists to resolve collisions, we merely choose a fixed constant k and require that $N/M < k$. In this case, the constant expected time for hash table operations is no larger than k.

Prime numbers figure prominently in the construction of many hash functions. There are a couple of reasons for this. An incremental probing strategy can reach all slots in the table if and only if the increment is relatively prime to the table size; an easy way to ensure this is to make the table size be a prime number. A prime number can also help to break up patterns in input data. For example, hash function $h_2()$ above would map the keys f000, f001, f002, ..., into $c, c+16,$ $c+32, \ldots$, where the constant c depends on the character set. If the table size were a power of 2, this collection of keys would collide in a small number of slots. When the table size is prime, however, this collection of keys is scattered throughout the table.

EXERCISES

1 Draw the contents of array planet[] produced by Program 8.1.

2 Program 8.1 reserves room for six more planets than are needed, simply to give fast search times. Revise it so that the table contains pointers to planets and allocates room for a planet structure only when necessary.

3 It is not really fair to say that perfect hash functions are hard to find: any key can be regarded as a number written in a suitably large base, and under this interpretation two different keys will hash to different values. Comment on the suitability of such hash functions for practical use.

4 Devise an incrementation function $incr()$ that causes Algorithm 8.1 to fail when the simpler statement "$try = (try+i+M) \bmod M;$" is used to move to the next position in the probe sequence.

5 Show that the expected number of probes to search in a hash table using the linear probing strategy does not depend on the order in which items were inserted into the hash table.

6 Write another simulation of hashing with linear probing that gathers statistics on the length of an *unsuccessful* search. How will you compute the average length of an unsuccessful search?

7 Plot the function shown in expression (8.2).

8 Explain the code for linked-list insertion in Program 8.3. Why does it call `calloc()` to allocate room for the new node?

9 In general, a probe strategy for collision resolution in an M-element hash table uses M hash functions $h_1()$, $h_2()$, ..., $h_M()$. An item with key k is stored in the $h_i(k)$th slot, where $i = \min\{\, j \mid \text{location } h_j(k) \text{ is empty}\}$. What properties should the function collection $\{\, h_i()\,\}$ have?

10 In *coalesced hashing*, the hash table has $M = m + c$ entries, and the hash function can yield only values between 0 and $m - 1$; the remaining c entries are called the *cellar*. When a collision occurs, the item is placed in the vacant slot with the largest address in the table; thus, the first c overflow items are stored in a single chain that grows upwards from the floor of the cellar; this chain can continue to grow up into the main part of the table. Implement coalesced hashing, and use simulation to decide a good value for c/M.

11 Algorithm 8.2 is alleged to delete an item from a hash table that uses linear probing. Show that it works.

12 Use a hash table to solve the problem in Section 1.1.

13 Comment on the suitability of each of the following as a hash function:

(a) $h(\sigma) = \sum_{i \geq 0} p_i^{\sigma_i}$, where p_i is the ith prime number;

```
delete(i)
/* delete item in position i of table[0:M−1] */
     int j, r
     while (1) {
          table[i] = 0 /* mark ith position empty */
          j = i
          while (1)
               i = (i−1+M) mod M
               if (table[i] == 0)
                    return
               r = hash(table[i].key)
               if (!(i ≤ r < j || r < j < i || j < i ≤ r))
                    break
          table[ j] = table[i]
```

ALGORITHM 8.2

An algorithm to delete an item from a hash table that resolves collisions with linear probing.

(b) $h(\sigma) = \sum_{i \geq 0} 2^i \sigma_i;$

(c) $h(\sigma) = \sigma_0 + \sigma_{|\sigma|-1};$

(d) $h(\sigma) = \Pi_{i \geq 0} \sigma_i;$

(e) $h(\sigma) = \sum_{i > 0} \sigma_{i-1} \sigma_i.$

14 Show how to use C's << operator to implement the hash function in Exercise 13(b).

REFERENCES

Most books call hashing with a probe strategy (Section 8.2) *open addressing*; an exception is

A. V. Aho, J. E. Hopcroft, and J. D. Ullman. *Data Structures and Algorithms*. Reading, Mass.: Addison-Wesley, 1983.

in which it is called *closed hashing*. Most books call hashing with linked lists (Section 8.3) *separate chaining*; Aho, Hopcroft, and Ullman call it *open hashing*.
Various hashing algorithms are analyzed in the following sources:

D. E. Knuth. *Sorting and Searching*. Vol. 3, *The Art of Computer Programming*. 2d printing. Reading, Mass.: Addison-Wesley, 1975.

G. H. Gonnet. *Handbook of Algorithms and Data Structures*. Reading, Mass.: Addison-Wesley, 1984.

R. L. Morris. "Scatter storage techniques." *Communications of the ACM* 11 (1968): 38–44.

The merits of various hash functions are discussed in

A. V. Aho, R. Sethi, and J. D. Ullman. *Compilers, Principles, Techniques, and Tools*. Reading, Mass.: Addison-Wesley, 1986.

G. D. Knott. "Hashing functions." *Computer Journal* 18 (1975): 265–278.

9

Sorted
Lists

Chapters 7 and 8 presented several ideas for how to search in a dictionary, but all of them can degenerate to brute-force sequential search in the worst case. In this chapter we shall see how to build search trees that obey *balance* conditions that keep them from becoming too scrawny. The balance conditions imply that a search in a tree on n items can be performed in $O(\log n)$ time. An obvious use for balanced search trees is to solve the dynamic dictionary problem when we cannot take the chance that the dictionary operations will take longer than time logarithmic in the size of the list.

A more important property of balanced trees, however, is that they let us implement a more powerful data type that supports several operations besides those in a standard dynamic dictionary. This data type is called a *sorted list*, though it has nothing to do with the ordered list data structure in Section 5.2. We can traverse a sorted list visiting the items in order according to their keys. Sorted lists also let us find the *bracketing pair* of an item with key k. The bracketing pair contains the two neighbors of k in the sorted list; if the list does not contain items with equal keys, then the bracketing pair contains the item in the list with the largest key smaller than k, and the item with the smallest key larger than k. Many applications need to find one or both members of an item's bracketing pair.

There are several ways to define balance conditions on trees. We shall see two kinds of balanced trees, then combine some ideas from each to define and implement a third variety. For each kind of balanced tree, we shall consider only how to insert and delete elements. Section 9.4 considers other operations on balanced trees.

193

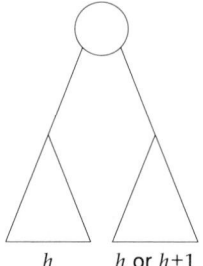

FIGURE 9.1

Abstract drawing of an AVL tree. Both subtrees of the root are themselves AVL trees.

9.1

AVL TREES

Define the *height* of a tree as the maximum depth of any leaf; a tree's height is the maximum length of any path from its root to a leaf. An AVL tree is a binary search tree that obeys the following rule on its shape:

> the height of the left and right subtrees of any node differs by at most one.

Figure 9.1 illustrates this rule schematically. The AVL tree in Figure 9.2 has height 4; its left subtree has height 3, and its right subtree has height 2. Since an AVL tree is a binary search tree, we can use Algorithm 7.4 to search in it.

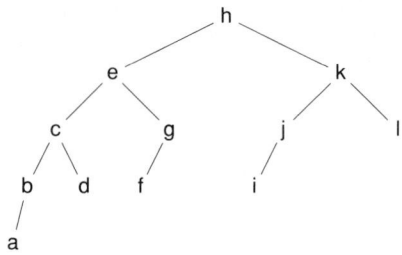

FIGURE 9.2

An AVL tree of height 4.

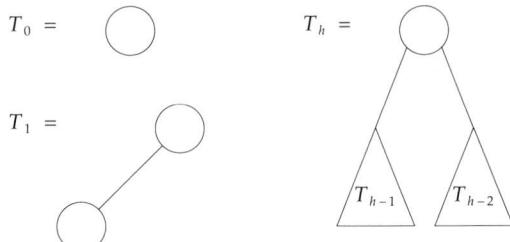

FIGURE 9.3

Formation rule for T_h, a sparsest AVL tree of height h. The tree in Figure 9.2 is an example of T_4.

Size of AVL Trees

The AVL rule is meant to prevent an AVL tree of n items from being so scrawny that some items lie at a depth larger than $O(\log n)$. To see that the AVL rule does this, let A_h be the minimum possible number of nodes in an AVL tree of height h. Because the subtrees of an AVL tree are also AVL trees, we can construct AVL trees of height h on A_h nodes according to the formation rules in Figure 9.3. Therefore, we can write the recurrence relation

$$A_h = A_{h-1} + A_{h-2} + 1, \ h \geq 0, \tag{9.1}$$

with the implicit understanding that $A_h = 0$ when $h < 0$.

The following solution to Equation (9.1) can be verified by induction:

$$A_h = \left[1 + \frac{2\sqrt{5}}{5}\right]\left[\frac{1+\sqrt{5}}{2}\right]^h + \left[1 - \frac{2\sqrt{5}}{5}\right]\left[\frac{1-\sqrt{5}}{2}\right]^h - 1. \tag{9.2}$$

Since $|(1-\sqrt{5})/2| < 1$, the second term shrinks as h becomes larger, and we can express the asymptotic behavior of A_h as a function of the first term alone: $A_h = \Theta(((1+\sqrt{5})/2)^h)$. From this we can conclude that the height of an AVL tree on n nodes is $O(\log n)$. Since any binary search tree on n nodes has height $\Omega(\log n)$, the height of an AVL tree on n nodes is $\Theta(\log n)$.

Insertion into an AVL Tree

To insert an item into a binary search tree, we search as if it were already in the tree; if the item is not present, this search leads us to a

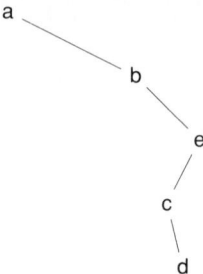

FIGURE 9.4

The scrawny binary search tree generated by inserting a, b, e, c, and d, in that order, into a binary search tree.

leaf of the tree, where we insert the new item as a child. This algorithm is also the first step to insert an item into an AVL tree. Sometimes, however, after we do this the tree does not obey the AVL rule, and we must take further steps to rebalance the tree.

We illustrate this by inserting the five letters a, b, e, c, and d, in that order, into an initially empty AVL tree. Without care to maintain the AVL property, this insertion order produces the scrawny binary search tree shown in Figure 9.4.

The first two insertions (of a and b) require no special treatment, and yield the AVL tree shown in Figure 9.5.

Figure 9.6a shows the tree that results immediately after inserting e; it does not obey the AVL rule, because the left subtree of the root is empty, while the right subtree has height two. To repair this violation, we rearrange the tree so that b is at the root and the symmetric ordering of the nodes is preserved, as shown in Figure 9.6b. This is an example of a *single rotation*.

When c is inserted into the tree in Figure 9.6b, the result is still an AVL tree. After d is inserted, however, the resulting tree no longer obeys the AVL rule (Figure 9.7a). To repair the violation, we rearrange the right subtree of the root as shown in Figure 9.7b, restoring the AVL

FIGURE 9.5

The AVL tree after insertion of a and b.

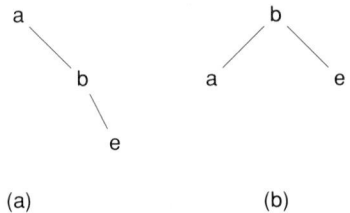

FIGURE 9.6

Inserting e into the AVL tree of Figure 9.5. Immediately after insertion, the tree appears as in (a); a single rotation corrects the violation, leaving the tree shown in (b).

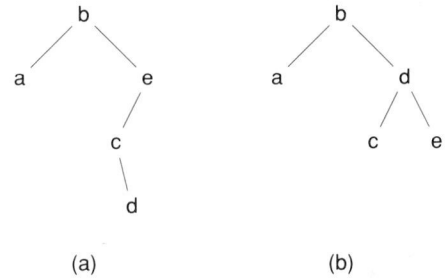

FIGURE 9.7

Insertion of d into an AVL tree. The tree shown in (a), immediately after the insertion, fails to obey the AVL property; a double rotation restores the property, as shown in (b).

property and preserving the symmetric order of the nodes. This is an example of a *double rotation*.

The construction of the AVL tree in Figure 9.7b shows the two basic kinds of operation that are needed to maintain an AVL tree: single and double rotations. (There are symmetric variants of both single and double rotation that apply when the tree is unbalanced in a different direction.) To demonstrate that single and double rotations suffice to maintain an AVL tree, we show how to use them to repair any violation of the AVL rule that is detected during a walk back up the tree from a newly inserted item. Consider the tree rooted at the first node we discover during this walk whose left and right subtrees violate the AVL rule. It must look like the tree shown in Figure 9.8a: since this tree was an AVL tree before the insertion, and insertion of a single

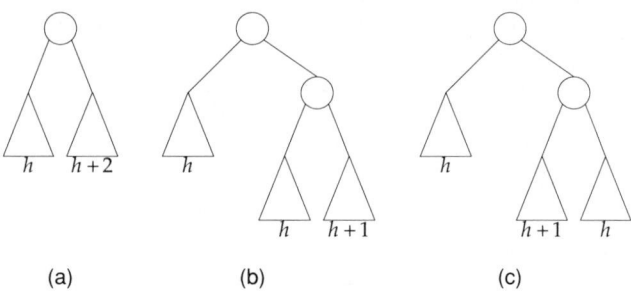

(a)   (b)   (c)

FIGURE 9.8

When a violation of the AVL rule is discovered after insertion into an AVL tree, the tree must have a node with subtrees that differ in height by two, as shown in (a). The taller subtree must itself have subtrees that differ in height by one as in either (b) or (c). There is a symmetric variant of each of these trees in which the taller subtree is on the left.

item can increase the height of a tree by at most one, the disparity in height between its left and right subtrees must be two.

Before the insertion, this tree was of height $h+2$; now it is of height $h+3$. The new leaf was added to the subtree that is now of height $h+2$; since this was also an AVL tree before insertion and remains an AVL tree now, its height was $h+1$ before the insertion. The root of the $h+2$-high subtree has subtrees of heights h and $h+1$, as shown in Figure 9.8b or c.

If the tree is as shown in Figure 9.8b, then Figure 9.9 shows how a single rotation restores the AVL property and preserves symmetric order on the nodes. If the tree is as shown in Figure 9.9c, then Figure 9.10 shows how a double rotation restores the AVL property and preserves symmetric order on the nodes. In either case the resulting tree has height $h+2$. Since this is the same as the height of the tree before the insertion, no more rotations will be needed during the rest of the walk toward the root. Figure 9.11 illustrates that the repairs needed after insertion can occur at some distance from the new leaf.

To analyze the time complexity of insertion into AVL trees, we observe first that we can perform a single or double rotation in constant time by rearranging pointers. Since the search path is of length $O(\log n)$ when the AVL tree contains n nodes, and we discover the need for rotations and perform them during a single walk along the search path, we can insert an item into an AVL tree on n nodes in $O(\log n)$ time.

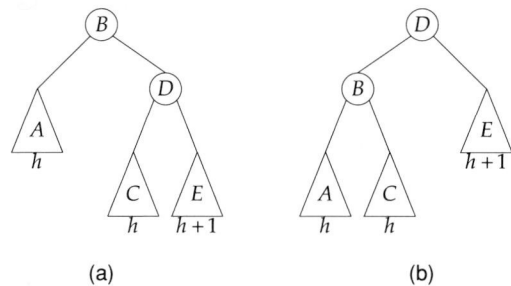

(a)   (b)

FIGURE 9.9

The pieces of the tree in Figure 9.8b are named in (a). The result of a single rotation is shown as (b). There is a symmetric variant of single rotation.

Deletion from an AVL Tree

As in the case of insertion, the first step in deleting an item from an AVL tree is the same as for any binary search tree: find the item and remove it. The rearrangement can cause the tree to lose the AVL property, so we must walk back up toward the root from the deepest node affected by the deletion to detect and repair any violations of the

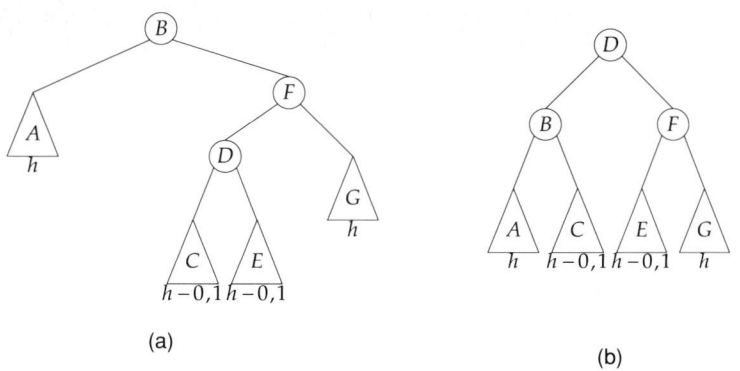

(a)   (b)

FIGURE 9.10

The tree in Figure 9.8c is drawn in more detail in (a); the height label "$h-0,1$" means either h or $h-1$; note that at least one of subtrees C and E has height h. A double rotation leaves the tree as in (b). There is a symmetric variant of double rotation.

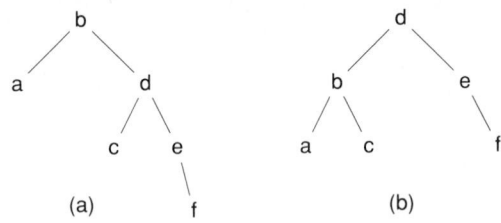

FIGURE 9.11

The tree in (a) results from inserting f into the AVL tree of Figure 9.7b; we must walk back up to the root before we discover a violation; a single rotation repairs it, as shown in (b).

AVL property. This walk proceeds much as in the case of insertion, with one important difference.

Suppose we discover a violation of the AVL rule at a node x; that is, the subtree rooted at x looks like Figure 9.8a. Since we have just deleted an item, the deletion must have occurred in x's child subtree of height h. Before we repair the imbalance, the tree rooted at x has height $h+3$; after the appropriate rotation, it has height $h+2$. Since rotation decreases the height of the tree rooted at x, we might discover that we need to repair more imbalances as we continue our walk toward the root. As an example of such propagating rotations, suppose we delete 1 from the AVL tree in Figure 9.2. During the walk to the root, we discover and repair a violation at the node that contains k, then discover another violation at the node that contains h. Figure 9.12 shows the two rotations that are needed to restore the AVL property.

Since the search path is of length $O(\log n)$, and we perform at most one rotation at each level of the tree, we can delete an item from an AVL tree on n nodes in $O(\log n)$ time.

9.2
2,4 TREES

There is no need to restrict ourselves to binary trees as candidates for search trees with good worst-case operation time. The trees in this section are not binary trees; nevertheless, the definitions of tree properties such as height and node depth have an obvious and natural interpretation on non-binary trees.

A *2,4 tree* is a tree with the following properties:

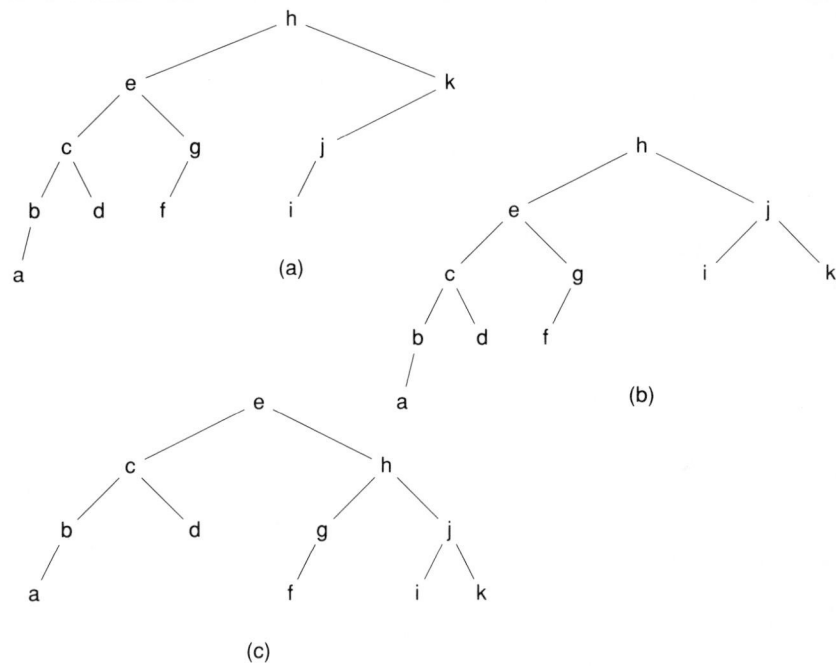

FIGURE 9.12

Figure (a) shows the tree of Figure 9.2 after l is deleted. To restore the AVL property, we must perform two double rotations, as shown in (b) and (c).

1 Every node (except possibly the root) has between two and four children. A node with k children is called a k-*node*.

2 All leaves lie at the same depth, the height of the 2,4 tree.

3 Items are stored in the leaves of the tree. Each internal node contains, for each of its children, the value of the largest key in the subtree rooted at that child.

4 The items in the leaves appear in order from left to right.

Figure 9.13 shows an example of a 2,4-tree. This tree on 22 items is of height three.

Properties 3 and 4 make searching in a 2,4 tree only slightly more complicated than searching in a binary tree. To search for an item given its key, we begin at the root and use the information at each node to decide which child of that node should be next on our search path. For instance, to find r in the tree of Figure 9.13, we would go from the root (e, j, y) to its rightmost child, because j < r < y. Next

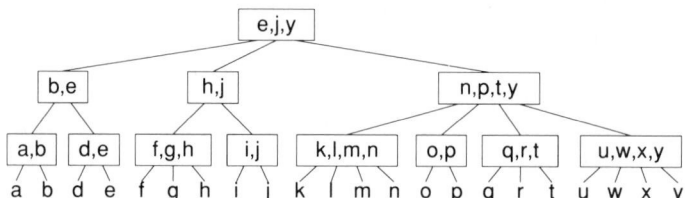

FIGURE 9.13

A 2,4 tree on 22 items. The left subtree of the root is a 2,4 tree on four items, while the right subtree is a 2,4 tree on 13 items.

we would go to the second from the right child of the 4-node n,p,t,y, because p < r < t. Finally, we would go to the middle child of the 3-node q,r,t, which contains the item with key r.

Size of 2,4 Trees

Properties 2, 3, and 4 mean that to search for any item in a 2,4 tree takes a number of steps proportional to the height of the tree. Property 1 implies that a 2,4 tree of height h, $h > 1$, has between 2^h and 4^h items at its leaves. Therefore, a search in a 2,4 tree on n items takes $\Theta(\log n)$ time.

Insertion into a 2,4 Tree

As in a binary search tree, insertion into a 2,4 tree begins with a search to locate where the item should be inserted, and insertion of that item. If the item is inserted at a 2-node or a 3-node, then the node becomes a 3-node or a 4-node, and we need only update the key information at internal nodes along the search path to the new item. For instance, if we insert c into the tree of Figure 9.13, the 2-node d,e becomes a 3-node; if we insert s into the same tree, the 3-node q,r,t becomes a 4-node.

If we insert an item into a 4-node, however, it becomes a 5-node, which violates property 1. Figure 9.14a shows the result of inserting v into the tree of Figure 9.13. There are many ways we could repair the tree. A uniform method is to split the 5-node into a 2-node and a 3-node; these legal nodes replace the 5-node as children of its parent. (See Figure 9.14b.) This can make the parent into a 5-node, as it does in this example (n,p,t,w,y), requiring it to split into a 2-node and a 3-node, as shown in Figure 9.14c. In the worst case, all nodes on the

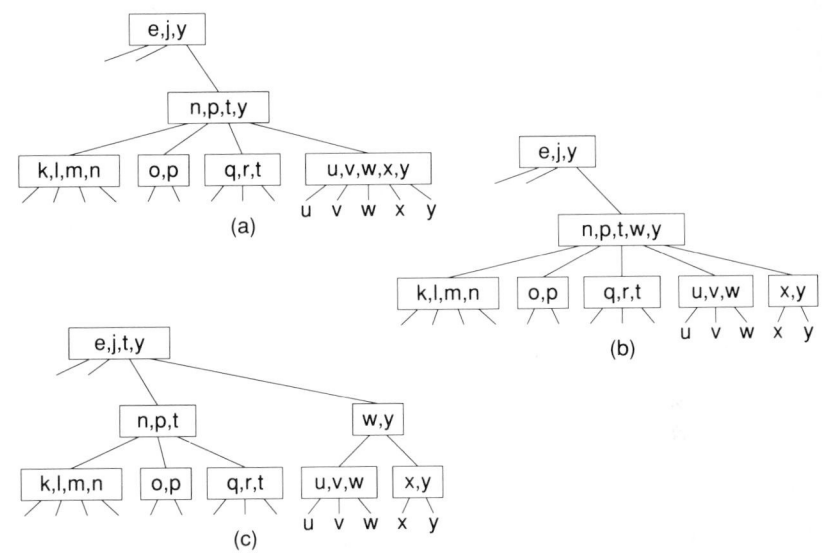

FIGURE 9.14

Insertion of the letter v into the 2,4 tree of Figure 9.13. Dangling edges indicate subtrees that do not change. The insertion creates a 5-node that contains keys u, v, w, x, y, shown in (a); when u, v, w, x, y splits into a 2-node and a 3-node, it creates a 5-node on keys n, p, t, w, y, shown in (b); when n, p, t, w, y splits into a 2-node and a 3-node, the root becomes a 4-node as shown in (c).

path from the root to the new leaf must split, and a new root must be created, leaving a tree that is one level taller than it was before.

Since the length of the access path is $\Theta(\log n)$, and a split requires $O(1)$ operations, we can insert an item into a 2,4 tree in $\Theta(\log n)$ time.

Deletion from a 2,4 Tree

Deletion from a 2,4 tree is more complicated than insertion. The first step is to search for the item. After the item is deleted we must repair any imbalance at its parent. If the parent is a 3-node or a 4-node, deleting an item leaves a 2-node or a 3-node, so we need only update key information in the nodes along the access path. For example, if we delete g or n from the tree in Figure 9.13, the tree still obeys the 2,4 property without rearrangement.

If the parent of the doomed node is a 2-node, however, deletion leaves it a 1-node. We must repair this violation of property 1. There are two possibilities: if the 1-node has a sibling with more than two children, then we can redistribute the children among the 1-node and its siblings. For instance, in Figure 9.13, if we delete i, we can move h from f,g,h to create two 2-nodes from a 3-node and a 1-node; if we delete p, we can move n or q from a neighbor to fill up the 1-node o.

If all siblings of the doomed item are also 2-nodes, however, then we have more nodes than items to distribute among them, so we coalesce the 1-node and one of the 2-nodes into a 3-node. This node replaces the 1-node and the 2-node as a child of their parent, and can make the parent into a 1-node. For example, if we delete b from the tree in Figure 9.13, and coalesce the two nodes, their parent becomes a 1-node, as illustrated in Figures 9.15a and b. Thus node coalescings can propagate up the access path, as illustrated in Figure 9.15c.

Deletion from 2,4 trees is complicated because at each step along the access path we must decide which of several cases applies to repair an imbalance. Since there is a fixed number of cases, however, and each case can be fixed in constant time, rebalancing costs $O(1)$ time per level. Property 1 guarantees that the length of the access path is $\Theta(\log n)$, so we can delete an item from a 2,4 tree on n nodes in $\Theta(\log n)$ time.

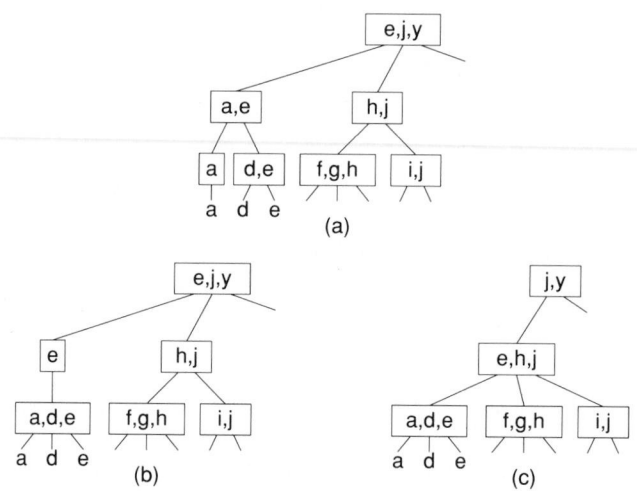

FIGURE 9.15

Deletion of the letter b from the 2,4 tree of Figure 9.13. Dangling edges indicate subtrees that do not change. Removing b leaves a 1-node containing key a, shown in (a); coalescing that with its sibling 2-node creates a 3-node, but leaves a 1-node parent e, as shown in (b); coalescing that node with its sibling h, j creates a 3-node and makes the root a 2-node, shown in (c).

9.3

IMPLEMENTATION: RED-BLACK TREES

In this section we shall implement a data structure for sorted lists that uses ideas from both AVL trees and 2,4 trees. *Red-black trees* are binary search trees like AVL trees, and we use rotations to maintain them. On the other hand, red-black trees can be interpreted as 2,4 trees; like 2,4 trees, red-black trees store items at their leaves and keep search information at internal nodes.

A red-black tree is a binary search tree whose nodes are colored either red or black in obedience to the following rules:

1   All leaves are black.

2   *Red rule*: Both children of any red node are black.

3   The path from the root to any leaf passes through the same number of black nodes; when this number is $h+1$, the red-black tree has *black height h*.

The keys in the internal nodes of a red-black tree obey the following condition: the key at a node is smaller than the key of any item in the node's right subtree, and is at least as large as the key of any item in the node's left subtree (it need not be equal to the largest item in the left subtree). You should take a moment to convince yourself that the conventional search algorithm for a binary search tree (Algorithm 7.4) continues to work when the keys at the internal nodes obey the stated condition. This flexible condition makes it easier to perform insertion and deletion in a red-black tree.

Figure 9.16 shows a red-black tree of black height two. By drawing all black nodes of the same black depth at the same horizontal level, we can see at a glance that the tree is red-black.

Relation to 2,4 Trees

It is convenient to insist that the root of a red-black tree be black, except possibly during an operation that modifies the tree. This convention yields a simple relationship between a red-black tree and a 2,4 tree. Take each black node together with its red children (if any), and replace the collection by the corresponding 2,4 tree node shown in Figure 9.17. The result is a 2,4 tree whose height is the same as the black height of the original red-black tree. We conclude that a red-black tree on n items has black height $\Theta(\log n)$. Since the red rule guarantees that a red-black tree of black height h has height at most $2h+1$, we can search for an item in a red-black tree on n items in $\Theta(\log n)$ time.

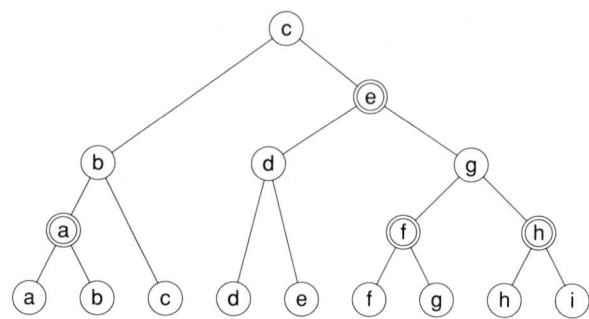

FIGURE 9.16

A red-black tree on nine items whose black height is two.

Declarations

Program 9.1a shows the declarations for our implementation of red-black trees. To keep the illustration simple, we use integers as items; the values of the identifiers PLUSINFINITY and MINUSINFINITY should be larger and smaller, respectively, than the values that will be stored in the red-black tree. To make it easy to change the types of

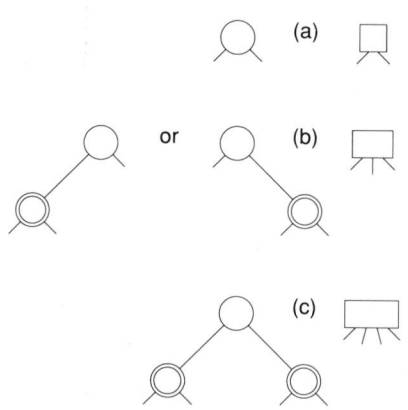

FIGURE 9.17

Correspondences between red-black tree node configurations and 2,4 tree nodes: (a) 2-node; (b) two forms of 3-node; (c) 4-node.

```
typedef int kind;
#define isleq(x,y)  ((x)<=(y))

typedef struct node node;
struct node {
    boolean red;
    kind key;
    node *link[2];
};
#define isred(p)   ((p)->red)
#define makered(p)  (p)->red = TRUE
#define makeblack(p)  (p)->red = FALSE
#define lchild(p)  ((p)->link[TRUE])
#define rchild(p)  ((p)->link[FALSE])
#define isleaf(p)  (lchild(p) == (p))
node *head;
#define root rchild(head)
```

PROGRAM 9.1a

Declarations for an implementation of red-black trees. The implementation also assumes that two constants, PLUSINFINITY and MINUSINFINITY, are defined.

---

items, the extreme values that serve as sentinels, and the inequality comparison, we refer to them through macro definitions.

A red-black tree node has a color, a search key value, and pointers to its left and right children; a node whose left child points to itself is a leaf. We test for the color of a node and whether it is a leaf using macro definitions. By storing the pointers to a node's children in an array, we can express very concisely the rotations needed to restore the red-black property; macro definitions let us write in terms of the more customary notions of left and right child.

Program 9.1b contains elementary functions we need in our implementation. Function newleaf() simply creates a leaf that contains its argument as the item. Function newnode() creates an internal node with its two arguments as children. It installs the child with smaller key as the left child, and it can store that key in itself to satisfy the condition on internal node keys.

Our implementation uses a header node head, whose right child is the root of the red-black tree under construction. To initialize the red-black tree, function init() creates the header node with two children that contain extreme key values, as shown in Figure 9.18.

```
node *newnode(node *c1, node *c2)
{
    node *result;
    result = (node *) malloc(sizeof(node));
    demand(result, out of memory in newnode);
    makeblack(result);
    demand((c1 && c2), newnode needs 2 children);
    if (isleq(c1->key, c2->key)) {
        lchild(result) = c1;
        rchild(result) = c2;
    } else {
        lchild(result) = c2;
        rchild(result) = c1;
    }
    result->key = lchild(result)->key;
    return result;
}

node *newleaf(kind x)
{
    node *result;
    result = (node *) malloc(sizeof(node));
    demand(result, out of memory in newleaf);
    makeblack(result);
    result->key = x;
    lchild(result) = rchild(result) = result;
    return result;
}

void init(void)
{
    head = newnode(newleaf(MINUSINFINITY),
        newleaf(PLUSINFINITY));
}
```

PROGRAM 9.1b

Node allocation and tree initialization functions for an implementation of red-black trees.

Insertion into a Red-Black Tree

Red-black trees are similar enough to 2,4 trees that you can probably see how to insert an item and repair imbalances during a walk back up

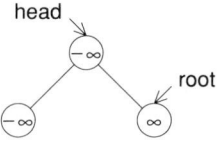

FIGURE 9.18

Data structure view of the "empty" red-black tree constructed by `init()`.

the access path to the root. It is also possible, however, to perform enough rebalancing operations on the way down to an insertion to obviate completely the backward traversal of the access path. To perform such a *top-down insertion*, we want our search for the new item's position to arrive at a leaf whose parent is black; if we can make this happen, then we can replace that leaf by a red internal node, one of whose children is the new item, as shown in Figure 9.19.

In pursuit of this goal, we try to toss red nodes up the tree as we walk down. The basic tool we use is the *color flip* illustrated in Figure 9.20. It pushes the red color one level up the tree while preserving the black height requirement.

The snag in this scheme is that a color flip can lead to a newly colored red node whose parent is also red, which violates the red rule. Ignoring symmetries, there are two ways this can happen, shown in Figure 9.21. If we apply the appropriate rotation (single for Figure 9.21a, double for Figure 9.21b) and swap the colors of nodes c and e, we get the tree in Figure 9.22. Since the trees rooted at b, d, f, and h are all red-black trees, the tree rooted at e is also a red-black tree.

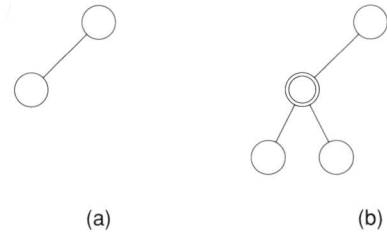

(a)   (b)

FIGURE 9.19

Insertion at a leaf that is a child of a black node is as easy as going from (a) to (b).

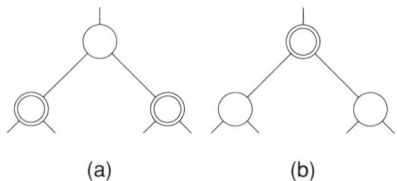

(a)   (b)

FIGURE 9.20

In the color flip operation, red coloring of a node is pushed one level up the tree by going from (a) to (b). Whether the root of this subtree is a right or left child of its parent is irrelevant.

Moreover, its black height is the same as the black height of a's old right subtree, so the whole search tree is once again a red-black tree.

We implement red-black tree insertion in several pieces. We already know that we shall need to store a portion of the access path; we can deduce how much from Figure 9.21. When we perform a color flip at a node (at g in Figure 9.21a, at e in Figure 9.21b) that requires subsequent repairs, we need to change a child of the great-grandparent of that node (the great-grandparent is a in both Figures 9.21a and b). Thus, we shall keep track of the four most recent nodes along the

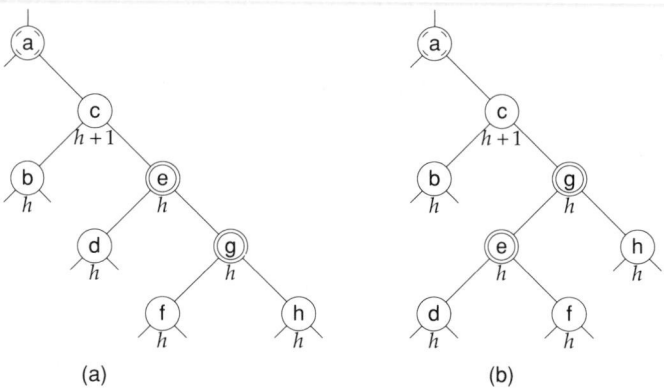

(a)   (b)

FIGURE 9.21

A color flip (at g in (a), at e in (b)) can lead to a path with two red nodes in a row. The black heights of all nodes but a are shown; a could be either black or red, so its black height could be either $h+1$ or $h+2$. There are three symmetric variants of each case.

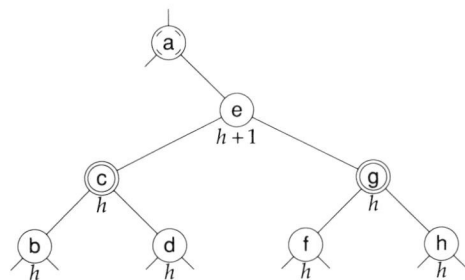

FIGURE 9.22

Both of the trees in Figure 9.21 can be rotated and recolored into this red-black tree.

access path, together with an indication for each node of which child it is of its parent. For instance, when we reach node e at depth i in Figure 9.21b, we shall have available the access path information shown in Figure 9.23. The data structure declarations for the access path appear at the start of Program 9.1c.

Function `singlerot()` in Program 9.1c performs a single rotation. Its argument is the index in the access path of the topmost node that will be affected by the rotation; that node's grandchild along the access path will become its child. To make this possible, the subtree that lies in symmetric order between the child and grandchild must be moved. For example, suppose we wish to perform a single rotation on the tree in Figure 9.21a. We would call `singlerot()` at a; hence, in `singlerot()`, `path(i).ptr` is a, `path(i+1).ptr` is c, and `path(i+2).ptr` is e. Three assignment statements effect the rotation: d becomes the right child of c, c becomes the left child of e, and finally e becomes the right child of a. After the rotation is finished, e

j	path(j).ptr	path(j).left
i-3	a	*irrelevant*
i-2	c	FALSE
i-1	g	FALSE
i	e	TRUE

FIGURE 9.23

The contents of the access path array when the current node is E on the tree in Figure 9.21b.

```
typedef struct frame frame;
struct frame {
    boolean left;    /* which child is *ptr of its parent? */
    node *ptr;
};
frame nodepath[4];
#define path(j) nodepath[(j)%4]

void singlerot(int i)
{
    demand(path(i).ptr->link[path(i+1).left] ==
        path(i+1).ptr, ptr i botch before singlerot);
    demand(path(i+1).ptr->link[path(i+2).left] ==
        path(i+2).ptr, ptr i+1 botch before singlerot);
    path(i+1).ptr->link[path(i+2).left]
        = path(i+2).ptr->link[!path(i+2).left];
    path(i+2).ptr->link[!path(i+2).left] = path(i+1).ptr;
    path(i).ptr->link[path(i+1).left] = path(i+2).ptr;
    /* partially repair node path */
    path(i+1).ptr = path(i+2).ptr;
    demand(path(i).ptr->link[path(i+1).left] ==
        path(i+1).ptr, ptr botch after singlerot);
}

void rotate(int i)
{
    if (path(i+3).left != path(i+2).left)
        /* need a double rotation */
        singlerot(i+1);
    singlerot(i);
}
```

PROGRAM 9.1c

Declaration of access path data structure and rotation functions for red-black trees.

replaces c in the access path. The demand()s in singlerot() ensure that the access path data structure contains sensible information before and after the single rotation.

Function rotate() in Program 9.1c performs an appropriate rotation—single or double as needed. Its argument is the index of the topmost node in the access path that will be affected by the rotation. If that node's grandchild and great-grandchild along the access path are both left or both right children, then a single rotation suffices to rebalance the tree. If, on the other hand, one of the node's grandchild and great-grandchild along the access path is a right child and the other is a left child, then a double rotation is needed, and is performed as two single rotations. For example, to perform the appropriate rotation on the tree in Figure 9.21b, `rotate()` calls `singlerot()` twice; the first call at c yields the tree in Figure 9.21a; the second call at a results in the tree of Figure 9.22.

Both `rotate()` and `singlerot()` are concerned exclusively with tree rearrangement: they do not adjust any node colors. Color-flipping and other recoloring is performed by `flipandfix()`, shown in Program 9.1d. The argument to `flipandfix()` is the index of a node along the access path that should be colored red. After `flipandfix()` does this recoloring, it checks whether the parent of the newly red node is also red. If so, it makes the node's grandparent red, performs the appropriate rotation, and colors the root of the original great-grandparent's new right subtree black. Finally, it resets the value of i that is returned by `flipandfix()`. This value represents the last node on the access path that is still guaranteed to belong to the access path after `flipandfix()` has done its job.

With these three functions in hand, we turn to the job of insertion. The current node in the search down the tree is stored in `path(i).ptr`; its parent, grandparent, and great-grandparent are in `path(i-1).ptr`, `path(i-2).ptr`, and `path(i-3).ptr`, respectively. Because we access members of `nodepath[]` through macro `path()`, these relationships are preserved when we add one to i and store a node and direction at `path(i)`. Function `insert()` starts with the current node set to the header node and walks down the tree as in standard tree search. When the current node is a red node with two black children, `insert()` calls `flipandfix()` to perform a color flip and any necessary rotation. Since a rotation changes a child of the color-flipped node's great-grandparent, we use the result of `flipandfix()` to reset the current node to that great-grandparent, which is guaranteed to belong to the access path. Once we have modified the access path to a node, we should make no more changes on that path; variable `maxi` ensures that we shall not attempt to modify a changed access path during subsequent traversals. When `insert()` reaches a leaf, it performs the tree manipulation shown in Figure 9.19 to add the new item, then calls `flipandfix()` to do the recoloring and any necessary rotation. While doing its job, `insert()` might have colored the root red; since this does nothing for the balance of the tree, and we promised above to keep the tree root black, `insert()` recolors the root black before it returns.

```
int flipandfix(int i)
{
    makered(path(i).ptr);
    makeblack(lchild(path(i).ptr));
    makeblack(rchild(path(i).ptr));
    if (isred(path(i-1).ptr)) {
        makered(path(i-2).ptr);
        rotate(i-3);
        makeblack(path(i-2).ptr);
        i = i-3;
    }
    return i;
}

void insert(kind x)
{
    int i = 0, maxi = 0;
    path(i).ptr = head;
    do {
        path(i+1).left = isleq(x, path(i).ptr->key);
        path(i+1).ptr = path(i).ptr->link[path(i+1).left];
        if (++i > maxi)
            maxi = i;
        if (i >= maxi && isred(lchild(path(i).ptr)) &&
            isred(rchild(path(i).ptr)))
            i = flipandfix(i);
    } while (!isleaf(path(i).ptr));
    path(i).ptr = path(i-1).ptr->link[path(i).left]
        = newnode(path(i).ptr, newleaf(x));
    flipandfix(i);
    makeblack(root); /* in case red flipped too high */
}
```

PROGRAM 9.1d

Functions for insertion into a red-black tree.

It is important to note that insert() preserves the red-black property of the tree at each step along the access path. We could stop at
any time and have a valid red-black tree. In particular, if we reach a
leaf and discover that the item being inserted is already present, and
we do not wish to store duplicate items in the tree, then we can simply
return from insert() without having to undo any of the adjustments
we made on the way down the tree.

```
void delete(kind x)
{
    int i = 0;
    node *cur;
    boolean curdir, rotoccurred;
#define sib path(i+1).ptr
#define sibdir path(i+1).left
#define cous path(i+2).ptr
#define cousdir path(i+2).left
    if (!isred(lchild(root)) && !isred(rchild(root)))
        makered(root);
    path(i).ptr = head;
    for (;;) {
        rotoccurred = FALSE;
        curdir = isleq(x, path(i).ptr->key);
        cur = path(i).ptr->link[curdir];
        if (isleaf(cur))
            break;
        sibdir = !curdir;
        sib = path(i).ptr->link[sibdir];
        if (!isred(path(i).ptr) && !isred(cur) && isred(sib)) {
            makered(path(i).ptr);
            makeblack(sib);
            singlerot(i-1); /* 3-node rotation */
            rotoccurred = TRUE;
        } else if (!isred(cur) && !isred(lchild(cur)) &&
            !isred(rchild(cur))) {
            demand(isred(path(i).ptr), no red to shove down);
            makered(cur);
            makeblack(path(i).ptr);
            if (!isred(lchild(sib)) && !isred(rchild(sib)))
                makered(sib);   /* reverse color flip */
            else {
                if (isred(lchild(sib)))
```

PROGRAM 9.1e(i)

The first part of a deletion function for a red-black tree.

Deletion from Red-Black Trees

The idea behind the deletion algorithm for red-black trees is just the opposite of the motivation for the insertion algorithm. We would be delighted to find the doomed item hanging as a leaf of a red node, because deletion in that case could simply reverse the steps of Figure 9.19. Thus, we would like to shove the red node coloring down the

```
                    cousdir = TRUE;
               else
                    cousdir = FALSE;
               cous = sib->link[cousdir];
               makeblack(cous);
               rotate(i-1);
               rotoccurred = TRUE;
               makered(path(i).ptr);
            }
         }
         if (rotoccurred)
            i--;
         else {
            i++;
            path(i).ptr = cur;
            path(i).left = curdir;
         }
      }
   makeblack(root); /* undo root reddening */
   if (cur->key == x) {
      /* replace parent of doomed node by its sibling */
      node **parenthook;  /* hook from grandparent to parent *
      parenthook = &(path(i-1).ptr->link[path(i).left]);
      *parenthook = path(i).ptr->link[!curdir];
      makeblack(*parenthook);
   }
}
```

PROGRAM 9.1e(ii)

The second part of a deletion function for a red-black tree.

---

tree along the access path to deletion. Program 9.1e attests that there are more cases for deletion than for insertion.

We begin by ensuring that we have a red node available to shove down: if neither child of the root is red, we color the root red. As we proceed along the access path, we look for possible transformations. In the simpler kind, the current node and its parent are black, but its sibling is red. Since we would like to drag that red node along with us down the access path, we perform a single rotation. One way to understand this transformation is to observe that it has no effect on the 2,4 tree that corresponds to the red-black tree. All it does is change the direction in which the 3-node leans, from one form in Figure 9.17b to the other.

The more involved case arises when we reach a black node with two black children and a red parent. Since we are determined to drag a red node down the access path with us, we color the node red and its parent black, and perform whatever adjustments are needed on its sibling to preserve the black height requirement. In the simplest case, the sibling is also black with two black children, so we can color it red; this corresponds to a reversal of the color flip operation used during insertion (going from (b) to (a) in Figure 9.20).

If the sibling has a red child, it can be colored black, and a single or double rotation will preserve the black height requirement. Figure 9.24 illustrates two cases. Either case applies if both children of the sibling are red.

Program 9.1e also stores a path of four nodes, but it is not the access path to the current node. The reason is that rotations involve siblings and cousins, not the current node itself. In `delete()` in Program 9.1e, `cur`, the current node in the search, is always a child of `path(i).ptr`, `path(i-1).ptr` is the parent of `path(i).ptr`, and

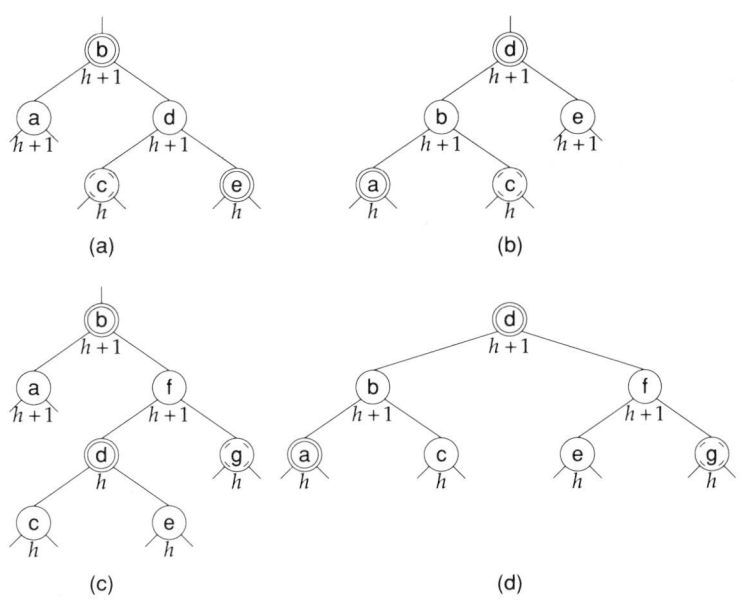

FIGURE 9.24

Two cases in node deletion when a black node's sibling has a red child. A single rotation and some recoloring takes (a) into (b). A double rotation and some recoloring takes (c) into (d). There is a symmetric variant of each case.

path(i+1).ptr is the sibling of cur. When necessary, path(i+2).ptr is a cousin of cur. The macro definitions at the start of delete() offer more familiar names for these elements of nodepath[]. As in insertion, if any rotation occurs, we move back up the access path to take the correct steps through the rearranged tree that hangs from path(i-1).ptr. When we reach the doomed leaf, we replace its red parent by its black sibling. We also make the root black.

9.4
FURTHER TOPICS

Because balanced trees offer good worst-case performance guarantees, they have been studied extensively for a wide variety of applications. The exercises explore other formation rules for balanced trees. In this section we shall see further topics related to balanced trees.

Other Operations

Although the chapter introduction mentioned the data type sorted list, so far we have not seen any operations on balanced trees besides the basic dictionary operations of search, insertion, and deletion. But balanced trees are flexible enough to support many other operations.

The chapter introduction mentioned the ordered traversal of a sorted list. When the list is stored in a binary search tree, an inorder traversal visits the items at the leaves in order. When items are stored at all nodes, this is the same inorder traversal we saw in Chapter 7. If items are stored only at the leaves, then we process items only when the traversal reaches a leaf. A similar traversal operation can be defined for a sorted list stored in a 2,4 tree: visit the children of each internal node in order. If the internal node's children are also internal, this rule causes all of its leaf descendants to appear in the right place in the traversal. If the internal node's children are all leaves, then we simply visit them in order. This traversal relies on property 2 of 2,4 trees, which implies that no node has both internal and external children.

Given a sorted list of items and a key value k, we might want to find the bracketing pair for k in the list. For example, given a list of lot boundaries as they appear along a street, we could use the bracketing pair to tell, for any point along the street, to which lot it belongs. In a balanced tree on n items, the elements of the bracketing pair for any key can be found in $O(\log n)$ time.

It can sometimes be useful to be able to catenate two sorted lists together into a single sorted list; obviously this is possible only if all elements on one list are less than all elements on the other. Many balanced tree schemes make it possible to catenate two lists to form a single list of n items in $O(\log n)$ time. For example, given two 2,4 trees H and K of heights h and k, respectively, suppose that $k \le h$ and that K should go to the right of H in the result of the catenation. To catenate H and K, find the node of depth $h - k$ on H's rightmost path and insert the root of K into that node; of course, we might have to propagate 5-node splittings up to the root to maintain the 2,4 property, but the result will be a valid 2,4 tree.

Self-Adjusting Trees

A disadvantage of many balanced tree schemes is that balance information must be kept at the nodes. This costs not only space beyond what is necessary to permit searching, but also time to keep the balance information current. Moreover, the algorithms for insertion and deletion are complicated by the many cases that arise. An attractive alternative is available for many applications.

Balanced trees offer a worst-case guarantee on the time required to perform each individual operation. If, instead, what matters is only the time to perform a sequence of dictionary operations, we can apply an amortized analysis and satisfy the time requirement more easily. *Self-adjusting trees* use a simple rule: whenever we find an item, we move it to the root of the tree using single and double rotations. Insertion, deletion, catenation, and splitting can also be defined using the same idea of moving a relevant node to the root of the tree by a sequence of rotations. The performance of self-adjusting trees is remarkable: a sequence of m operations on a collection of initially empty trees can be performed in $O(m + \sum_{j=1}^{m} \log n_j)$ time, where n_j is the number of items in the tree or trees involved in the jth operation. This is no worse than the time bound we would get using any of the balanced tree schemes in this chapter.

a,b Trees

A natural generalization of 2,4 trees has important applications for searching large sorted lists. All internal nodes of an a,b tree (except possibly the root) have between a and b children; an a,b tree also obeys rules 2 through 4 for 2,4 trees. An a,b tree on n items has height between $\log_a n$ and $\log_b n$. To make it possible to generalize the algorithms for insertion and deletion from 2,4 trees to a,b trees, we need only require that $2a \leq b+1$; then insertion can proceed by node splitting, and deletion by node coalescing, just as in the case of 2,4 trees.

When a sorted list is so large that it cannot be stored entirely in main memory, a,b trees are worth considering. Typically we choose b so that a b-node fits into a single page, and choose $a = \lfloor b/2 \rfloor$. If, say, $b = 200$, then an a,b tree on one million items will be of height at most three, so any search for an item will cause at most three page faults.

9.5
SUMMARY AND PERSPECTIVE

This chapter includes no data gathered from the implementation of red-black trees, because the mathematical analysis shows that the operations execute in $O(\log n)$ time when the tree contains n items. We leave it as an exercise to discover how large the constant lurking in the $O(\ )$ is.

The tree data structures in this chapter share two key properties that make their worst-case time for dictionary operations logarithmic in their size. First, of course, they obey formation rules that force them to be of height $\Theta(\log n)$ when they contain n items. A second, more subtle, property of these data structures is that the operations that preserve their formation rules are *local*: the rebalancing made necessary by an insertion or a deletion can affect only nodes that are on or a constant distance away from the access path; this property is crucial to ensure that rebalancing, as well as search, can be performed in time proportional to the height of the tree.

Notes on Implementation

As ingenious as these schemes for maintaining a balanced search tree are, they contain several pitfalls to trap the unwary programmer who plans to implement them.

The rebalancing operations for both AVL trees and 2,4 trees are easy to describe to another person, when we can draw pictures and dismiss symmetrical variants or similar cases with a brief comment. An implementation must handle all necessary cases explicitly and correctly.

Likewise, an implementation must cope with exceptional boundary conditions. For instance, in a 2,4 tree on one item, the root has only one child; this is the reason for exempting the root from the requirement that every node have between two and four children. A naive program must take account of this special case in many places. An attractive alternative is to write the program so that the tree always contains two sentinel items, $-\infty$ and $+\infty$, even when it is "empty." This can also avoid anomalies associated with deleting the smallest or largest item in the tree.

Finally, it is tempting to try to write insertion and deletion functions recursively. After all, searching is succinctly expressed as a recursive algorithm and the formation rules for balanced trees ensure that all subtrees of any node are themselves balanced trees. In general, however, to change a tree we must be able to reach ancestors along the access path and siblings and cousins one or two away from the access path, so it is better to maintain the sequence of nodes along the access path explicitly.

Because of the difficulty of implementing balanced trees, before we embark on such a project, we need to ask at least two questions: Is such a stringent worst-case performance bound really *needed*? Is the data set large enough that the possible asymptotic superiority of balanced search trees over a simpler data structure is likely to be apparent?

If we do decide to implement a balanced tree scheme, there is a variety from which to choose. The ideas behind the versions seen in Sections 9.1 through 9.3 can be combined in many other ways; for example, we can define an AVL tree in which all items reside at the leaves, or a 2,4 tree with items at internal nodes. Any implementation should make liberal use of a routine to dump the contents of the tree, as well as demand()s to test for correctness.

Because space is often at a premium when balanced trees are used, many programs that implement them employ various techniques that use less space than a naive implementation would. Program 9.1 uses one such technique to obviate a bit that tells whether a node is a leaf. If we wanted to use red-black trees to store large items, we might modify Program 9.1 so that the right-child field of each leaf points to the item that logically resides at that leaf. As another example for red-black trees, we can often find an unused bit at each node to store the node color, so that we need not use an entire node field; for example, if we know that all key values are positive, then we might use the sign bit of the key field to test whether a node is red or black. The use of such tricks makes it imperative that we access the fields of tree nodes through macro definitions, as we did in Program 9.1.

EXERCISES

1 Verify that Equation (9.2) solves Equation (9.1).

2 Exactly how does Equation (9.2) imply an upper bound on the height of an AVL tree of n nodes?

3 Show that any binary tree on n nodes has height $\Omega(\log n)$.

4 Explain why the subtrees in the subtree of height $h+2$ in Figure 9.8a cannot both have height $h+1$.

5 To maintain an AVL tree, one must know the relative heights of the subtrees of each node. Show how one can keep the height of each node in an AVL tree current by suitable operations during the walk toward the root.

6 The rebalancing operations for an AVL tree need to know only the relative heights of the subtrees of each node in an AVL tree. Show how to perform the rebalancing operations when the only balance information stored at each node is -1, 0, or $+1$, indicating, respectively, that the left subtree is one taller than the right, that both are the same height, or that the right subtree is one taller than the left.

7 It is possible to maintain a 2,4 tree by keeping at each internal node the values of the largest items in all but the rightmost subtree of the node. Thus, a 2-node contains one key value, a 3-node contains two key values, and a 4-node contains three key values.

(a) Show that if this is done, each key appears in exactly one internal node.

(b) Show how to search in a 2,4 tree maintained this way.

(c) Show how to keep this search information current during the backwards traversal of the access path.

8 Draw the 2,4 tree that corresponds to Figure 9.16.

9 Explain why the colors of all nodes but a in Figure 9.21 are fixed. In particular, how do we know that b must be black?

10 What are the symmetric variants of the trees in Figure 9.21?

11 The index i in the red-black tree function `insert()` does not increase monotonically from 0 to the depth of some leaf: some calls to `flipandfix()` can cause it to decrease by 3, which means that we trace over some nodes more than once. Show that, such retracing of steps notwithstanding, `insert()` uses $\Theta(\log n)$ time to insert an item into a red-black tree on n items.

12 In Figures 9.24a and c, how do we know when we reach a that b must be red?

13 Show how to catenate two sorted lists represented as red-black trees.

14 Explain why we must require that $2a \leq b+1$ in a,b trees.

The following exercises can be done with any kind of balanced tree. Compare how easy it is to solve these exercises on different kinds of balanced trees. It would be especially interesting to do these exercises for a variant of balanced trees not considered in the text; for example, try 2,4 trees that store items at internal and external nodes.

15 Implement a balanced tree data structure. Experiment to find out how large must it become before it runs faster than a program that uses an unbalanced search tree.

16 Write a function that checks whether a tree is balanced.

17 Given i, we would like to find the ith item in a sorted list stored in a balanced tree. What information should be stored at the nodes to permit us to find the ith out of n items in $O(\log n)$ time?

18 Show how to traverse the items in a balanced tree in order.

19 Show how to find the bracketing pair for a key value in a balanced tree.

20 Sometimes it is useful to keep the leaves of a balanced tree linked together in symmetric order. Show how to maintain such *leaf-level links* with no increase in asymptotic complexity.

21 Given a key value k, show how to split a balanced tree into two balanced trees, one of which contains all items $\leq k$ in the original tree, and the other of which contains the rest of the items.

Weight-balanced trees with parameter α obey the following formation rule: for any node, let $\#_l$ be the number of items in its left subtree, and $\#_r$ be the number of items in its right subtree; then $\alpha \leq (\#_l + 1)/(\#_l + \#_r + 1) \leq 1 - \alpha$.

22 Show that if $1/3 < \alpha \leq 1/2$, a weight-balanced tree with parameter α must be a perfectly balanced tree with $2^k - 1$ nodes for some value of k.

23 Show that a weight-balanced tree on n items can be searched in time $O(\log n)$.

24 Suppose that each item in a dictionary has an associated *weight*, that tells how likely the item is to be sought. The weight of a tree is the sum of the weights of the items it contains. Generalize weight-balanced trees to define a tree that permits particularly efficient searching for a given set of weights.

REFERENCES

Because of the practical importance of searching problems, there is an enormous literature on balanced trees.

AVL-trees are also called height-balanced trees. They first appeared in
G. M. Adel'son-Vel'skii and E. M. Landis. "An algorithm for the organization of information." *Doklady Akademiia Nauk SSSR* 146 (1962): 263–266. Translation in *Soviet Math.* 3 (1962): 1259–1263.

Non-binary balanced trees include the special case of 2,4 trees.

R. Bayer and E. McCreight. "Organization and maintenance of large ordered indexes." *Acta Informatica* 1 (1972) 173–189.

The simplest non-binary balanced tree scheme is the 2,3 tree, which is discussed in Chapter 4 of

A. V. Aho, J. E. Hopcroft, and J. D. Ullman. *The Design and Analysis of Computer Algorithms*. Reading, Mass.: Addison-Wesley, 1974.

The more general *a,b* tree is also called a *B-tree*. These trees are studied in the following reference, which shows that one can update a weak *a,b* tree top-down using $O(1)$ operations.

K. Mehlhorn. *Sorting and Searching*. Vol. 1, *Data Structures and Efficient Algorithms*. New York: Springer-Verlag, 1984.

Red-black trees were introduced in

L. J. Guibas and R. Sedgewick. "A dichromatic framework for balanced trees." In *Proc. 19th Ann. Symp. on Theory of Computing* (1978): 8–21.

A variant of red-black trees permits fast searching from between leaves; parts of such *finger search trees* have been described by many authors; a summary appears in the appendix of

R. E. Tarjan and C. J. Van Wyk. "An $O(n \log \log n)$-time algorithm for triangulating a simple polygon," *SIAM Journal on Computing* 17 (1988): 143–178.

Weight-balanced trees were introduced in

J. Nievergelt and E. M. Reingold. "Binary search trees of bounded balance." *SIAM Journal on Computing* 2 (1973): 33–43.

Self-adjusting trees are described in

D. D. Sleator and R. E. Tarjan. "Self-adjusting binary search trees." *Journal of the ACM* 32 (1985): 652–686.

The following references describe two data structures for sorted lists that offer good expected running times, with the expectation independent of the distribution of the input keys:

C. R. Aragon and R. G. Seidel. "Randomized search trees." *Proc 30th Ann. Symp. on Foundations of Computer Science"* (1989): 540–545.

W. Pugh. "Skip lists: a probabilistic alternative to balanced trees." *Communications of the ACM*, to appear June, 1990.

10

Priority Queues

Just as people face waiting lines in many situations, the data being manipulated by a program often must spend some time "waiting in line" before they are processed. Programmers must devise and maintain the data structures in which data items wait for service. In Chapter 4, we saw two data types that give rules for waiting lines and some data structures that we could use to store data in a waiting line. Data items can be arranged according to far more intricate rules than these, however.

Recall for a moment our discussion in Section 4.1 of strategies for paying bills. We discussed two rules that the pile of unpaid bills could obey: oldest-first or FIFO, and newest-first or LIFO. Even as you read about them, it may have occurred to you that both of these strategies are flawed. For instance, if you pay bills in a strict FIFO order, you might renew a magazine subscription only to find that you no longer have enough money left for some large expense like tuition or housing. On the other hand, if you pay bills according to a strict LIFO rule, then a large bill on top of the stack could prevent you from paying older and smaller unpaid bills underneath it. In short, paying bills based on their time of arrival may be easy to understand, but it fails to do justice to common sense: we would like to pay bills in order of *importance*, so that we make sure to pay for vital goods and services before we pay for luxuries.

This chapter presents the *priority queue* data type that organizes data items in a waiting line according to some measure of their importance. The first three sections describe the basic data type and an elegant and practical data structure for priority queues. Next we shall see an application that uses a priority queue of binary trees. The chapter concludes with a description of some other priority queue operations.

10.1
THE DATA TYPE PRIORITY QUEUE

Many applications require that we organize data items in a waiting line according to their importance. For scarce resources, money can be an index of importance: for a printer in high demand, users may have the option of offering to pay more in order to move their jobs ahead in the print queue. We also access data based on importance when we administer a shared resource: in timesharing environments, the computer may be working on many jobs at once, devoting a few milliseconds in turn to each job; by assigning jobs a measure of importance, we can designate long-term jobs as less important so that they use little time when there is any other demand on the computer.

Figure 10.1 shows the data type *priority queue*, a set of operations with which we can maintain and serve data items in a waiting line in order of their priority (the "importance" of the preceding discussion). Each item in a priority queue has a key that indicates its priority. Often, priority is related inversely to key size, so that an item with small key has higher priority than one with a large key. This coincides with the common usage that "Grade A" is usually better than "Grade B," even though "A" is lexicographically smaller than "B."

The sorted lists of Chapter 9 could be used as data structures for priority queues: each item's priority would serve as its search key, and the sorted list would keep the items in sorted order. They would allow us to perform all of the operations in Figure 10.1 on a priority queue of n items in $O(\log n)$ time. It turns out, however, that priority queues can be stored in a much simpler data structure that meets or beats this time bound, as we shall see in Section 10.2.

---

empty( ) — are any items waiting on the priority queue?
findmin( ) — return an item with smallest priority
insert(item, key) — insert an item with the priority given by key
deletemin( ) — remove an item with smallest priority

FIGURE 10.1

Operations for the data type priority queue.

10.2
HEAPS

The *heap* data structure for priority queues is based on binary trees that obey certain rules. (This heap has nothing to do with Chapter 6's heap of dynamically allocated space.) As in Chapter 9, one rule governs the location of items in the tree, and the other rule regulates the overall shape of the tree. Because we ask less of priority queues than of sorted lists, however, the rules for constructing heaps are simpler than they are for balanced search trees.

Heap Order

First we shall consider the rule that governs the position of items in the tree. We say that a tree is *heap ordered* if the key at each node in the tree is no larger than the keys at its children. (A tree need not be binary to be heap ordered.) An example of a heap ordered binary tree appears in Figure 10.2. Several observations about heap ordered trees suggest why they are useful as a data structure for priority queues.

First, the item with the smallest key must reside at the root of the tree; this makes it trivial to implement *findmin*( ). Second, if we change the priority of one item in a heap ordered tree, then we can restore the tree to heap order fairly easily.

If the changed item's key is now smaller than the key in its parent, we can restore the heap order by letting the item rise in the tree along the path to the root; the items past which the changed item rises move

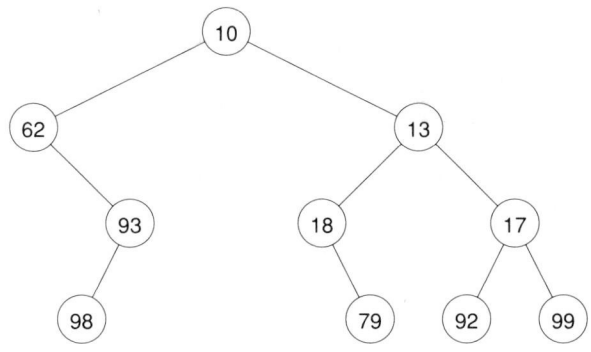

FIGURE 10.2

A heap ordered binary tree that contains 10 items.

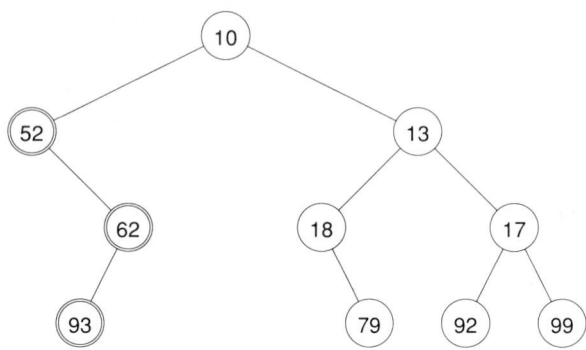

FIGURE 10.3

In the tree of Figure 10.2, when the item with priority 98 changes to priority 52, it floats up two levels in the tree. The nodes affected by the rise have dark borders.

down one level in the tree. (See Figure 10.3.) This procedure works because the changed item resides at the root of a heap-ordered subtree both before and after the changed item rises one level. When the changed item stops rising, either it is the child of a node whose key is smaller, or it is the root. In either case, when the changed item stops rising the entire tree is heap ordered again.

On the other hand, if the changed item's key is now larger than the key at one of its children, then we can restore the heap order by letting the item fall in the tree. At each step in its fall, the changed item swaps places with the item among its children whose key is minimum. (See Figure 10.4.) Thus, both before and after the changed item falls, the entire tree *minus the subtree rooted at the changed item* is heap ordered. The changed item falls in the tree until either it becomes the parent of nodes whose keys are all at least as large as its key, or it becomes a leaf. In either case, the entire tree is heap ordered when the changed item stops falling.

The algorithms to change an item's priority can be used to implement priority queue operations. To perform *insert*( ), we append the item as a leaf of the tree, and let it rise as necessary to restore the heap order. To execute *deletemin*( ), we replace the item at the root by the item at any leaf and let it fall in the tree as necessary to restore heap order.

Notice that when we change an item's key and restore the heap order to the tree, the item *either* rises toward the root *or* falls toward the leaves; it moves in only one direction. Furthermore, if h is the

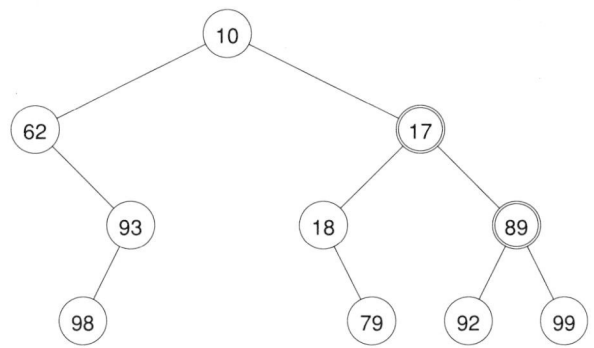

FIGURE 10.4

In the tree of Figure 10.2, when the item with priority 13 changes to priority 89, it falls one level in the tree. Nodes affected by the fall are shown with dark borders.

height of the tree, the changed item cannot move more than h levels away. This observation suggests a strategy. If we can restrict the binary tree to be of height $O(\log n)$ when it contains n nodes, then we can perform a priority queue operation and still maintain the heap order in $O(\log n)$ time. The *heap shape* property makes this possible.

Heap Shape

We begin the definition of heap shape by numbering the nodes of the complete infinite binary tree according to these rules:

- The root is numbered 1.
- If a node is numbered k, its left child is numbered $2k$ and its right child is numbered $2k+1$.

(See Figure 10.5.) The node numbered k appears in the tree at depth $\lfloor \log_2 k \rfloor$, at a position $k - 2^{\lfloor \log_2 k \rfloor}$ from the left on that level. Thus, the nodes numbered 1 through n form a subtree of height $\lfloor \log_2 n \rfloor$; this subtree has the *heap shape property*.

A heap ordered binary tree on n nodes that has the heap shape property is called a *heap*. Figure 10.6 shows an example, which we shall use to illustrate the priority queue operations of Figure 10.1. As we have already noted, the heap order lets us perform *findmin( )* in $O(1)$ time by looking at the root. To modify the heap by *deletemin( )* or *insert( )*, we apply the above observations about changing the prior-

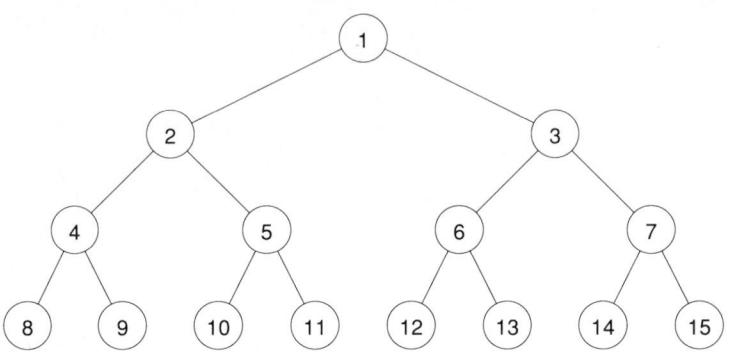

FIGURE 10.5

The first four levels of the full infinite binary tree with heap numbered nodes.

ity of an item in a heap-ordered tree, restricting the operations to work at the rightmost leaf on the bottom level of the heap.

To perform *deletemin*( ), we move the item at the node numbered n to the root and let it fall down the tree until the entire tree has been restored to heap order. Thus, when we execute *deletemin*( ) on the tree in Figure 10.6, we put 99 at the root (where 10 used to be), then let it fall down the tree; Figure 10.7 shows the result after 99 has fallen two levels to a leaf of the tree. To insert a new item, we put it into tree position $n+1$ and let it rise in the tree until the entire tree is restored

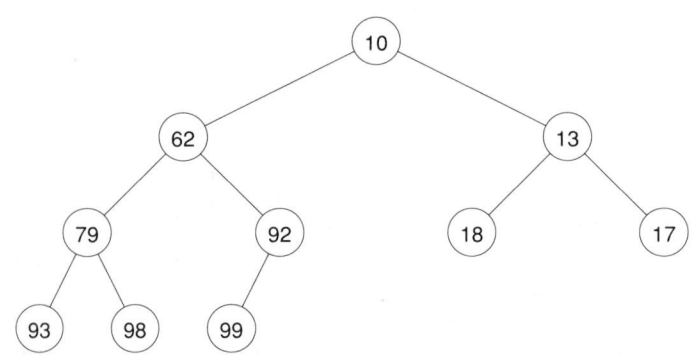

FIGURE 10.6

This heap contains the same items as the heap ordered binary tree in Figure 10.2.

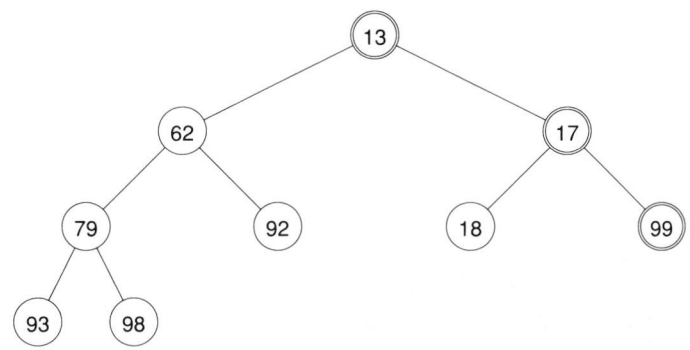

FIGURE 10.7

To remove the item with smallest key from the tree in Figure 10.6, we move the rightmost item on the bottom level to the root, then let it fall in the tree to restore heap order. The nodes affected by the fall have dark borders.

to heap order. Figure 10.8 shows the result of adding 89 to the tree of Figure 10.6; it rises only one level. Because the height of the tree is $O(\log n)$, and items move in only one direction, both of these operations can be performed in $O(\log n)$ time.

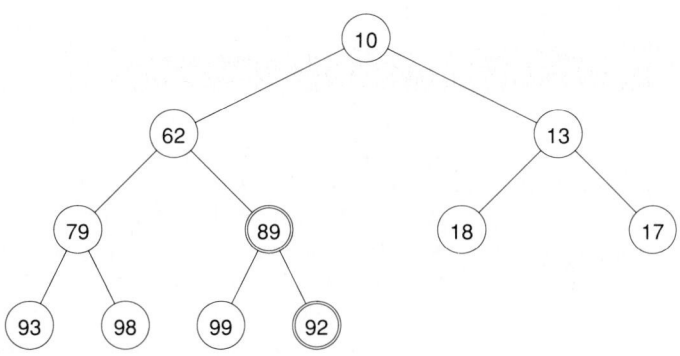

FIGURE 10.8

When an item with key 89 is inserted into the heap of Figure 10.6, the bottom level gets a new rightmost leaf, then the item rises to its proper place in the heap. Nodes visited during the rise have dark borders.

i	0	1	2	3	4	5	6	7	8	9	10
$heap[i]$	$-\infty$	13	62	17	79	92	18	99	93	98	$+\infty$

FIGURE 10.9

The heap of Figure 10.7, stored in an array.

Implicit Representation

We could store a heap in a binary tree data structure like the one in Figure 7.7. However, the node numbering shown in Figure 10.5 can be used to store a heap in an *implicit* (or pointerless) data structure. An elegant way to express the idea of this data structure is to imagine the heap stored in an infinite array as shown in Figure 10.9, which contains the same heap as Figure 10.7. The item at the tree node numbered i is stored at index i in array $heap[\ ]$. Outside of indexes 1 through n, $heap[0]$ contains $-\infty$ and $heap[n+1]$, $heap[n+2]$, . . . contain $+\infty$.

With the heap shape numbering scheme, we can reach the parent of $heap[k]$ at $heap[\lfloor k/2 \rfloor]$, the left child at $heap[2k]$, and the right child at $heap[2k+1]$. The positions outside the heap serve as sentinels so that the heap order property holds; this can be expressed as

$$\text{for all } i \geq 0, \ heap[i] \ \leq \ \min(heap[2i], heap[2i+1]).$$

10.3
IMPLEMENTATION OF HEAPS

When we implement heaps we must store them in arrays of finite length, and we cannot be quite so cavalier about assuming that infinite quantities of the appropriate sign are stored in array locations outside the heap proper. We have to make sure that no item rises past the root or falls past the leaves as the heap order is restored. In this section we shall write a package with which one can maintain a heap on any type of item whose priorities are integers.

Program 10.1a shows declarations and two simple heap functions. To use our package for a particular item type we need only `typedef` `item` appropriately. We shall write the package so that it aborts the program when someone tries to insert an item and the heap is full; a more robust implementation would grow the heap to fit.

Any C array has a slot whose index is zero. (Thus, the heap declared in Program 10.1a has room for only `MAXHEAP-1` items.) If a

```
typedef struct heapslot heapslot;
struct heapslot {
    int key;
    item thing;
};

heapslot heap[MAXHEAP];
int heapnum;

boolean empty(void)
{
    return heapnum == 0;
}

item findmin(void)
{
    demand(!empty(), findmin not allowed on empty heap);
    return heap[1].thing;
}
```

PROGRAM 10.1a

Declarations and simple functions for a heap of items. A user of this package must also declare a value for MAXHEAP.

suitable sentinel value is available to serve as $-\infty$, we can use the initialization function shown in Program 10.1b. This makes it slightly easier to implement operation *insert*( ), which is also shown in Program 10.1b.

In function insert(), we maintain the invariant at the while-test that cur is the index in heap of the newly inserted item, and that parent is the index of cur's parent. The demand() condition, that parent belong to the heap proper, fails only if the sentinel value ("$-\infty$") is larger than the key of some item stored in the heap.

Even if no suitable sentinel value exists to serve as $-\infty$ in heap[0], *insert*( ) is relatively simple to write because at each step in the rise of the new item there are only two possibilities—either it stops or it changes places with its parent. By contrast, when an item is falling in the heap, as in *deletemin*( ), there are three possibilities: the item can stop, change places with its left child (if it has one), or change places with its right child (if any). This trichotomy, together with the need to avoid running off the end of the heap, makes it trickier to write a function that implements *deletemin*( ).

```
void initheap(void)
{
    heapnum = 0;
    heap[0].key = MINUSINFINITY;
}

void swap(heapslot *s1, heapslot *s2)
{
    heapslot temp;
    temp = *s1;
    *s1 = *s2;
    *s2 = temp;
}

void insert(item thing, int key)
{
    int cur, parent;
    demand(heapnum < MAXHEAP, heap overflow);
    cur = ++heapnum;
    heap[cur].key = key;
    heap[cur].thing = thing;
    parent = cur/2;
    while (heap[parent].key > heap[cur].key) {
        demand(parent > 0, inserted item rising past root);
        swap(&heap[parent], &heap[cur]);
        cur = parent;
        parent = cur/2;
    }
}
```

PROGRAM 10.1b

Initialization and insertion functions for a heap. A user would also have to define the sentinel value MINUSINFINITY.

Program 10.1c shows one version of deletemin(). Each time we enter the while-loop, child is the index of the left child of cur. After the first if, child is the index of the child of cur whose key is the smaller of the two. If the second if-test succeeds, the new item must fall a level in the tree and we must prepare for the next level, but if the test fails we are done.

```
void deletemin(void)
{
    int cur, child;
    demand(!empty(), deletemin not allowed on empty heap);
    heap[1] = heap[heapnum--];
    cur = 1;
    child = 2;
    while (child <= heapnum) {
        if (child < heapnum &&
            heap[child+1].key < heap[child].key)
            child++;
        if (heap[cur].key > heap[child].key) {
            demand(child <= heapnum, falling past leaves);
            swap(&heap[cur], &heap[child]);
            cur = child;
            child = 2*cur;
        } else
            break;
    }
}
```

PROGRAM 10.1c

Function to delete the smallest item in a heap.

10.4
HUFFMAN TREES

In this section we shall see how to use priority queues to construct compact binary encodings—binary codes that represent sequences of characters in far fewer bits than the encodings commonly used for variables of type char. On the way to this result we shall see a relation between binary codes and binary trees, as well as a generalization of the notion of path length.

Most computers represent characters using a 7-bit code; two common ones are ASCII (the American Standard Code for Information Interchange) and BCDIC (the Binary Coded Decimal Interchange Code). For example, in ASCII the seven bit *codeword* 1000001 represents the character A, and 1010001 represents a. Because all codewords are of the same length, it is easy to store, retrieve, and otherwise manipulate characters that are encoded in such 7-bit codes; indeed, the char data type is especially intended to make these operations convenient. On the other hand, when all codewords are of the

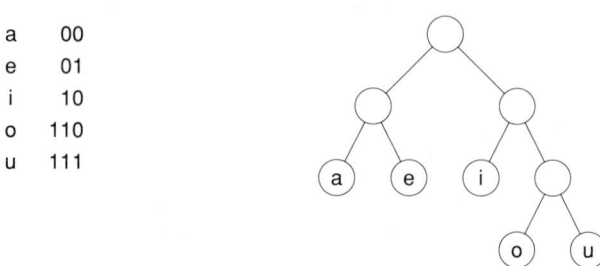

FIGURE 10.10

A code for the vowels a, e, i, o, and u, together with the corresponding binary tree.

same length a code can use many more bits than are necessary to represent a sequence of characters. We can save bits by encoding frequent symbols in short codewords and infrequent ones in long codewords.

A natural relationship between binary codes and binary trees illustrates the construction of codes with codewords of different lengths. Any binary tree can be used to derive a binary code for the items at its leaves. To encode a leaf ℓ, traverse the path from the root to ℓ; each time you go from a node to its left child, write 0; each time you go to the right, write 1. The string of bits you wrote down on the way to ℓ is the codeword for the item at ℓ. Thus, the binary tree of Figure 10.10 encodes each of the five vowels as shown. (A 7-bit code like ASCII or BCDIC corresponds to a complete binary tree of height 7.)

The requirement that the encoded items reside at the *leaves* of a binary tree is important. To see why, consider the binary tree and its associated code in Figure 10.11. There are at least two ways to decode

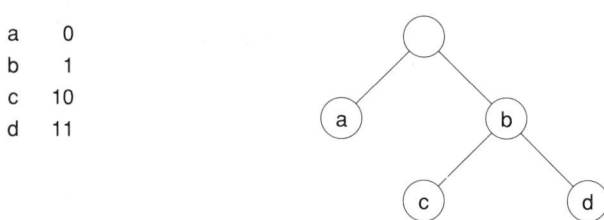

FIGURE 10.11

An ambiguous code: the codeword for b is a prefix of the codewords for c and d. The corresponding binary tree shows that b does not reside at a leaf.

the bit sequence 1001: one possibility is cab; another is baab. The ambiguity arises because the codeword for b is a prefix of the codewords for c and d, so when we see a 1 we do not know whether to decode it as b or to wait for the next bit and decode the two together as c or d. The requirement that all encoded items reside at the leaves ensures that no codeword can be a prefix of another; such a code is said to be *prefix-free*.

We want to construct a code that is more than prefix-free, however. We want the code to get the most mileage out of the bits it uses to represent a sequence of characters. To encode frequent characters in fewer bits than rare characters, frequent items should appear at a smaller depth in the code tree than items that are rarely used. A generalization of path length gives us the tool we need to compare how well two trees meet this objective.

For this generalization of path length, we associate a *weight* with each item. The weight measures how often we shall need to encode the associated item. If the weight of the item at leaf ℓ_i is w_i, then the *weighted external path length* of tree T is

$$\sum_{\ell_i \text{ a leaf of } T} w_i \times depth(\ell_i).$$

If two trees contain the same set of items at their leaves, then the tree with smaller weighted external path length corresponds to a better code for the given distribution of weights. For a given set of items and weights, a tree with the minimum weighted external path length is a *Huffman tree*.

Forest–Setup Step:
> Construct a forest of one–node trees.
> Each tree contains a single item.
> The weight of each tree is the weight of the item it contains.

Tree–Building Step:
> Until the forest contains only one tree,
>> remove two trees of smallest weights from the forest,
>> make them children of a new node whose weight is the sum of their weights,
>> and add the new tree to the forest.

ALGORITHM 10.1

Huffman's algorithm to construct the tree of minimum weighted external path length on a set of weighted items.

```
typedef struct node node;
struct node {
    node *left, *right;
    int freq;
    char let;
};

typedef node *item;

main()
{
    getfreqs();
    printtree(makehuff(), 0);
    exit(0);
}
```

PROGRAM 10.2a

Declarations and main program to construct a Huffman tree.

Huffman gave the simple algorithm shown as Algorithm 10.1 to construct his namesake trees. The forest-setup step builds the pieces out of which the Huffman tree will be constructed by the tree-building step. The tree-building step requires that we be able to find and remove the smallest tree in the forest, and to add a tree to the forest. Evidently we can use a priority queue of binary trees to implement Huffman's algorithm.

We begin our implementation of Huffman's algorithm by defining the nodes of a binary tree shown in Program 10.2a. The typedef, which says that an item is a pointer to a node, lets us use the heap implementation of Program 10.1 for our priority queue. The main() function in Program 10.2a calls two functions, getfreqs() to set up the forest and makehuff() to build the tree.

To set up the forest, getfreqs(), shown as Program 10.2b, puts each character and its weight into a one-node tree, then puts the tree into the heap. When getfreqs() is finished, the heap contains a forest of one-node trees, and we are ready to build the tree.

To build the tree, makehuff() in Program 10.2c deletes the two smallest trees, makes them the children of a new node, and adds the new tree back to the heap. When the first deletion leaves the heap empty, the algorithm is done and makehuff() returns the root of the Huffman tree.

```c
node *newnode(node *left, node *right, int freq, char let)
{
    node *result;
    result = (node *) malloc(sizeof(node));
    demand(result, out of memory in newnode);
    result->left = left;
    result->right = right;
    result->freq = freq;
    result->let = let;
    return result;
}

void getfreqs(void)
{
    FILE *data;
    char let;
    int freq;
    initheap();
    data = fopen("alpha.freq", "r");
    while (2 == fscanf(data, "%c %d\n", &let, &freq))
        insert(newnode(NULL, NULL, freq, let), freq);
}
```

PROGRAM 10.2b

Function to read letters and associated weights, and construct a forest for Huffman tree construction.

Figure 10.12 shows the output of Program 10.2 when its input is the five most frequent and five least frequent letters in English together with their frequencies. The codeword for e is 01, while the codeword for z is 111101.

Now we consider the time complexity of Huffman's algorithm. When the input contains n weighted items, the forest-setup step inserts n items into the heap; each time through the while-loop, the tree-building step replaces two items by one item, so it does not cause the heap to grow beyond n items. Therefore we can bound the time for each single heap operation by $O(\log n)$; this bound is quite weak, since many of the heap operations are on a heap of many fewer than n items, but it is strong enough to allow us to prove a good time bound for the whole algorithm. Since the algorithm performs *insert*( ) and *deletemin*( ) $2n - 1$ times each, its total running time is $O(n \log n)$.

```
node *makehuff(void)
{
    node *lc, *rc;
    int freq;
    while (!empty()) {
        lc = findmin();
        deletemin();
        if (empty())
            return lc;
        rc = findmin();
        deletemin();
        freq = lc->freq + rc->freq;
        insert(newnode(lc, rc, freq, '0'), freq);
    }
    return NULL;
}
```

PROGRAM 10.2c

The workhorse of Huffman tree construction.

Application

A large file whose contents are unlikely to change is an excellent candidate for Huffman coding. We can derive frequency statistics directly from the file, then construct a Huffman code that is *minimal*: it uses no more bits than any other code that always uses the same codeword for each character. When we store the file in Huffman-coded form, we must include a description of the Huffman tree that was used to encode it.

10.5
OTHER OPERATIONS

The operations shown in Figure 10.1 are basic to the definition of the data type priority queue. This section describes some other common operations on priority queues.

Changing Priorities

The heaps described in Section 10.2 and implemented in Section 10.3 allow items to enter with a priority that is fixed for the duration of their stay in the queue. For many applications, we need to be able to

```
                                    3 k
                           6
                                       1 z
                           3
                                       2 j
                    14
                                    3 q
                           8
                                    5 x
             88
                    74 o
       181
             93 t
 466
             130 e
       285
             77 r
       155
             78 n
```

FIGURE 10.12

Output from a run of Program 10.2 on the five most frequent and five least frequent letters in English. The numbers are the weights of each node. (Source for the weights at the leaves: A. Sinkov, *Elementary Cryptanalysis: A Mathematical Approach*, Washington, D.C.: Mathematical Association of America, 1966.)

change the priority of an item in a priority queue. For example, a user might want to raise the priority of a job that has been running in the background so it will finish sooner. If we already know where an item is (so that we need not search through the heap for it), then changing its priority is straightforward in any priority queue data structure that is heap ordered: we simply allow the changed item to rise or fall as described in Section 10.2.

Bottom-Up Heap Construction

Suppose we have n weighted items in an array x, and we want them to be heap ordered. We could do it using *insert*( ) $n-1$ times: before the ith *insert*( ), $x[1:i]$ is a heap; after the ith *insert*( ), $x[1:i+1]$ is a heap. This method, akin to that used in Program 10.2, requires $O(\sum_{k=1}^{n-1} \log k) = O(n \log n)$ time.

It is possible to do the job faster by proceeding through array $x[\,]$ in the opposite direction—from n down to 1. The method relies on the observation that the subtree rooted at each node in a heap is itself a heap. To turn the array into a heap, we process the items in the array from $x[n]$ down to $x[1]$; when we treat the ith item, we transform the subtree of which it is the root into a heap by letting it fall in that subtree as far as necessary. This algorithm works because when we reach item $x[i]$, the subtrees rooted at its children (if it has any) are themselves heap ordered. We call this algorithm *bottom-up heap construction* because it starts at the leaves of the would-be heap and works upwards toward the root.

To compute the time required by this algorithm we shall count the maximum possible number of comparisons and swaps it makes when $n = 2^k - 1$. We count comparisons and swaps as the algorithm proceeds, from position n down to position 1. All 2^{k-1} nodes at depth $k-1$ are leaves, hence trivially the roots of heaps, so they require no comparisons or swaps. The 2^{k-2} nodes at depth $k-2$ cannot move down more than one level before they become leaves, so they can require no more than one comparison and swap. In general, the 2^{k-i} nodes at depth $k-i$ cannot move down more than $i-1$ levels in the tree. Thus, the total number of comparisons and swaps to turn an array of $n = 2^k - 1$ items into a heap is

$$2^{k-1} \times 0 + 2^{k-2} \times 1 + \cdots + 2 \times (k-2) + 1 \times (k-1)$$

$$= \sum_{i=1}^{k} 2^{k-i}(i-1)$$

$$= \sum_{i=0}^{k-1} 2^i(k-(i+1))$$

$$= \left[\sum_{i=0}^{k-1} 2^i k\right] - \left[\sum_{i=0}^{k-1} 2^i(i+1)\right]$$

$$= \left[k(2^k-1)\right] - \left[(k-1)2^k + 1\right]$$

$$= 2^k - (k+1).$$

This analysis leads easily to the more general conclusion that for any n, we can turn n items in an array into a heap in a bottom-up fashion in $O(n)$ time.

Combining Priority Queues

Sometimes we must maintain a collection of priority queues, occasionally combining two priority queues into a larger queue. The array-based heap data structure offers no particular advantage for this job: even with bottom-up heap construction it takes $O(n)$ time to combine two heaps of size $n/2$. If we knew that all items in one priority queue would be larger than all items in the other, then we could use a sorted list structure from Chapter 9 and combine two priority queues of size $n/2$ into a single queue of size n in $O(\log n)$ time. The exercises explore two data structures that are simpler than balanced trees but permit more general merging in logarithmic time.

10.6
SUMMARY AND PERSPECTIVE

Priority queues appear frequently in applications. Besides the literal waiting-lines discussed in Section 10.1, one common use is in geometric algorithms that sweep across the plane examining line segments to search for intersections. When a line sweeps across the plane, it must stop whenever line segments begin or end, and whenever two segments cross; a priority queue is a natural data structure in which to store the locations at which the sweeping line must stop so that it always sweeps to the next closest stop.

The heap data structure is elegant, simple, and useful. The biggest limitation it imposes is its fixed size. In C, we can avoid this limitation by reallocating the array that contains a heap whenever it is about to overflow; of course, the insertion operation that causes this action will take more than logarithmic time, but a careful choice of chunk size can usually make this a problem of minor importance. Data structures for priority queues of dynamic size are interesting, but they appear much less frequently in practice than heaps.

EXERCISES

1 One advantage of a FIFO scheme for managing a print queue is that every job is eventually printed. Devise a sequence of print requests with the property that some requests are never fulfilled if the requests are maintained in a priority queue.

2 Choose a sorted list data structure for a priority queue and show how to perform the *findmin*( ) operation on it.

3 Where is the second smallest item in a heap? The third smallest item?

4 The text explains informally why the algorithm to restore heap order when an item's key becomes smaller is correct. State formally the invariant assertion whose truth is maintained while the item whose priority has changed rises in a heap ordered tree.

5 State the invariant assertion whose truth is maintained as an item whose priority has changed falls in a heap ordered tree.

6 Revise `insert()` to allocate a larger array when the heap becomes full.

7 Write a version of `insert()` that works in the absence of a suitable sentinel value.

8 Another way to implement `deletemin()` is to use a function or macro that returns a value of $+\infty$ given an index that lies outside the heap. Assuming that a suitable sentinel value exists, write such a version of `deletemin()`.

9 Revise `deletemin()` to return the value of the item being deleted.

10 Even if a code is not prefix-free, some strings might not be ambiguous. For example, a string of all zeroes is unambiguous in the code of Figure 10.11. Is it possible to find an unambiguous string using any non-prefix-free code? How many must exist?

11 Radio operators use Morse code to communicate. Although Morse code is usually expressed in dots and dashes (or "dits" and "dahs"), we can use binary notation to write it down. In Morse code, e is represented by 0 and a is represented by 01. Obviously Morse code is not prefix-free. How, then, can it be used to communicate?

12 Given three items with weights p, q, and r, with $p \geq q \geq r$, draw a Huffman tree for the items.

13 A trivial way to construct a prefix-free code is to represent the ith item as $1^{i-1}0$—that is, $i-1$ ones followed by a single zero. In effect, we use the ones to count in unary, and the zeroes as spaces between the codewords.

(a) Draw the tree that corresponds to this code.

(b) Can you construct a frequency distribution for which this code is the optimum?

14 Show that both subtrees of the root of a Huffman tree are themselves Huffman trees for the weighted items at their leaves.

15 Prove that Huffman's algorithm does indeed produce a tree whose weighted external path length is minimum.

16 Complete Program 10.2 by writing function `printtree()`.

17 Sometimes a Huffman-encoded file is longer than the original file. How can this happen?

18 Implement bottom-up heap construction.

19 Show that for $k \geq 0$,

$$\sum_{i=0}^{k-1} 2^i = 2^k - 1.$$

20 Show that for $k \geq 0$,

$$\sum_{i=0}^{k-1} 2^i(i+1) = (k-1)2^k + 1.$$

21 Show how the proof that bottom-up heap construction for $n = 2^k - 1$ uses $O(n)$ time can be used to show that bottom-up heap construction can be performed in linear time for any n.

The next set of exercises concerns a data structure for priority queues. *Binomial trees* are defined by the following rules:

B_0 is a single node; for $k \geq 0$,

$$B_{k+1} =$$

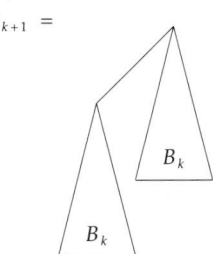

That is, to construct B_{k+1}, take two copies of B_k, and make one copy of B_k the leftmost child of the root of the other copy of B_k.

22 Determine the following quantities about B_k for $k \geq 0$: the number of children of the root of B_k; the number of nodes in B_k; the height of B_k.

A *binomial forest* is a collection of binomial trees in which no two trees have the same size.

23 Show that for any n, there is exactly one binomial forest that has n nodes.

A binomial forest of heap ordered binomial trees is a *binomial queue*.

24 Show how to perform *findmin*( ) on a binomial queue of n items in $O(\log n)$ time.

The formation rule for binomial trees implies that we can merge two binomial trees of the same size into a single binomial tree in $O(1)$ time.

25 Show how to merge two binomial forests of m and n nodes to form a single binomial forest of $m + n$ nodes in $O(\log(m+n))$ time. (*Hint*: consider an analogy with binary arithmetic.)

The above result on merging two binomial queues means that we can implement *insert*( ) into a binomial queue of n items as the merging of two binomial queues of sizes n and 1.

26 Show that if we delete the root of a binomial tree B_k, the result is a binomial forest of binomial trees $B_{k-1}, B_{k-2}, \ldots, B_1, B_0$.

27 Use Exercise 26 to show how to perform *deletemin*( ) on a binomial queue of n nodes in $O(\log n)$ time.

28 Show that if we start with n one-node binomial trees, any sequence of $n-1$ merges can be used to form an n-node binomial forest in $O(n)$ time.

29 Implement a binomial queue.

The next few exercises concern another data structure for priority queues. Given a binary tree, its *left height* is the maximum depth of any descendant of the left child of the root. A *leftist tree* is a binary tree such that for each node, the left height of its right child is no larger than the left height of its left child.

30 Draw the shortest and tallest leftist trees with 10 nodes.

The *right path* of a binary tree is defined by the nodes that can be reached from the root by passing only through right edges.

31 Show that the length of the right path of a leftist tree of n nodes is $O(\log n)$.

32 Use the preceding result to show how to merge two leftist trees on m and n nodes in $O(\log (m+n))$ time.

33 Use this merging technique to show how to implement *findmin*( ), *insert*( ) and *deletemin*( ) on a leftist tree of n nodes so that each operation uses $O(\log n)$ time.

REFERENCES

The heap data structure was invented by Williams:

    J. W. J. Williams. "Algorithm 232: heapsort." *Communications of the ACM* 7 (1964): 347–348.

Bottom-up heap creation was described in

    R. W. Floyd. "Algorithm 245: treesort 3." *Communications of the ACM* 7 (1964): 701.

Column 12 of the following reference gives a careful yet informal presentation of heaps:

    J. Bentley. *Programming Pearls*. Reading, Mass.: Addison-Wesley, 1986.

Huffman's algorithm appears in

    D. A. Huffman. "A method for the construction of minimum-redundancy codes." *Proceedings of the Institute of Radio Engineers* 40 (1952): 1098–1101.

A variant of Huffman coding that can be used when the data must be compressed as it is read appears in

J. S. Vitter. "Design and analysis of dynamic Huffman codes." *Journal of the ACM* 34 (1987): 825–845.

Binomial queues were presented in

J. Vuillemin. "A data structure for manipulating priority queues." *Communications of the ACM* 21 (1978): 309–315.

The complete analysis of binomial queues appears in

M. R. Brown. "Implementation and analysis of binomial queue algorithms." *SIAM Journal on Computing* 7 (1978): 298–319.

Leftist trees were invented by Crane:

C. A. Crane. *Linear Lists and Priority Queues as Balanced Binary Trees*. Ph.D. diss., Stanford University, 1972.

The following book is probably more accessible than Crane's dissertation. Its Chapter 3 also discusses a generalization of heaps to trees whose nodes may have up to d children:

R. E. Tarjan. *Data Structures and Network Algorithms*. Philadelphia: Society for Industrial and Applied Mathematics, 1983.

Another data structure for priority queues appears in

M. J. Fischer and M. S. Paterson. "Fishspear: a priority queue algorithm." In *Proc. 25th Ann. Symp. on Foundations of Computer Science* (1984): 375–386.

11

Sorting

Problems that involve putting items into order, or *sorting*, arise frequently in practice. Sometimes we sort merely for our convenience, as when we alphabetize a list before we print it. At other times we sort to set up a more efficient data structure, as when we sort an array so we can use binary search on it. And many times we sort to facilitate further processing; for instance, it is much easier to find duplicate items in a list that is sorted than in one that is out of order.

Because the need to sort is so common, and because the problem is so simple to state, sorting has been studied extensively. This chapter presents several kinds of sorting problem, and several kinds of solution. An important lesson is that there is no single best way to solve all sorting problems.

11.1
SETTINGS FOR SORTING

People have been sorting for centuries, whether to keep a list in alphabetical order or to arrange their hands in card games. To understand why this routine task is challenging for a computer, imagine that we are playing a game in which we must sort using the limited capabilities available to a computer.

To begin the game, we enter a room in which a line of cards lies in a single row on a table. Each card has an encoded key, perhaps on a magnetic stripe; in a departure from the search problem of Chapter 7, we shall not assume that the keys are distinct. A comparison machine hums quietly in one corner; when we insert two cards into the comparison machine, it tells us whether the key on the first card is less than the key on the second card. We enter the room with a small number of markers that we can place on a card to show that it is interesting in some way; we decided how many markers to bring *before* we entered the room, hence before we knew how many cards we would have to sort.

To play the sorting game, we are allowed to perform two kinds of operations on the row of cards:

- *swap*: Exchange the position of two cards in the row;

- *binary key comparison*: Choose two cards; insert them into the comparison machine, which tells whether the first card contains the smaller of the two keys; return the cards to their places in the row. (This is a different key comparison operation from the one in Chapter 7: if two cards have equal keys, the comparison machine reports that the first does not have a smaller key.)

The object of the sorting game is to put the cards into sorted order by key. We would like to do this using as few binary key comparisons and swaps as we can.

The sorting game probably doesn't sound like much fun. Indeed, it would seem terribly frustrating to most of us, who would like to *see* the key on each card. Nevertheless, this game models nicely the situation faced by any algorithm to solve the general sorting problem. In this problem, we are never allowed to see the items' keys, so our solution must rely on binary key comparisons. The items to be sorted in the general sorting problem reside in an array, so we can reach any item in $O(1)$ time. The problem also requires that the sorting occur *in place*, using only $O(1)$ additional storage for items (not counting the memory occupied by the n items); this requirement is modeled by the markers we bring into the room.

In Sections 11.2 and 11.3 we shall see four algorithms to solve the general sorting problem. To evaluate them we shall count both the number of binary key comparisons (hereafter, "comparisons") and the number of swaps they make. We need to know both numbers to make a sensible choice of algorithm for a particular application. For example, it can cost much more to compare two strings than two integers. If we were sorting large structures whose keys depended on several members, comparisons would be even more costly; on the other hand, it is also expensive to swap large structures.

Section 11.4 presents some other approaches to sorting that apply in many practical situations, even though they either use operations on keys that are more general than binary key comparisons or they do not sort in place. After all, the sorting game is not the only game in town.

11.2
TWO SIMPLE SORTING ALGORITHMS

We begin our study of strategies for the sorting game with two elementary sorting algorithms. The worst-case running time of both algorithms is far from the best possible solution to the general sorting problem, but both are useful in some practical situations.

Insertion Sort

One simple strategy for sorting is analogous to the way many people sort their hands when playing cards: pick up one item at a time and move it into place among the items already picked up and sorted. Algorithm 11.1 describes this *insertion sort* more formally, and Figure 11.1 illustrates the idea: the region of the array that is sorted grows from the low end of the array until it encompasses the entire array.

The correctness of Algorithm 11.1 follows directly from the invariant assertion. Figure 11.2 depicts the operation of insertion sort on a small array.

The running time of insertion sort depends on how out of order its input is. In the worst case, the array is in reverse sorted order, so at each iteration the inner loop must swap the inserted item all the way to the low end of the array, and the number of both comparisons and swaps is

$$\sum_{i=1}^{n-1} \sum_{j=1}^{i} 1 = \sum_{i=1}^{n-1} i = \frac{n(n-1)}{2} = \Theta(n^2).$$

```
/* sort items in array x[0:n−1] */
for (i = 1; i < n; i++)
    for (j = i; j > 0 && x[ j] < x[ j−1]; j−−)
        swap the contents of x[ j] and x[ j−1]
    /* ASSERT:  x[0:i] is a sorted permutation of X[0:i] */
```

ALGORITHM 11.1

Insertion sort. The inequality $x[j] < x[j−1]$ uses whatever binary comparison operator is appropriate for the items in $x[ ]$. As in Program 3.9, the invariant assertion uses $X[ ]$ to refer to the original contents of array $x[ ]$.

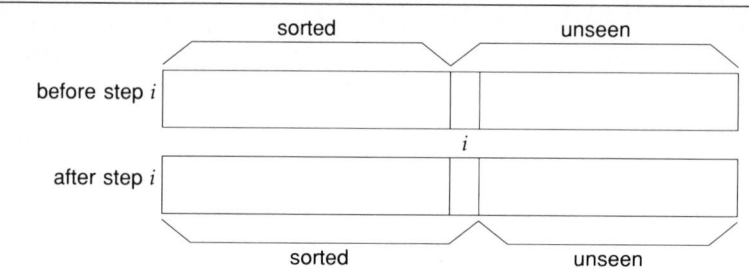

FIGURE 11.1

Illustration of the invariant for insertion sort: during step i, the ith item is inserted into its correct place among the first i items in the array.

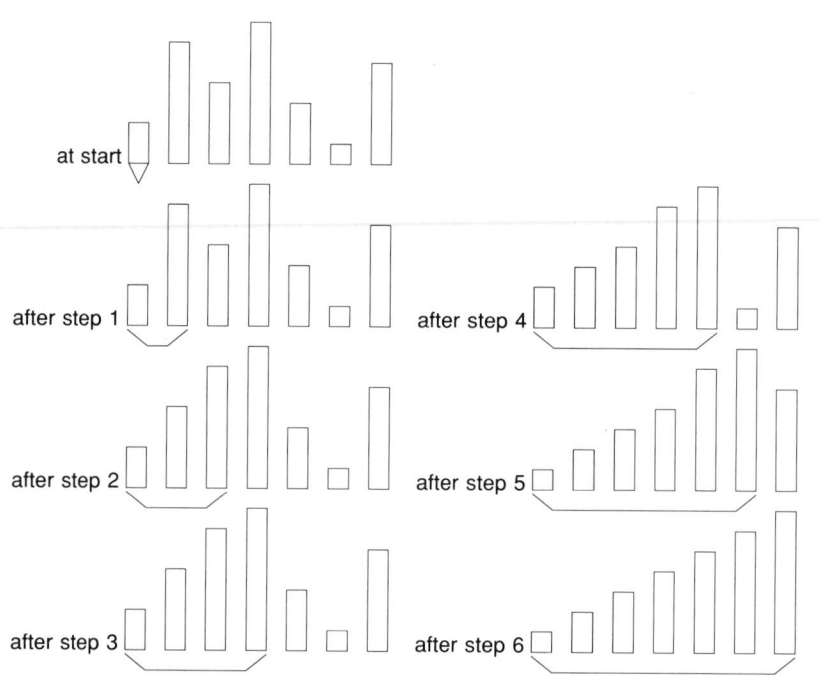

FIGURE 11.2

Progress of insertion sort on an array of seven items. The bracket indicates the portion of the array that is known to be sorted.

```
void isort(int n)
{
    int i, j;
    item t;
    for (i = 1; i < n; i++) {
        t = x[i];
        j = i;
        while (--j >= 0 && isless(t, x[j]))
            x[j+1] = x[j];
        x[j+1] = t;
        /* ASSERT: x[0:i] is a sorted permutation of X[0:i] */
    }
}
```

PROGRAM 11.1

An implementation of insertion sort. Function isless() returns TRUE if its first argument has a smaller key than its second argument.

(Here and below, we count only comparisons between keys, not comparisons on the values of array indexes.) On the other hand, when the array is sorted, the inserted item never moves at all, so insertion sort uses $n-1$ comparisons and no swaps. Thus, insertion sort is a good choice when the array is almost sorted.

The implementation of insertion sort shown as Program 11.1 is not a direct transcription of Algorithm 11.1. Indeed, it violates the rules of the sorting game in two minor ways for reasons of efficiency. At each step it makes a copy of the item being inserted, because it is usually faster to examine the value of a scalar variable than to examine an array element. The existence of this copy of the new item also means that the while-loop can simply shove the larger items one slot over in the array, rather than swap the inserted item back one slot at a time; if the item being inserted moves down k slots in the array, this uses k copy operations on elements rather than the $3k$ we would use with swaps.

Selection Sort

The smallest key in a sorted array is in slot 0, the next smallest in slot 1, and so on. In *selection sort* we sort by finding the smallest key in $x[0:n-1]$ and swapping it with $x[0]$. Then we find the smallest key in $x[1:n-1]$, which is the second smallest in $x[0:n-1]$, and swap it with $x[1]$. In effect, the correct answer grows from the low end of the array

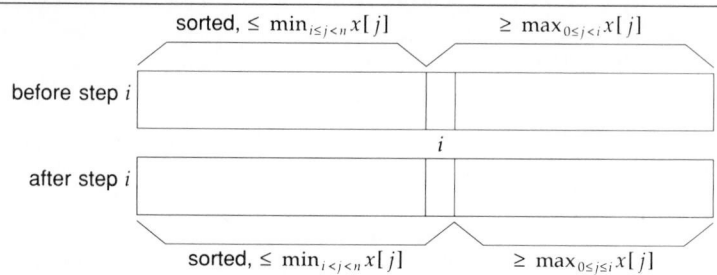

FIGURE 11.3

Illustration of the progress of selection sort.

```
/* x[0:n-1] to be sorted */
for (i = 0; i < n; i++)
    small = i;
    for (j = i+1; j < n; j++)
        if (x[j] < x[small])
            small = j
    swap the contents of x[i] and x[small]
    /* ASSERT: x[0:i] contains the smallest i items in X[0:n-1], sorted */
```

ALGORITHM 11.2

Algorithm for selection sort.

as illustrated in Figure 11.3. Algorithm 11.2 shows a simple selection sort that uses sequential search at each step to locate the item with the smallest key, then swaps it with the item that resides where it should be. Figure 11.4 shows the progress of selection sort on the same array as was sorted in Figure 11.2.

The time complexity of Algorithm 11.2 is simple to analyze because the number of comparisons and swaps it uses does not depend on the contents of the input array. The number of comparisons is

$$\sum_{i=0}^{n-1} \sum_{j=i+1}^{n-1} 1 = \sum_{i=0}^{n-1} (n-i-1) = \sum_{i=0}^{n-1} i = \frac{n(n-1)}{2}.$$

The number of swaps is $n-1$; this could be reduced if we avoided swapping when $i = small$.

Thus, selection sort uses $\Theta(n^2)$ comparisons but only $O(n)$ swaps to sort an array of n items. It can be very useful when the swaps are

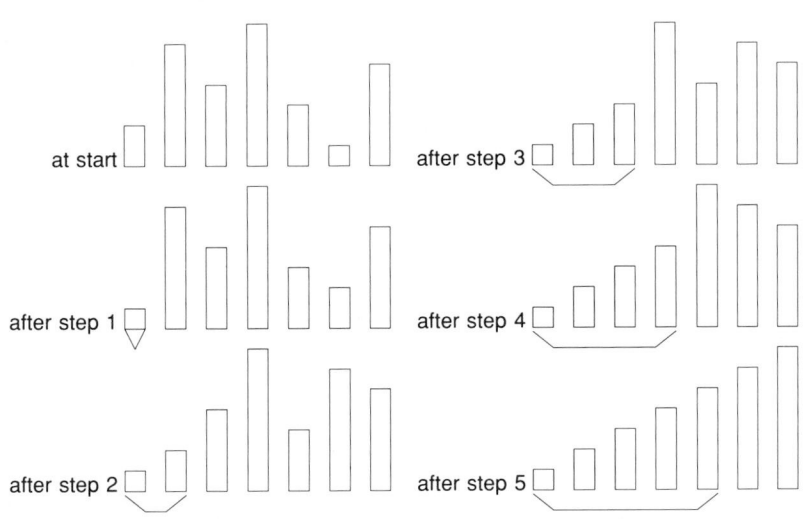

FIGURE 11.4

In this picture of selection sort applied to the input array of Figure 11.2, the bracket shows the portion of the array that is known to contain the correct final result. Thus, even though the array is sorted after step 5, straight selection sort would perform step 6, only to find that slot 6 already contains the correct item.

costly or inconvenient. For instance, if we were sorting wild animals among cages, the swaps would be much riskier than the comparisons, and we would probably choose selection sort in order to minimize the number of swaps required.

11.3
TWO EFFICIENT SORTING ALGORITHMS

Both of the sorting algorithms in Section 11.2 use $\Omega(n^2)$ time in the worst case to sort an array of n items. This section presents two algorithms whose time complexity asymptotically beats this time bound.

Heapsort

Heapsort is a version of selection sort in which we use heap-like operations to find and move the smallest remaining element at each step. It is convenient to arrange the heap so that the item with maximum key has highest priority. As the heap shrinks, the items with large keys fill

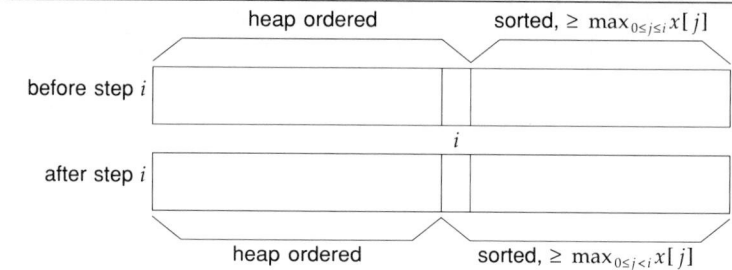

FIGURE 11.5

The progress of heapsort.

in the array from the high end, as illustrated in Figure 11.5. Algorithm 11.3 describes heapsort, and Figure 11.6 illustrates its operation on our sample array.

We know from Section 10.5 that we can turn $x[0:n-1]$ into a heap in $O(n)$ time. The sorting step uses $n-1$ explicit swaps, and whatever swaps and comparisons are needed to restore the heap order. Since the heap order can be restored each time in $O(\log n)$ steps, the sorting step uses $O(n \log n)$ swaps and comparisons. Thus, heapsort runs in $O(n \log n)$ time.

Heapsort is the first general purpose sorting algorithm we have seen that has a worst case time bound better than $O(n^2)$. This does not mean, however, that we should simply use heapsort all the time. One reason is that simpler sorts are easier to write and perfectly acceptable on short arrays. Another reason is that the running time of

---

/* $x[1:n]$ contains items to be sorted */
Heap Creation Step:
    Turn $x[1:n]$ into a heap using priority inversely related to key.
Sorting Step:
    for ($i = n; i > 1; i--$)
        swap the contents of $x[i]$ and $x[1]$
        restore heap order to $x[1:i-1]$ by letting $x[1]$ fall
        /* ASSERT: $x[1:i-1]$ is a heap */
        /* ASSERT: $x[i:n]$ contains the largest $n-i+1$ items in $X[1:n]$, sorted */

ALGORITHM 11.3

Algorithm for heapsort. Note that, since heaps are best defined with the item of highest priority in slot 1, this pseudo-code assumes that the items to be sorted also start in slot 1.

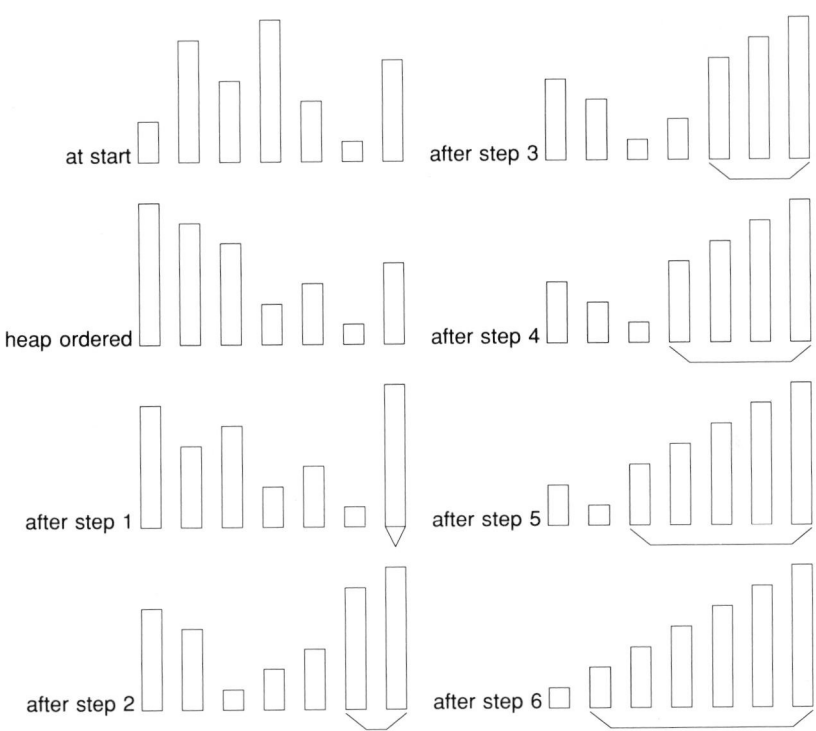

FIGURE 11.6

The operation of heapsort. The bracket shows the portion of the array that is known to be correct. The unbracketed part of the array is a heap.

heapsort is almost independent of the input order. If the input is sorted already, heapsort laboriously turns the array into a heap and then restores it to sorted order. If the input is in reverse sorted order, then it is already a heap, but the kth sorting step uses $\Theta(\log(n-k))$ operations since the element placed at the root must fall to the leaves each time. In both cases, heapsort uses $\Theta(n \log n)$ time.

Quicksort

Quicksort names a family of related algorithms that sort using a recursive divide-and-conquer strategy. Algorithm 11.4 shows the outline of quicksort, and Figure 11.7 shows schematically the progress of one recursive call. Algorithm 11.4 just might be the vaguest description of an algorithm that we have seen yet: it does not describe how either the

/* Elements to be sorted are in x[low:high] */
Split selection Step:
    Choose an element s in x[low:high].
Partition Step:
    Partition x[low:high] using s so that for some i,
    x[i] = s, x[low:i−1] are all ≤ s, and x[i+1:high] are all ≥ s.
Recursive Step:
    Call quicksort recursively on x[low:i−1] and x[i+1:high].

ALGORITHM 11.4

Outline of the quicksort family of algorithms. (Figure 11.7 explains the partition step.)

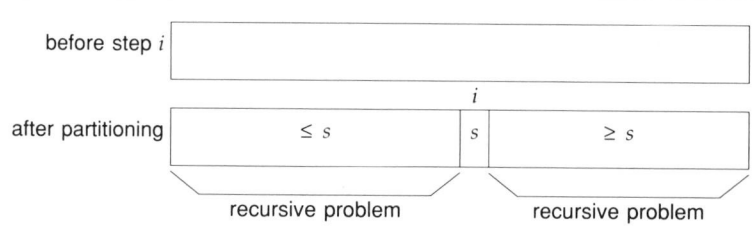

FIGURE 11.7

Quicksort after partitioning on the element s.

split selection or the partition steps should be performed. We discuss the partition step first, since it is straightforward.

Within each recursive call, the main work is to partition the array. Program 11.2a shows how to do this in linear time. Function divide() uses a function passed as a parameter to determine which element of x[low:high] should serve as the splitting value. It stashes the splitting value in x[low], then moves low and high together, maintaining the invariant illustrated in Figure 11.8. When we enter the loop, low moves forward to the next element larger than s, then high moves backward to the next element smaller than s. If the indexes have not met or crossed during this motion, we swap the items and continue. Once the indexes meet, we put s into its rightful position and return the index of that location (so that we know what subarrays to process recursively).

With the partition operation in hand, the quicksort function itself is simple and short, as shown in Program 11.2b. It partitions the array,

```
int divide(int low, int high, int (*fsplit)(int, int))
{
    int split;
    if (low >= high)
        return low;
    split = (*fsplit)(low, high);
    demand(low <= split && split <= high, fsplit botch);
    swap(&x[low], &x[split]);
    split = low;
    low++;
    for (;;) {
        /* ASSERT: x[LOW:low-1] <= x[split] */
        /* ASSERT: x[high+1:HIGH] >= x[split] */
        while (low < high && !isless(x[split], x[low]))
            low++;
        while (high > low && !isless(x[high], x[split]))
            high--;
        if (low < high)
            swap(&x[low], &x[high]);
        else
            break;
    }
    if (isless(x[split], x[low]))
        low--;
    swap(&x[low], &x[split]);
    return low;
}
```

PROGRAM 11.2a

Function to partition an array. The parameter function fsplit() is used to decide which element should be used to split.

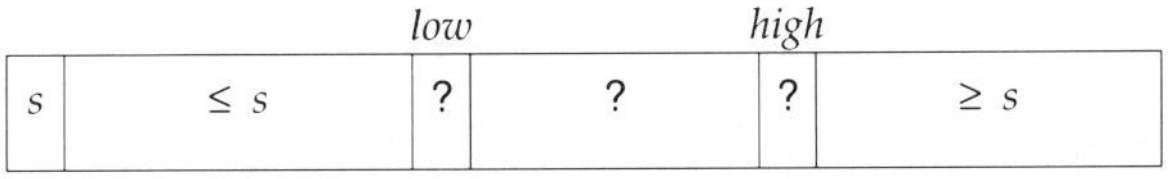

FIGURE 11.8

The invariant maintained by function divide() in Program 11.2a. The splitting element s is stored in the array slot indexed by the original value of low. The question marks indicate that we know nothing about how the values in the interval compare to s.

```
void quicksort(int low, int high, int (*fsplit)(int, int))
{
    int split;
    split = divide(low, high, fsplit);
    if (split > low)
        quicksort(low, split-1, fsplit);
    if (split < high)
        quicksort(split+1, high, fsplit);
}
```

PROGRAM 11.2b

Quicksort function that uses function `divide()` in Program 11.2a.

then calls itself recursively on any non-empty subarrays left after the partitioning.

Choosing the Splitting Element for Quicksort

When we choose the element that will be used to partition the array at each recursive step, we hope to partition the array into subarrays that are about the same size. If we succeed perfectly and always partition the array into subarrays of equal size, then the total running time will obey the recurrence

$$T(1) = 1;$$
$$T(n) = n + 2T(n/2), \text{ for } n > 1, \tag{11.1}$$

because the work of partitioning takes linear time. The solution to Equation (11.1) is $T(n) = n \log_2 n$, so we would have another $O(n \log n)$-time sorting algorithm. Unfortunately, if we choose the splitting element badly so that one subarray is always empty, then the running time of the algorithm will obey the recurrence

$$T(1) = 1;$$
$$T(n) = n + T(n-1), \text{ for } n > 1, \tag{11.2}$$

to which the solution is $T(n) = \Theta(n^2)$. Evidently the choice of splitting element matters a great deal to the performance of quicksort.

A simple rule for choosing the splitting element is always to choose x[low]—the element at the lowest index in the subarray. This works well on a randomly ordered array of items. If the array is already in order, however, this splitting rule leads to the quadratic behavior reflected by Equation (11.2).

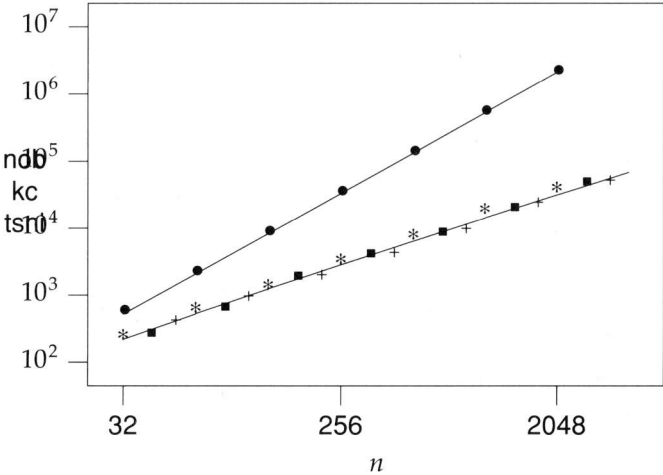

FIGURE 11.9

The number of comparisons quicksort was observed to use under different splitting rules on different input:

-     sorted input, split at low position, arrays of size 2^k
- *   random input, split at low position, arrays of size 2^k
- ■   random input, split at random position, arrays of size $\lfloor 4 \times 2^k /3 \rfloor$
- +   sorted input, split at random position, arrays of size $\lfloor 5 \times 2^k /3 \rfloor$

The two lines show the functions $2n \log_e n$ and $n(n+1)/2$, which give the theoretical predictions for the number of comparisons in the two essentially different situations.

Another rule for choosing the splitting element is to pick an element randomly from the range `low:high`. In practice, this works well on both randomly ordered input and sorted input. Figure 11.9 compares the performance of these two splitting rules on these two kinds of input.

The exercises mention some other rules for choosing the splitting element. The danger in devising elaborate rules for splitting is that the time we spend choosing the splitting element can become a significant fraction of the total sorting time.

Early Termination of Recursion in Quicksort

Program 11.2b implements a purely recursive form of quicksort: function `quicksort()` is called n times on an array of length n. We know, however, that asymptotically efficient methods are not always fastest for small problems. One way to use this observation is to terminate the recursion before the problems get very small. To do this, simply change the if-tests in quicksort() so that the recursive call is not made unless the subarray is larger than some chosen value m.

When such a truncated quicksort is finished, the array is not in sorted order. Every element is within m of its final destination, however, so insertion sort is an excellent way for this hybrid scheme to finish sorting.

Heapsort vs. Quicksort

Since heapsort is guaranteed to run in $O(n \log n)$ time, while quicksort runs in $O(n \log n)$ time only on average, why would anyone ever use quicksort? It turns out that quicksort is much faster on average than heapsort. Figure 11.10 compares the number of binary comparisons used by heapsort and by quicksort using some randomness; heapsort consistently uses more binary comparisons than quicksort. An even stronger statement applies to the number of swaps used by the two sorts.

On the other hand, quicksort has a hidden cost not shared by heapsort: its recursive calls use stack space. On average the stack never contains more than $O(\log n)$ recursive calls, but in the worst case it can contain $\Omega(n)$. The following rule ensures that the stack need never contain more than $O(\log n)$ recursive calls: after partitioning the array, process the smaller subarray first.

11.4
TWO USEFUL SORTING IDEAS

The sorting game in Section 11.1 models a very general sorting problem, but sometimes its rules do not reflect accurately the constraints we face in a particular situation. In this section we shall see two problems that lie outside the rules of the sorting game. The first problem requires that we sort under more stringent rules, while the second problem can be solved under easier rules.

Merging

The sorting game requires that we be able to reach each item in $O(1)$ time. One situation that obviously violates this condition is when the

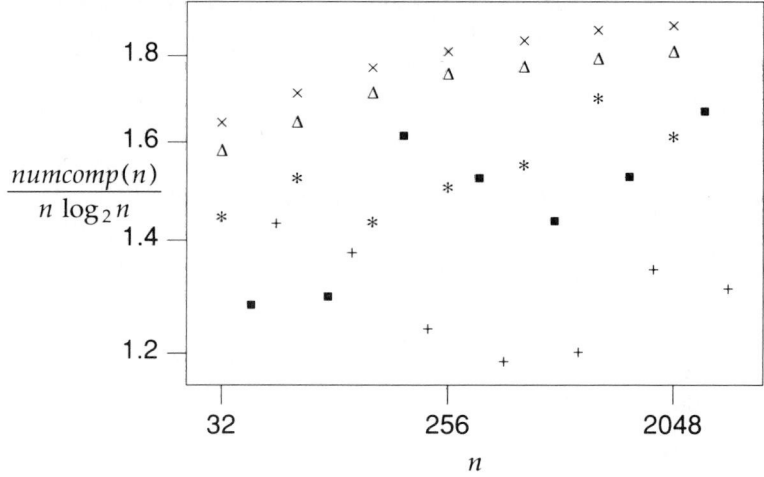

FIGURE 11.10

The expression $numcomp(n)$ is to the number of comparisons heapsort and quicksort used under the following conditions:
- ×   heapsort, sorted input, arrays of size 2^k
- Δ   heapsort, random input, arrays of size 2^k
- ∗   quicksort, random input, split at low position, arrays of size 2^k
- ■   quicksort, random input, split at random position, arrays of size $\lfloor 4 \times 2^k / 3 \rfloor$
- +   quicksort, sorted input, split at random position, arrays of size $\lfloor 5 \times 2^k / 3 \rfloor$

The graph shows the constant hidden in the notation $O(n \log n)$.

items reside in a linked list. Several approaches for sorting in such a situation rely on the easier operation of *merging*.

Given two sorted linked lists, we can merge them into a single sorted linked list in linear time. All we need to do is traverse both lists, pausing at each stage to append the smaller element to the merged result; when we reach the end of one list, we attach the remainder of the other list as the end of the merged result in $O(1)$ time with a final pointer change. This process is similar to the unite() function in Program 5.1, with some rule about how to break ties.

Linear-time merging is the basis of several sorting algorithms. The idea of a divide-and-conquer algorithm that sorts by merging is straightforward. Say we wish to sort a list of length n. If we had two sorted lists of length $n/2$, we could merge them into a sorted result in $O(n)$ time. To form the two half-length sorted lists, we apply this idea recursively. Since such recursive applications must terminate at (trivially sorted) single nodes in $O(\log n)$ steps, the whole algorithm uses $O(n \log n)$ steps to perform the merging at all recursive steps. An obvious implementation of this idea uses $\Omega(n)$ space to store pointers (in addition to the nodes themselves).

We can reduce the additional space required for pointers to $O(\log n)$ using a simple data structure in which to store sorted sublists that are partial results in the algorithm. This data structure might be called a *binomial comb*: it consists of an array *list*[ ] of pointers, such that *list*[i] is either null or points to the head of a sorted linked list of 2^i nodes. To add a sorted linked list of 2^k nodes to a binomial comb, we try to place a pointer to its head in *list*[k]; if that slot already points to a list, we remove that list from the comb, merge it with the new list to form a single list of 2^{k+1} nodes, and add this new larger list back to the comb. (Adding this list forces another merge if there is already a list in slot $k+1$.)

Algorithm 11.5 sorts a linked list using merging and a binomial comb. To analyze the time complexity of Algorithm 11.5, note that each time we touch a node, it belongs to a list that is being merged as we maintain the binomial comb. Furthermore, each time a node is involved in a merge, the linked list to which it belongs moves forward one slot in the array. Since the node cannot move past *list*[$\lceil \log_2 n \rceil - 1$], it cannot be touched more than $\lceil \log_2 n \rceil$ times. Thus the total number of times all nodes are touched is at most $n \lceil \log_2 n \rceil$, from which we conclude that Algorithm 11.5 runs in $O(n \log n)$ time.

A simple variation of this algorithm can run faster on linked lists that contain long sequences that are already sorted. Instead of breaking the original linked list into single nodes and adding them one at a time to the binomial comb, we use any ordering already present in the list. That is, we repeatedly break off the longest possible sorted chain

---

/* The linked list to be sorted contains n nodes. */
Comb Initialization Step:
    Allocate space for an array list[0: $\lceil \log_2 n \rceil - 1$] *of list head pointers.*
List Decomposition Step:
    One at a time, remove each node from the list, and add it to the binomial comb.
Final Step:
    Sweep through the comb from list[0] *through list*[$\lceil \log_2 n \rceil - 1$] *to create*
    a single sorted linked list.

ALGORITHM 11.5

An algorithm to sort a linked list using linear-time merging.

from the head of the linked list, adding that chain to a comb that contains partially sorted results.

Computing on Keys

Suppose someone gave you a pile of about 100 index cards containing bibliographic citations and asked you to alphabetize them by author name. Would you consider doing the job using any of the sorts we have seen so far? Probably not. Instead, you might make piles for different initial letters, and distribute the cards into the piles. If each pile were small enough after this step, you could sort them at a glance or using a simple insertion sort. If some piles were still too large for these methods, you could distribute their cards into piles based on second letter.

This strategy does not apply to the sorting game, because it assumes that we are able to see the sort keys and perform some computation on them. But in many practical situations it can be used to good effect. The simple idea described above resembles using the initial letter as a hash function to index into a table of separate chains, and using insertion sort to keep each hash chain ordered.

Suppose that we can devise a hash function that distributes the n items to be sorted evenly among k classes, and the classes themselves are ordered: if $i < j$, then any item in class i is less than any item in class j. Then this strategy would use $O(n)$ time to distribute the items into classes, and $O((n/k)^2)$ time to put each class into order using insertion sort. The total time to distribute the items and perform k insertion sorts would be $O(n + n^2/k)$. If we choose $k = \Omega(n)$, a constant fraction of n, then this sort would run in $O(n)$ time.

11.5
SUMMARY AND PERSPECTIVE

The question "Which sort should I use?" often meets the glib reply "Use the system sort," since most computer systems make such a program available as a general utility. The system sort is often the correct answer too, because using it requires none of the effort of constructing and debugging a program. On the other hand, the system sort may be inconvenient to use from deep within a program.

Sometimes when we write a program, we know enough at a particular point to choose a good sorting method. When we cannot commit ourselves confidently to a particular sorting method, we should at least perform the sorting in a separate function so that we can easily determine if sorting is important to the running time and change the method if necessary.

The preceding sections did not mention several topics that are related to sorting and that can be important in practice.

Stability

Suppose that two items a and b with the same sort key appear at positions $x[i_a]$ and $x[i_b]$ in the input to a sorting algorithm, with $i_a < i_b$. A sorting algorithm is said to be *stable* if the items appear in the same order in its output; that is, if a and b appear in the output at positions $x[j_a]$ and $x[j_b]$, then $j_a < j_b$.

We can make any sort stable by including with each item its original position in the input, and using this value to decide the answer to binary key comparisons when the sort keys are equal. Some sorting algorithms, however, are naturally stable: they sort stably with no extra care. For example, Program 11.1 is a stable insertion sort. Unfortunately, neither of the efficient sorting algorithms of Section 11.3 is naturally stable.

External Sorting

If all of the items to be sorted do not fit into primary memory, then each of the methods in this chapter is vulnerable to serious problems of performance caused by excessive paging. Such large sorting problems often require special consideration to find a suitable sorting method. A simple hybrid idea that is often effective is to break the input into chunks that will fit into primary memory, sort each chunk, then merge the chunks using a generalization of the merging operation described in Section 11.4; such a *multiway merge* naturally uses a priority queue to store as many items as there are chunks.

Lower Bounds

You may have noticed that all of our solutions to the sorting game need $\Omega(n \log n)$ binary comparisons in the worst case to sort n items. One way to see that it is impossible to do better than this is to consider the following related but artificial problem. Given a set of n distinct items, the problem is to use binary comparisons to discover which permutation of them would bring the items into sorted order. This problem is equivalent to the sorting problem, in that if we know the permutation, we can sort the items, and if we perform some minor bookkeeping before we sort the items, then we can report what permutation was used to sort them.

There are $n!$ possible permutations of n distinct items, and our job is to find the correct one using binary comparisons. Suppose we construct a binary search tree on the permutations. At each internal node, we store a binary comparison "$x[i] <? x[j]$." All permutations in which $x[i] < x[j]$ is true are leaves of the left subtree of the node, while all permutations in which $x[i] < x[j]$ is false are leaves of the right subtree of the node. Since our binary search tree has $n!$ leaves, it has height $\Omega(\log n!) = \Omega(n \log n)$, so at least one permutation requires $\Omega(n \log n)$ binary comparisons to determine that it is the correct answer.

In the folklore of sorting you may read that any sorting algorithm must take $\Omega(n \log n)$ time to sort n items. This broad statement is false: for instance, we can sort based on key computation in linear time, as described in Section 11.4. If our only tool in sorting is binary key comparisons, however, then the preceding argument shows that no one can devise a sorting algorithm that beats the $\Omega(n \log n)$ lower bound.

EXERCISES

1 Show that $\Omega(n)$ comparisons are necessary to verify that an array is sorted.

2 Show that it takes $\Omega(n)$ swaps in the worst case to sort an array.

3 What are the contents of array x[] during the execution of the while-loop in Program 11.1?

4 Both Algorithm 11.1 and Program 11.1 use sequential search to find where the item being inserted should be added to the sorted portion of the array. But we could use binary search to determine the destination of the new item. How many comparisons and swaps would such *binary insertion sort* use?

5 Verify the correctness of selection sort.

6 Implement selection sort.

7 Write a smart swap function that does not perform the interchange if it would in fact change nothing. How much difference does it make to the performance of insertion sort or selection sort?

8 Implement heapsort so it sorts a traditional C-style array of n items $x[0:n-1]$.

9 Experiment to determine the average performance of heapsort.

10 Verify that divide() in Program 11.2a works.

11 Show that the following algorithm partitions array $x[low:high]$ around $x[low]$:

```
mid = low − 1
for (i = low; i ≤ high; i++)
    if (x[i] < x[low])
        mid++
        interchange the contents of x[mid] and x[i]
    interchange the contents of x[low] and x[mid]
```

12 Show that the solution to Equation (11.1) is $T(n) = n\log_2 n$.

13 Predict the performance of quicksort using each of the two splitting rules on arrays in reverse sorted order. Experiment to verify your prediction.

14 Show that the expected number of comparisons used by quicksort when it sorts a random array of distinct elements is $2n\log_e n$.

15 Experiment to determine the best value at which to terminate recursion in a quicksort program running on your system.

16 Another splitting rule for quicksort is to split around the median of three (or an odd number more) elements of the subarray. This approach guarantees that neither recursive subproblem will be empty, and also lends itself naturally to the early termination of recursion. Experiment to see if this approach leads to improved running times.

17 Why does recurring on the smaller subarray guarantee that the stack for quicksort need contain only $O(\log n)$ recursive calls?

18 The *median* of n numbers is the $((n+1)/2)$th largest if n is odd, and the average of the $(n/2)$th and $(n/2+1)$th if n is even. Show how to modify quicksort to find the median of an array of n numbers in $O(n)$ expected time.

19 What can you say about the average number of swaps used by heapsort and quicksort?

20 Implement a version of linear-time merging that is allowed to destroy the component linked lists. Implement a non-destructive version of linear-time merging that leaves the component linked lists intact.

21 Write a function to merge two binomial combs.

22 Implement Algorithm 11.5. Can you do it without knowing n (and without running down the list to discover n)?

23 How long does Algorithm 11.5 take to sort a linked list that is already in order?

24 Describe a comb-like data structure that would be appropriate for the modified version of Algorithm 11.5 that exploits any order already present in the input linked list. Does the running time of the modified algorithm depend on where the partially sorted lists are added to the comb? Implement the suggested modification of

```
/* items to be sorted are in x[0:n−1] */
for (i = 0; i < n; i++)
    for (j = 0; j < i; j++)
        if x[j+1] < x[j]
            interchange x[j] and x[j+1]
```

ALGORITHM 11.6

Bubble sort.

Algorithm 11.5 using your data structure, and report on its performance.

25 If $x[0:n−1]$ contains the input to a sorting algorithm, and $y[0:n−1]$ is extra space that the algorithm can use, show how to use linear-time merging to sort $x[0:n−1]$ in $O(n \log n)$ time.

26 *Decimal radix sort* uses key computations to sort k-digit integers. It maintains two sets of ten queues A and B (often called *buckets*) labelled 0 through 9. To begin, insert each integer into the A bucket labelled by its units digit. At the ith step, move the A buckets to the corresponding B buckets, then go through the B buckets from 0 through 9, inserting each integer into the A bucket labelled by its 10^i digit. Show that this algorithm produces sorted output. What is its time complexity?

27 Find out what algorithm the system sort on your system uses. Can you devise input that causes it to perform badly? How "natural" is that input?

28 Show that Program 11.1 is a stable sort.

29 Show that Algorithm 11.2 is not a stable sort.

30 Implement a stable efficient sort.

31 Implement an external sort procedure like the one described in the text.

32 Given an array $x[0:n−1]$ and a permutation $p_0, p_1, \ldots, p_{n−1}$ of the numbers 0 through $n−1$, show how to reorder the array so that for $0 \le i < n, x[p_i] = X[i]$, where $X[i]$ means the original contents of the array. How much space does your solution use?

33 With what information would you augment the items so a sorting algorithm could report what permutation it applied to the input?

The following exercises are about Algorithm 11.6.

34 Devise an invariant assertion to show that Algorithm 11.6 works.

35 How many comparisons and swaps does Algorithm 11.6 use?

36 Can you construct any input on which Algorithm 11.6 uses fewer comparisons than insertion sort?

REFERENCES

Sorting is the subject of Chapter 5 of

> D. E. Knuth. *Sorting and Searching*. Vol. 3, *The Art of Computer Programming*. 2d printing. Reading, Mass.: Addison-Wesley, 1975.

Heapsort appeared in:

> J. W. J. Williams. "Algorithm 232: heapsort." *Communications of the ACM* 7 (1964): 347–348.

Smoothsort is a sorting algorithm that is intended to improve the performance of heapsort on lists that are almost in order:

> E. W. Dijkstra. "Smoothsort, an alternative for sorting in situ." *Science of Computer Programming* 1 (1982): 223–233.

Quicksort appeared as two short pieces:

> C. A. R. Hoare. "Algorithm 63: partition." *Communications of the ACM* 4 (1961): 321.

> C. A. R. Hoare. "Algorithm 64: quicksort." *Communications of the ACM* 4 (1961): 321.

An introductory discussion of quicksort appears in:

> C. A. R. Hoare. "Quicksort." *Computer Journal* 5 (1962): 10–15.

Robert Sedgewick's 1975 Stanford University Ph.D. dissertation studied many variations on quicksort:

> R. Sedgewick. *Quicksort*. New York: Garland, 1980.

A non-recursive quicksort appears in

> B.-C. Huang and D. E. Knuth. "A one-way, stackless quicksort algorithm." *BIT* 26 (1986): 127–130.

Exercise 11 about alternative partitioning code for quicksort is from Column 10 of

> J. L. Bentley. *Programming Pearls*. Reading, Mass.: Addison-Wesley, 1986.

The following reference discusses one person's experience in implementing a sorting algorithm for general use:

> J. P. Linderman. "Theory and practice in the construction of a working sort routine." *Bell System Technical Journal* 63 (1984): 1827–1843.

12

Applying Data Structures

Program 1.2 maintains a checkbook by keeping track of the total amounts deposited to or withdrawn from various accounts. Although it was useful as a vehicle to demonstrate the role of algorithms and data structures in determining the performance of programs, Program 1.2 leaves a lot to be desired as a tool for maintaining a record of accounts. If an account name is misspelled, Program 1.2 creates a new account with the misspelled name. If the dollar amount of a transaction is entered incorrectly, Program 1.2 accepts it without any reservation.

In this chapter we shall write two programs that maintain accounts using the time-honored method of double-entry bookkeeping to detect many errors in the input and to provide more general information about the sources and uses of funds. These programs use several of the data structures and algorithms in the preceding chapters, though you might choose other techniques when faced with a similar problem. One of the goals of the chapter is to show how we can confine the details of the data structures to one part of the program, so that we can change them quickly if necessary.

12.1
DOUBLE-ENTRY BOOKKEEPING

To set up a double-entry bookkeeping system, we first establish *accounts*, much as we did in Chapter 1. In general, accounts represent sources and uses of money. Traditional bookkeeping distinguishes four kinds of accounts:

- *Asset*: money that is available to spend; examples are cash and checking.
- *Expense*: money that has been spent; examples are food and shelter.
- *Liability*: money owed; examples are outstanding balances for loans and on credit cards.
- *Income*: money received; examples are salary and interest on savings.

The method of double-entry bookkeeping is inspired by the observation that every transaction must affect at least two accounts in compensating ways. For instance, when you buy a can of soda, its cost should be reflected in both an increase in the expense account for food and a decrease in the asset account for cash on hand. When you deposit a paycheck to your checking account, the income account for salary increases, as do the amounts in the asset account for checking and in expense accounts for taxes withheld.

The calendar year is the most common *accounting period*. At the beginning of an accounting period, some asset and liability accounts may have a non-zero balance left over from the preceding year, but the expense and income accounts should have zero balances. During the accounting period, we enter transactions as they occur. To close the books at the end of an accounting period, we transfer the balances in asset and liability accounts to the books for the next accounting period and start the process all over again.

Types of Accounts

The four kinds of accounts are classified into types as depicted in Figure 12.1. The balances in real accounts survive through changes in accounting period, while those in nominal accounts start each accounting period at zero. For example, at the very beginning of the year, your checking account may contain a positive balance and you may still owe money on a loan; on the other hand, you have not yet earned or spent any money.

The distinction between debit and credit is more arbitrary than the distinction between real and nominal accounts. Table 12.1 shows the traditional classification. You just have to remember it: the vernacular meanings of "credit" and "debit" would scarcely lead most people to classify a savings account as a "real debit" but an outstanding loan as a "real credit."

	Debit	Credit
Real	Asset (e.g, Cash)	Liability (e.g., Loan) Net Worth
Nominal	Expense (e.g., Food)	Income (e.g., Salary)

TABLE 12.1

How accounts are usually divided among four categories. (The text explains the special account "net worth.")

Balancing Accounts

The fundamental rule that governs double-entry bookkeeping is that debits must always balance credits:

$$DEBITS = CREDITS. \tag{12.1}$$

This equation has several implications for the process of double-entry bookkeeping. Before any transactions occur, the nominal accounts all contain zero balances. Therefore the real accounts must obey the following equation:

$$ASSETS = NET\ WORTH + LIABILITIES. \tag{12.2}$$

We can consider Equation (12.2) to be a definition of net worth. Figure 12.1 shows a display of the values in real accounts in the format of a *balance sheet*. The value of net worth shown on a balance sheet usually

```
                    Dr                  Cr
Checking         1000.00
Savings          2000.00

Loan                                 1500.00
Net Worth                            1500.00

Total            3000.00             3000.00
```

FIGURE 12.1

A sample balance sheet. The heading "Cr" means "credit balance"; "Dr" means "debit balance."

```
Move $1500 from savings into checking.
Borrow $3500 more and deposit it into checking.
Pay $3000 tuition from checking.
Pay $2500 room and board from checking.
Deposit net of $400 income into checking; taxes = $50.
Buy books with $300 from checking.
```

FIGURE 12.2

Six transactions that occur soon after the beginning of the year reflected in the balance sheet of Figure 12.1.

is not changed by subsequent transactions; it would be more accurate to call it the net worth at the start of the accounting period.

The invariant expressed by Equation (12.1) also governs every transaction that occurs in a double-entry bookkeeping system. We can use the two example transactions above to illustrate how this works. When we buy a soda, the real debit account for cash decreases, and the nominal debit account for food increases. When a paycheck is deposited into a checking account, the nominal credit account for income increases, and the debit accounts for checking (real) and taxes (nominal) increase by the same amount. Since each transaction obeys Equation (12.1), at any time during a sequence of transactions we can stop to verify that

$$ASSETS + EXPENSES = NET\ WORTH + LIABILITIES + INCOME;$$

when we perform the sequence of transactions shown in Figure 12.2 on the balance sheet of Figure 12.1, the result is the *trial balance* shown in Figure 12.3. From the trial balance we can see the balances in all accounts: how much money we still have in assets, how much we now owe in liabilities, how much we spent, and how much we earned. The grand totals show that Equation (12.1) still holds.

The Problem

We shall write two programs that use double-entry bookkeeping to maintain a system of accounts. Each program should read the account classifications from one file and the transactions from a second file, and produce a trial balance.

We can use the example of Figures 12.1, 12.2, and 12.3 to test a scheme for setting up the files of accounts and transactions. Figure 12.4 shows a simple way to encode the accounts. Each line refers to one account; it contains a short code name for the account; a 1 or 2

	Dr	Cr
Checking	550.00	
Savings	500.00	
Tuition	3000.00	
Room & Board	2500.00	
Books	300.00	
Tax	50.00	
Loan		5000.00
Net Worth		1500.00
Income		400.00
Total Real	1050.00	6500.00
Total Nominal	5850.00	400.00
Grand Totals	6900.00	6900.00

FIGURE 12.3

Trial balance sheet showing the balances in real and nominal accounts after the transactions of Figure 12.2 have occurred.

---

that tells whether the account is real or nominal, respectively; and a -1 or 1 to tell whether the account type is debit or credit, respectively; the rest of the line contains an English name for the account.

Figure 12.5 shows an equally simple way to encode transactions. A sequence of non-blank lines represents a single transaction. Lines that

---

```
chk 1 -1 Checking
sav 1 -1 Savings
loan 1 1 Loan
net 1 1 Net Worth
tuit 2 -1 Tuition
r&b 2 -1 Room and Board
inc 2 1 Income
tax 2 -1 Tax Withheld
book 2 -1 Books
```

FIGURE 12.4

Encoding of classifications for the accounts shown in the trial balance in Figure 12.3.

```
#beginning balances
chk 1000
sav 2000
loan 1500
net 1500

#Move $1500 from savings into checking.
sav -1500
chk 1500

#Borrow $3500 more and deposit it into checking.
loan 3500
chk 3500

#Pay $3000 tuition from checking.
tuit 3000
chk -3000

#Pay $2500 room and board from checking.
r&b 2500
chk -2500

#Deposit net of $400 income into checking; taxes = $50.
inc 400
chk 350
tax 50

#Buy books with $300 from checking.
book 300
chk -300
```

FIGURE 12.5

The transactions shown in Figure 12.2, encoded using the account codes of Figure 12.4.

start with the symbol # are ignored; they may contain comments, the date, or other information. The remaining lines in a transaction contain the code name for an account and an amount to be debited or credited to that account. The first transaction in Figure 12.5 encodes the balance sheet of Figure 12.1: thus our encoding is general enough that we need not devise a separate mechanism with which to initialize the balances in real accounts.

The trial balance that is output by our program could be presented in many ways. To avoid a lengthy digression on formatting, we shall

```
chk                      550.00
sav                      500.00
loan                    5000.00
net                     1500.00
tuit                    3000.00
r&b                     2500.00
inc                      400.00
tax                       50.00
book                     300.00
#REAL DEBITS            6500.00
#NOMINAL DEBITS          400.00
#REAL CREDITS           1050.00
#NOMINAL CREDITS        5850.00
#TOTAL DEBITS           6900.00
#TOTAL CREDITS          6900.00
```

FIGURE 12.6

The trial balance of Figure 12.3, formatted as a single input transaction.
Comment lines show partial totals for the various categories of accounts.

follow the simple technique used in Chapter 1, and format the trial balance so that it is suitable as input to our program. Figure 12.6 shows the trial balance of Figure 12.3 as it could be output by the program.

12.2
BASIC SOLUTION

Our solution begins with the following straightforward outline:

Read the names and classifications of accounts.
Process each transaction.
Print the trial balance in the appropriate format.

In the first step, we build a dictionary with room to store account balances. In the second step, we must search for accounts in the dictionary by name, and alter information associated with the named accounts. In the third step, we print the appropriate information for each account in the dictionary. In this section we shall write a base program that performs this outline in terms of the operations in a data type.

```
typedef double money;    /* in dollars */
extern money readmoney(char *);
extern void writemoney(money);

#define abs(x)    ((x)>0?x:-(x))
#define iszero(x)    (abs(x) < 0.01)
```

PROGRAM 12.1a

Declaration of how amounts of money will be stored.

File `account.h`

We begin in Program 12.1 with a header file whose contents reflect some decisions common to any of our solutions. First we must decide how to store money amounts. It is easiest to keep money in floating-point numbers, as in the declaration in Program 12.1a. To make it easy to change the way money amounts are stored, we shall always access those amounts through functions `readmoney()` and `writemoney()`.

```
#define RE 1
#define NOM 2
#define DR 1
#define CR -1
/* For function dumpaccts() to work correctly, the
/* values of these four constants must have this property:
/* if renom is one of {RE, NOM} and sign is one of {DR, CR},
/* then the value of the expression renom + sign
/* (1) determines the values of renom and sign; and,
/* (2) lies between 0 and 3, inclusive. */

typedef struct account account;
struct account {
    char name[NAMELEN];
    int renom;   /* should be RE or NOM */
    int sign;    /* should be DR or CR */
    money balance;
    char title[TITLELEN];
};
```

PROGRAM 12.1b

Declaration of the account structure, omitting the definitions of MAXACCT, NAMELEN, and TITLELEN since they are completely arbitrary.

We use the macro iszero() to declare that a money amount whose absolute value is smaller than one cent is a roundoff error and should be treated as zero.

Program 12.1b shows the declarations associated with the structure that will store an account. The defined constants RE, NOM, DR, and CR denote the category to which each account belongs. The values assigned to these constants seemed natural: sign should certainly be either 1 or -1, so the appropriate definitions of DR and CR are obvious; RE and NOM need only be different, so 1 and 2 work just fine. (They also coincide with the numbers in Figure 12.4.) This assignment of values to constants turns out to be useful, because it lets us encode both aspects of an account's type in a single expression. This important property is carefully documented immediately after the constants are defined.

Finally, Program 12.1c declares a structure in which to store pointers to functions that implement the necessary data type operations. We explain here briefly what the member functions do; their purpose should become clearer when we write the base program that uses them. Function install() accepts the name and classification of an account and installs the account in the table. Function setup() will be called after all account names and classifications have been read; it arranges the table so that find() can search for an account by name. We use function nextacct() to traverse the table of accounts; the first time we call it, it returns a pointer to an account; each subsequent time, it returns a pointer to another (unvisited) account; when all accounts have been visited, nextacct() returns NULL to signal that all accounts have been seen.

```
typedef struct table table;
struct table {
    void (*install)(char *, int, int, char *, table *);
    void (*setup)(table *);
    account *(*find)(char *, table *);
    account *(*nextacct)(table *);
};

extern table *opentable(void);
```

PROGRAM 12.1c

Declaration of a structure that contains pointers to functions we shall need to implement our base solution, and the existence of a function to create such a structure.

```
void main(int argc, char **argv)
{
    FILE *infile;
    char *filename = "accounts";
    table *ledger;
    while (argc > 1 && argv[1][0] == '-')
        switch (argv[1][1]) {
        case 'a':
            filename = argv[2];
            argc -= 2;
            argv += 2;
            break;
        default:
            fprintf(stderr, "unknown flag %c\n", argv[1][1]);
            argc--;
            argv++;
            break;
        }
    ledger = opentable();
    readaccts(filename, ledger);
    (*ledger->setup)(ledger);
    if (argc > 1) {
        int i;
        for (i = 1; i < argc; i++) {
            infile = fopen(argv[i], "r");
            demand(infile, could not open input file);
            process(infile, ledger);
        }
    } else {
        infile = stdin;
        process(infile, ledger);
    }
    dumpaccts(ledger);
    exit(0);
}
```

PROGRAM 12.1d

Function `main()` for the base program.

Program 12.1c also declares that a function `opentable()` exists. We shall call it when we need to create a table of accounts.

File base.c

The file that contains the base program #includes the header file account.h. We shall discuss the functions in base.c from the top down. Program 12.1d shows function main(). It lets us choose whether to specify the name of a file that contains the names and classifications of accounts (via the −a flag) or to use the information in the default file accounts. The program can read transactions either from a sequence of files named on the command line or from the standard input. Most C programs use both flags and file indirection in ways like these.

The six steps in main() elaborate the outline at the beginning of the section: (1) parse any flags on the command line; (2) call opentable() to create a structure ledger that contains pointers to the table functions; (3) call readaccts() to read the file of accounts and install them in the table; (4) call the table setup function to make searching possible; (5) call process() on the appropriate input files; (6) call dumpaccts() to print the contents of the table of accounts. The base program includes functions readaccts(), process(), and

```
void readaccts(char *filename, table *ledger)
{
    char buf[2*TITLELEN];
    char namebuf[NAMELEN], titlebuf[TITLELEN];
    int renom, sign;
    FILE *acctfile = fopen(filename, "r");
    demand(acctfile, could not open file of accounts);
    while (fgets(buf, 2*TITLELEN, acctfile)) {
        sscanf(buf, "%s %d %d %[^\n]s",
            namebuf,
            &renom,
            &sign,
            titlebuf
        );
        demand(renom == RE || renom == NOM, bad renom);
        demand(sign == 1 || sign == -1, bad sign);
        (*ledger->install)(namebuf, renom, sign,
            titlebuf, ledger);
    }
}
```

PROGRAM 12.1e

Function to read account classifications and install them in the table.

dumpaccts(); each accepts ledger as an argument, because each needs to use one or more table functions.

Program 12.1e shows function readaccts(). It parses each line in the named file, checks that the real/nominal and debit/credit classifications make sense, then calls the table function to install the account in the table.

Program 12.1f shows a pair of functions with which to process a file of transactions. To process a transaction file, we need to peel off sequences of non-blank lines until we hit the end of the file. The principal function, single(), reads the lines for a single transaction, updates the balances in the appropriate accounts, and maintains a run-

```
/* process a single transaction from transfile */
void single(FILE *transfile, table *ledger)
{
    char buf[TITLELEN];
    char namebuf[NAMELEN];
    money amt, balance = 0;
    account *pacct;
    while (fgets(buf, TITLELEN, transfile)) {
        if (buf[0] == '#')
            continue;
        if (buf[0] == '\n')
            break;
        sscanf(buf, "%s", namebuf);
        amt = readmoney(buf + strlen(namebuf));
        pacct = (*ledger->find)(namebuf, ledger);
        demand(pacct, account not found);
        balance += pacct->sign * amt;
        pacct->balance += amt;
    }
    demand(iszero(balance), unbalanced transaction);
}

/* read transfile, processing one transaction at a time. */
void process(FILE *transfile, table *ledger)
{
    while (!feof(transfile))
        single(transfile, ledger);
}
```

PROGRAM 12.1f

Two functions that process a file of transactions.

```
#define lineout(string, amount)\
    printf("%*s", -2*NAMELEN, string);\
    writemoney(amount);\
    printf("\n");

void dumpaccts(table *ledger)
/* Recall that this relies on the values of RE, NOM, DR, CR. */
{
    account *pacct;
    money total[4], drtotal, crtotal;
    int i;
    for (i = 0; i < 4; i++)
        total[i] = 0;
    while (pacct = (*ledger->nextacct)(ledger)) {
        lineout(pacct->name, pacct->balance);
        total[pacct->renom + pacct->sign] +=
            pacct->balance;
    }
    lineout("#REAL DEBITS", total[RE+DR]);
    lineout("#NOMINAL DEBITS", total[NOM+DR]);
    lineout("#REAL CREDITS", total[RE+CR]);
    lineout("#NOMINAL CREDITS", total[NOM+CR]);
    drtotal = total[RE+DR] + total[NOM+DR];
    lineout("#TOTAL DEBITS", drtotal);
    crtotal = total[RE+CR] + total[NOM+CR];
    lineout("#TOTAL CREDITS", crtotal);
    demand(iszero(drtotal - crtotal), major balance failure);
}
```

PROGRAM 12.1g

Function to produce the output trial balance in input format.

ning total, balance, that will be zero at the end of the transaction if
Equation (12.1) is satisfied. The controlling function, process(), calls
single() until the input file is exhausted.

Program 12.1f shows function dumpaccts(). It uses the table
function nextacct() to traverse the table of accounts, printing the
balances in a single giant transaction. During this traversal it also
accumulates totals for the four types of account, using the encoding
mentioned above to index array total[]. After it has dumped the
contents of all accounts, it prints the accumulated totals as comments
on the transaction, and verifies that Equation (12.1) holds.

Although we have built a fair amount of machinery, we do not yet have a program that does anything, because we have not written the table functions. In the next two sections we shall see two ways to write them, and discuss how they perform.

12.3

SOLUTION I

Solution I keeps the ledger of accounts in an array. We might do this to keep the program simple, or because we do not trust the version of malloc() available to us. Since we know from Program 1.2 that simple sequential search can lead to expensive accounting programs, we shall use binary search to find account names.

We store the declarations of the table functions and the associated data structures in file binsch.c. All of the variables and all but one of the functions in this file are declared to be static, so they cannot be called by any function that is not itself declared in binsch.c. The exception to this information hiding is opentable(), which the base program must call directly.

Program 12.2a shows the declaration of the array of accounts and a function to install an account in that array. After it checks that there is

```
static account acct[MAXACCT];
static int numaccts;

static void install(char *name, int renom, int sign,
    char *title, table *ledger)
{
    demand(numaccts < MAXACCT, too many accounts);
    strcpy(acct[numaccts].name, name);
    acct[numaccts].renom = renom;
    acct[numaccts].sign = sign;
    strcpy(acct[numaccts].title, title);
    numaccts++;
}
```

PROGRAM 12.2a

Declaration of a array of accounts and a function to install a new account in the array.

```
static void setup(table *ledger)
{
    int i;
    qsort(acct, numaccts, sizeof(account), acctcmp);
    for (i = 1; i < numaccts; i++)
        demand(strcmp(acct[i-1].name, acct[i].name),
            duplicate account names);
}
```

PROGRAM 12.2b

Function to sort the array of accounts by name.

room for the account, function `install()` copies the members into the next available space.

Function `setup()` in Program 12.2b uses the library function `qsort()` to sort the array of accounts by name so that we can use binary search on it. (If `qsort()` were not available, we could use the quicksort in Program 11.2.) Once the array is sorted by name, we check for duplicate names. This simple check will warn of an obvious error in the input; of course the problem statement does not require this care, and the reckless can be omit this test and live dangerously.

Function `find()`, in Program 12.2c, is a revised version of Program 7.1b that searches in the array of accounts for a named account.

Program 12.2d shows function `nextacct()`. Its static variable `last` tells the array index of the last account that it returned.

Finally, Program 12.2e shows function `opentable()`, which allocates room for a structure of type `table`, then stores pointers to the four table functions that appear in Programs 12.2a through 12.2d. Since we need to call this function from `main()`, we do not declare it to be static to file `binsch.c`.

Theoretical and Experimental Analysis

If there are n accounts, `setup()` can be expected to run in $O(n \log n)$ time. If there are m transactions, and each transaction refers to $O(1)$ accounts, `process()` will run in $O(m \log n)$ time. Functions `readaccts()` and `dumpaccts()` each run in $O(n)$ time. Thus, we expect that Solution I will run in $O((m+n) \log n)$ time.

To test Solution I, we generated 1000 (= n) random account names and 10000 (= m) random transactions on two accounts each. It ran in about ten seconds on a DEC VAX™ 8550. A profile reveals that the

```
static account *find(char *name, table *ledger)
{
    int lo = 0, mid, hi = numaccts - 1;
    while (lo <= hi) {
        /* ASSERT:  name must lie in acct[lo:hi] */
        int cmpresult;
        mid = (lo + hi)/2;
        cmpresult = strcmp(acct[mid].name, name);
        if (cmpresult < 0)
            lo = mid + 1;
        else if (cmpresult > 0)
            hi = mid - 1;
        else
            return acct + mid;
    }
    return NULL;
}
```

PROGRAM 12.2c

Function that uses binary search to find an account by name.

program spends more than half of its time performing input and output. One possibility for improving its performance, however, is suggested by the fact that Solution I spends about 15% of its time in function qsort (); if we could avoid sorting the array, we might be able to write a faster program.

```
static account *nextacct(table *ledger)
{
    static int last = 0;
    if (last >= numaccts) {
        last = 0;
        return NULL;
    }
    return acct + last++;
}
```

PROGRAM 12.2d

Function with which we can walk through the table of accounts.

```
table *opentable(void)
{
    table *ledger;
    ledger = (table *) calloc(1, sizeof(table));
    ledger->install = install;
    ledger->setup = setup;
    ledger->find = find;
    ledger->nextacct = nextacct;
    return ledger;
}
```

PROGRAM 12.2e

The only function in file `binsch.c` that is not declared to be static. The base program calls it to create a table.

12.4

SOLUTION II

Solution II keeps the ledger of accounts in a hash table. We shall store the declarations of table functions and associated data structures in file `hasch.c`. Once again, all functions but `opentable()` are declared to be static to that file. In fact, we can use the same program `opentable()` as Program 12.2e.

The installation function in Program 12.3a builds a single linked list of accounts.

Program 12.3b shows function `setup()`. It allocates a hash table whose size depends on the number of accounts, then traverses the linked list built by `install()`, installing each account in the hash table as it goes. Since there is no ordering requirement on the linked lists in each hash slot, this function is easy to write: it uses a simple search to check for duplicates, then installs the name at the head of the list.

Program 12.3c shows function `find()`, which uses the hash function `hash()` in Program 12.3b to search the hash table for the named account.

Program 12.3d shows function `nextacct()`, which we can use to traverse the linked list of accounts in its original order.

```
typedef struct acctnode acctnode;
struct acctnode {
    acctnode *next;  /* in input */
    acctnode *link;  /* in hash chain */
    account data;
};
static acctnode dummy, *last = &dummy;
static int numaccts;

static void install(char *name, int renom, int sign,
    char *title, table *ledger)
{
    acctnode *new = (acctnode *) calloc(1, sizeof(acctnode));
    demand(new, out of memory);
    strcpy(new->data.name, name);
    new->data.renom = renom;
    new->data.sign = sign;
    strcpy(new->data.title, title);
    last->next = new;
    last = new;
    numaccts++;
}
```

PROGRAM 12.3a

Declaration of the structures with which Solution II hooks accounts together into a single linked list (through next members) and into hash chains (through link members).

Theoretical and Experimental Analysis

As before, let n be the number of accounts and m be the number of transactions. Since the hash table grows with n, the expected time to insert or to find an account is $O(1)$, so setup() runs in $O(n)$ expected time and process() runs in $O(m)$ expected time. Since functions readaccts() and dumpaccts() still run in $O(n)$ time, we expect that Solution II will run in $O(m+n)$ time.

Solution II takes about seven seconds to process the same 1000 accounts and 10000 transactions as we used to test Solution I. This cuts almost one-third off the execution time of Solution I. Solution II spends about three quarters of its time doing input and output, so it would be hard to improve its performance further by making changes to the data structures and algorithms.

```
static int hash(char *name)
{
    int result = 0;
    while (*name)
        result = (result << 1) + *name++;
    result %= numaccts;
    return result < 0 ? result + numaccts : result;
}

static acctnode **hashtab;
static void hashin(acctnode *a, table *ledger)
{
    acctnode *p;
    int h = hash(a->data.name);
    for (p = hashtab[h]; p; p = p->link)
        demand(strcmp(p->data.name, a->data.name),
            duplicate names)
    a->link = hashtab[h];
    hashtab[h] = a;
}

static void setup(table *ledger)
{
    acctnode *p;
    hashtab = (acctnode **) calloc(numaccts, sizeof(acctnode));
    demand(hashtab, no memory for hash table);
    for (p = dummy.next; p; p = p->next)
        hashin(p, ledger);
}
```

PROGRAM 12.3b

Functions to install accounts in a hash table for Solution II.

12.5
SUMMARY AND PERSPECTIVE

The programs in this chapter illustrate why Chapter 4 defines a data type as a set of operations. Each of the functions in these programs accepts a table as an argument; this table is not an array of data, but a collection of functions with which we can manipulate the data in a data structure whose inner workings are unknown to us.

One of the goals of this chapter was to separate the data structures and algorithms that maintain a table of accounts from the program that

```
static account *find(char *name, table *ledger)
{
    acctnode *p;
    int h = hash(name);
    for (p = hashtab[h]; p; p = p->link)
        if (!strcmp(p->data.name, name))
            return &p->data;
    return NULL;
}
```

PROGRAM 12.3c

Function to find an account by name in a hash table for Solution II.

manipulates the information in those accounts. The separation lets us plug in different data structures and algorithms, but it does not conceal completely the way accounts are stored. For example, readaccts() follows a pointer to an account to change its data; a more complete separation might require another table function post() that posts a balance change to an account. In general it is hard to draw the line between operations on the data structure and operations on the data.

These two programs produce different output: the trial balance produced by Solution I is sorted by account key, while accounts in the trial balance produced by Solution II appear in the same order as they did in the file that describes accounts. If the problem specification

```
static account *nextacct(table *ledger)
{
    static acctnode *prev = NULL;
    if (prev == NULL) {
        prev = dummy.next;
        return &prev->data;
    }
    prev = prev->next;
    if (prev)
        return &prev->data;
    else
        return NULL;
}
```

PROGRAM 12.3d

Function to return a pointer to the next unvisited account.

were more specific about how the output should appear, we might want to modify the data type to reflect this. For example, if we wanted accounts printed in their input order, Solution I would need to preserve that order somewhere, then sort by key to permit binary search to work.

Other Separation Methods

Often, a program of modest size can separate data structures from operations on data simply by keeping related functions together in files and not declaring them to be static to the file. If we did this in our solutions, then any function could call the table functions even if it were not given a pointer to `ledger`. Thus, we would not have to keep `ledger` around at all, much less pass it as an argument to every function in sight.

When a large program uses several data structures, however, the technique shown here is more robust. Each data structure will probably have (at least) functions to install items in it and to search it. If we rely on different files to separate data structures from data operations, then we have to invent different names for these functions for each data structure. When we pass data types to functions, however, then each function has available exactly the functions it needs to do its job.

The Payoff of Data Structures and Algorithms

Another lesson of this chapter is the importance of knowing what to expect when we use efficient data structures and algorithms. Chapters 1 through 11 could easily leave the impression that data structures and algorithms are the only keys to good programming, that worst-case running time is the most important consideration, and that really good methods have a $O(\log n)$ lurking somewhere in their asymptotic analysis. The profiles of our programs show clearly that such factors as the speed of input and output can play an important, and even dominant, role in the performance of programs.

EXERCISES

1 Let $NET\ WORTH_i$ be the net worth at the beginning of period i. Show that

$$NET\ WORTH_{n+1} = NET\ WORTH_n + INCOME - EXPENSES,$$

where $INCOME$ and $EXPENSES$ are the balances after the transactions in accounting period n.

2 What net worth would one bring forward to the next accounting period from the trial balance in Figure 12.3?

The following exercises refer to both Solutions I and II.

3 Write functions `readmoney()` and `writemoney()` to complete one of Solutions I and II. Now change the `typedef` of `money`; does anything in the program have to change besides `readmoney()` and `writemoney()`?

4 What does the program do if a transaction line contains leading spaces? What if an account description contains leading spaces? Modify the program to handle leading spaces and tabs in either place.

5 Modify the program so that account descriptions can include symbolic expressions such as NOM DR rather than the implementation-specific 1 -1.

6 Add the appropriate pieces to the program to make it count the number of transactions processed. Does your modification count two consecutive blank lines as a transaction?

7 The program stops processing when it detects an unbalanced transaction. Modify it so that it merely ignores unbalanced transactions. This means that account balances should not be modified until the transaction is known to obey Equation (12.1).

8 Modify the program so that it can read a transaction file in which several account–amount pairs appear on a single line of a transaction.

9 Change the program to print a trial balance in which all accounts of each type appear together, and within each type the accounts appear in order of decreasing balance.

10 Write a program that reads a trial balance and produces a printout more like Figure 12.3. How different need this program be from Solutions I and II?

REFERENCES

Bookkeeping is covered in the first chapter of most accounting books. One particularly accessible introduction appears in

C. B. Nickerson. *Accounting Handbook for Non-Accountants*. 3d ed. New York: Van Nostrand Reinhold, 1985.

The mathematical principles of double-entry bookkeeping are explained in the following article:

D. P. Ellerman. "The mathematics of double-entry bookkeeping." *Mathematics Magazine* 58 (1985): 226–233.

The following books show by example how to construct useful programs:

B. W. Kernighan and P. J. Plauger. *Software Tools*. Reading, Mass.: Addison-Wesley, 1976.

B. W. Kernighan and P. J. Plauger. *Software Tools in Pascal*. Reading, Mass.: Addison-Wesley, 1981.

This reference offers a useful overview of some tools that one can use to speed up programs:

J. L. Bentley. *Writing Efficient Programs*. Englewood Cliffs, N.J.: Prentice-Hall, 1982.

The C++ language is designed to make it more natural to separate data structures from data operations:

B. Stroustrup. *The C++ Programming Language*. Reading, Mass.: Addison-Wesley, 1986.

Part III

Advanced Topics

13

Acyclic Graphs

In Parts I and II we did not consider that items might bear any relation other than a linear ordering among themselves. Instead, we concentrated on arranging data so that we could search for matching items (using some kind of dictionary) or so that the right item would be available at the right time (using some kind of queue).

A graph is a combinatorial structure that can be used to model more general relationships among data items. We defer to Chapter 14 a formal definition of *graph*, but informally we can think of a graph as a set of nodes and some arrows that go between them. An *acyclic* graph has the property that if we start at any node and step through the graph following arrows, then we can never return to our starting point. We shall see two kinds of acyclic graphs and several problems about them in this chapter.

13.1
ROOTED TREES

A rooted tree is an acyclic graph that has two properties: one distinguished node is called the root, and there is a unique path from the root to any other node. Rooted trees are used to represent many kinds of relationships; examples include family trees in genealogy, taxonomic charts in biology, and organization charts in business. Figure 13.1 depicts part of a family tree from Greek mythology. In this rooted tree, each person's children appear in child nodes of the person's node, in contrast to the ancestor tree of Figure 7.8.

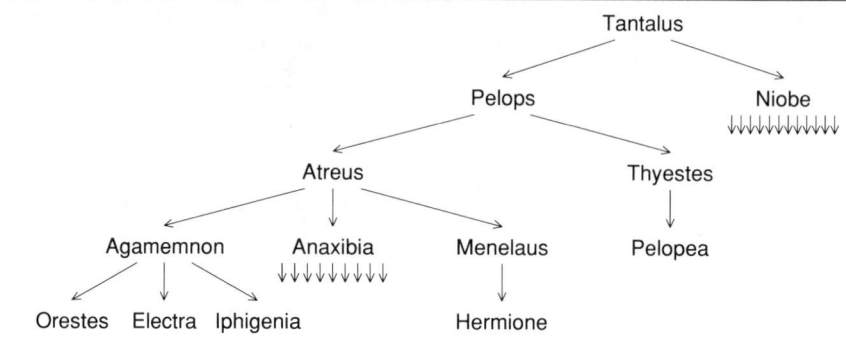

FIGURE 13.1

Part of the family tree of Atreus; the unlabelled arrows indicate that Anaxibia had nine children. Niobe had at least 12 children; Hesiod says she had 20. (Source: Aeschylus, *Oresteia*)

Most terminology from binary trees carries over naturally to rooted trees. Thus, we say that Tantalus appears at the root of the tree, that Hermione and Pelopea appear at leaves of the tree, and that Agamemnon's children are Orestes, Electra, and Iphigenia.

A drawing of a rooted tree imposes an ordering on the children of each node, from left to right across the page. Sometimes this ordering has a natural interpretation, as in many family trees where the children of each node appear in order from eldest to youngest. Sometimes this ordering has no particular importance, as in most organization charts. Whatever the significance of this ordering, however, its mere existence allows us to define two natural traversal orders on rooted trees. In a *preorder* traversal, we visit the root, then traverse in preorder the sub-trees rooted at each of its children in order. In a *postorder* traversal, we traverse in postorder the subtrees rooted at each child of the root in order, then visit the root. Figure 13.2 shows the results of these two traversals on the tree in Figure 13.1. Unless a rooted tree has a search order like the one for 2,3 trees in Section 9.2, there is no natural traversal order for rooted trees that corresponds to inorder on a binary tree.

Rooted trees differ in a fundamental way from binary trees: while the children of a node may be ordered, they are not otherwise distinguished. When a node has one child, that child is merely an only child, not a left or right child. This has some interesting implications for the data structures we use to represent rooted trees.

If we knew the maximum number of children that any node in a rooted tree could have, it would be tempting to allocate static space in each node in which to store that many pointers. Such a solution

preorder: Tantalus, Pelops, Atreus, Agamemnon, Orestes, Electra, Iphigenia, Anaxibia, Anaxibia's children, Menelaus, Hermione, Thyestes, Pelopea, Niobe, Niobe's children

postorder: Orestes, Electra, Iphigenia, Agamemnon, Anaxibia's children, Anaxibia, Hermione, Menelaus, Atreus, Pelopea, Thyestes, Pelops, Niobe's children, Niobe, Tantalus

FIGURE 13.2

The results of two traversal orders on Atreus's family tree.

would be inappropriate for a couple of reasons. Obviously, if the maximum number of children were large but the average number of children were small, this scheme would use a lot of unnecessary space. For instance, in Figure 13.1 the maximum number of children is twelve but the average is smaller than four. This scheme also requires that we take pains to treat all nodes with k children in the same way: it should not matter whether pointers to the k children are stored contiguously in one or the other end of the static array, or are scattered throughout the array in no discernible pattern.

Thus, if we use static tree nodes we must cope with pointers that can be sprinkled haphazardly throughout largely wasted space. Static tree nodes also suffer the disadvantage that they cannot represent trees whose nodes can have an unlimited number of children. For these reasons, it is more common to store a rooted tree using the *eldest child–eldest younger sibling* method illustrated in Figure 13.3. In words, the child link from a node p points to its eldest child q; through its sibling link, q heads a linked list of the children of p.

In the eldest child–eldest younger sibling data structure, each node contains two distinguished pointers. If you imagine picking up this data structure by the root and shaking it out so that child pointers go left and sibling pointers go right, you will see why this data structure is also called the *natural binary tree* of a rooted tree. The traversal orders on the natural binary tree bear a useful relationship to the traversal orders on the rooted tree it represents. A preorder traversal of either tree gives the same result. An inorder traversal of the natural binary tree is the same as a postorder traversal of the corresponding rooted tree. You can verify this on the trees of Figures 13.1 and 13.3. The general results follow from a simple induction argument.

In general, the root of a tree that is represented in the eldest child–eldest younger sibling data structure has a pointer to its eldest child, but no pointer to its younger sibling, since it *has* no younger

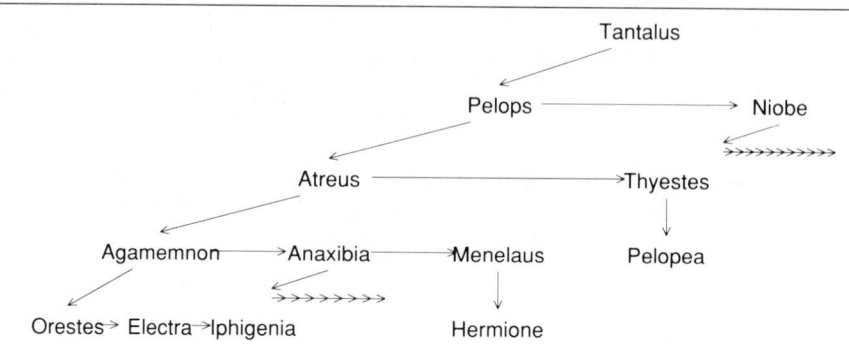

FIGURE 13.3

Data structure for the family tree of Figure 13.1. Arrows that point down represent links to eldest children; horizontal arrows point from each node to its eldest younger sibling.

sibling. Sometimes it is convenient to use this guaranteed null pointer to link a collection of trees together. Naturally, the result is called a *forest*.

Although they are a very specialized kind of acyclic graph, trees are useful in many applications when we can impose the tree property on relationships among data items. For example, many computers permit their users to organize their data in hierarchies of files: a directory can contain files and also other directories; these file systems are naturally represented as trees. Unfortunately, the trees that we see in real-world uses in genealogy, biology, and business often admit exceptional relationships that cause them to lose their graph-theoretic tree property. The exercises suggest some ways this can happen in family trees.

13.2
DISJOINT SETS

In this section we shall consider a rather abstract problem. Variations of this problem need to be solved to implement several important algorithms, including one in Section 14.4.

We wish to maintain a collection of disjoint subsets of the integers 0 through $n-1$. Initially, each integer is considered to belong to a singleton set. We are going to perform a sequence of operations of two types on these sets:

- *union*(x, y) — form the union of the set that contains x and the set that contains y;

- *find*(x) — report the set to which x belongs once all preceding *union*( )'s in the sequence have been performed.

To provide a convenient framework in which to state the algorithms and their time complexity, we make three technical assumptions:

1   We shall perform $n - 1$ union operations; none of these will be performed on two elements that belong to the same set.

2   We shall perform n find operations.

3   The result of a find operation is a unique or *canonical* element of the set: at any time, for any set in the collection, if we perform a find operation on any element in the set, the result should be the canonical element for that set.

Assumption 1 means that after all of the union operations are completed, there will be a single set that contains n integers. Assumption 3 is natural when we are using the find operation only to tell whether two elements belong to the same set.

Union-Find Trees

We can solve this problem by maintaining each set as a rooted tree; the root of each set's tree serves as the set's canonical element. Since we never need to traverse all of the elements in any set, we can store these trees in a simple data structure called a *union-find forest*. This is an array *parent*[ ] of n integers whose contents are defined by the following rule: if i lies at the root of the rooted tree for its set, then *parent*$[i] = i$; otherwise *parent*$[i]$ is the value at the parent of i in the rooted tree. In general many different rooted trees can represent the same set; Figure 13.4 shows an example of a collection of disjoint sets and a corresponding union-find forest.

Algorithm 13.1 shows how to perform *find*( ) and *union*( ) operations on union-find trees. We perform *find*( ) on a union-find tree by following parents from the item until we reach the root of the tree to which it belongs. For example, if we *find*(3) in the trees of Figure 13.4, we would pass from 3 through its parent (5) and its grandparent (8) before reaching the canonical element (7) for its set. The time required for a *find*( ) is proportional to the depth at which the found element lies in the tree.

To perform a *union*( ), we *find*( ) the roots of the trees that contain each element, then make one root the parent of the other; Algorithm 13.1 makes the arbitrary choice that the root of the second tree

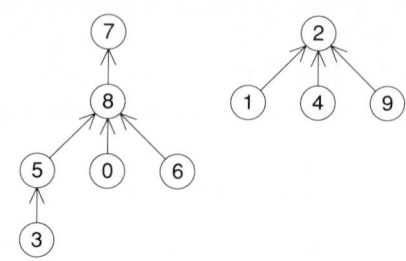

	i	0	1	2	3	4	5	6	7	8	9
$parent[i]$		8	2	2	5	2	8	8	7	7	2

FIGURE 13.4

A pair of rooted trees for the two disjoint sets { 0,3,5,6,7,8 } and { 1,2,4,9 }.

becomes the canonical element for the whole set. Since only one element of $parent[\ ]$ changes when a $union(\ )$ occurs, $union(\ )$ takes constant time in addition to the time for the two $find(\ )$ operations it performs.

If the ith operation is $union(i-1, i)$, for $1 \le i < n$, then after the last $union(\ )$ operation the union-find tree has height $n-1$. If now we perform n $find(\ )$ operations on its bottom element, the cost of the whole sequence of operations is $\Theta(n^2)$.

```
/* All variables are integers; parent[i] stores a rooted tree:
/* parent[i] is the contents of the parent of the node that contains i. */

find(x)
    while (parent[x] ≠ x)
        x = parent[x]
    return x

union(x, y)
    px = find(x)
    py = find(y)
    parent[px] = py
```

ALGORITHM 13.1

Simple $union(\ )$ and $find(\ )$ operations on union-find trees.

```
typedef struct element element;
struct element {
    int weight;
    element *parent;
};

void unite(element *x, element *y)
{
    x = find(x);
    y = find(y);
    demand(x != y, union on common set members);
    if (x->weight < y->weight)
        swap(&x, &y);
    y->parent = x;
    x->weight += y->weight;
}
```

PROGRAM 13.1a

Structure declaration and a function that performs weighted union. (The
function is named `unite` because `union` is a reserved word in C.) To gain
some generality in the program, we store pointers to parents rather than
integers.

Weighted Union

Part of the reason for the poor worst-case performance of Algorithm
13.1 is that it lets us build a long, skinny union-find tree. We can
avoid this with a more careful algorithm to perform *union()*. Instead
of always making the second element's root the root of the merged
result, we can insist that the tree with fewer elements always become a
child of the root of the tree with more elements, as shown in Program
13.1a. When we use this *weighting rule*, no union-find tree of n nodes
can have height greater than $\lceil \log_2 n \rceil$. To see this, consider any element. Its depth in the tree can increase only when the root of its tree
becomes the child of the root of another tree. The weighting rule
ensures that this happens only when the resulting tree contains at least
twice as many elements as it did before the *union()*; this can happen at
most $\lceil \log_2 n \rceil$ times. Since this weighting rule implies that no node
can have depth greater than $\lceil \log_2 n \rceil$, and *find()* does a constant
amount of work at each level of the tree, the cost of each *find()* is
$O(\log n)$. Since each *union()* uses two *find()*s and $O(1)$ other work,
the cost of the entire operation sequence is $O(n \log n)$.

```
element *find(element *x)
{
    element *canon, *p;
    p = x;
    while (p->parent != p)
        p = p->parent;
    canon = p;
    p = x;
    while (p->parent != canon) {
        p = p->parent;
        x->parent = canon;
        x = p;
    }
    return canon;
}
```

PROGRAM 13.1b

Find operation with path compression.

Path Compression

Path compression is another approach to modifying union-find trees. Taking a cue from self-organizing lists, we arrange for *find( )* to modify the tree structure: in this case, *find(x)* makes all nodes on the path from *x* up to the child of the root point to the root, as shown in Program 13.1b. Thus, once we have found an element, it and all of its ancestors on the path from it to the root are able to reach the root directly in a single operation; subsequent *find( )*s on any element of the set can be performed faster. The worst-case time complexity of this strategy, like that of weighted union, is $O(n \log n)$.

Applying Both Improvements

Since weighted union and path compression are independent ideas, both can be used together. Obviously the resulting algorithm has time complexity $O(n \log n)$, the same as it would if we used either idea alone. In fact, its complexity is much smaller than this, but we need to define some functions to express it.

We begin with an iterated power function. Let $\eta(1) = 2$, and $\eta(i) = 2^{\eta(i-1)}$ for $i > 1$. The function $\eta(k)$ is often called a stack of k twos. It grows very quickly: $\eta(2) = 2^2 = 4$, $\eta(3) = 2^{2^2} = 16$, $\eta(4) = 2^{2^{2^2}} = 65536$, and $\eta(5) = 2^{2^{2^{2^2}}} = 2^{65536}$.

Next we define an iterated logarithm function. Let $\log_2^{(1)} n = \log_2 n$, and $\log_2^{(i)} n = \log_2 \log_2^{(i-1)} n$ for $i > 1$. As i increases, the iterates of the binary logarithm grow more and more slowly. The first iterate is just $\log_2 n$, whose growth is illustrated in Figure 2.3. The second iterate, $\log_2^{(2)} n = \log_2 \log_2 n$, is less than 7 for all $n < 2^{2^7} \approx 3.4 \times 10^{39}$.

Finally, we define a function that tells how many times we must iterate the binary logarithm before the result is no more than one: $\log_2^* x = \min\{ i \mid \log_2^{(i)} x \le 1 \}$. This function grows much more slowly than any iterate of the binary logarithm. By definition, we have $\log_2^* \eta(i) = i$, so $\log_2^* n$ is no more than 5 as long as $n < 2^{65536}$.

It is possible to prove that when the disjoint set algorithm uses both weighted merging and path compression, it requires $O(n \log^* n)$ time in the worst case. Even this time bound, however, is not the best one possible.

Let us define the function $A(i,j)$ for $i,j > 0$ as follows:

$$A(1,j) = 2^j, \ j \ge 1;$$

$$A(i,1) = A(i-1,2), \ i \ge 2;$$

$$A(i,j) = A(i-1, A(i,j-1)), \ i,j \ge 2.$$

Table 13.1 shows how quickly $A(i,j)$ grows as we increase i and j. Since $A(1,j) = 2^j$, the first row of Table 13.1 contains a function that grows exponentially. The second row is an iterated power function: $A(2,j) = \eta(j+1)$. The third row begins with $A(3,1) = 16$, and then each entry is a stack of twos whose height is determined by the entry to its left. Since $A(3,2) = A(2,16)$, we know that both are $\eta(17)$; it follows that $A(3,3) = A(2,\eta(17))$ is a stack of $\eta(17)+1$ twos; it is hard even to write down $A(3,4)$. The fourth row contains such stupendously large numbers that we can write only its first entry: $A(4,1) = A(3,2)$.

$i \backslash j$	1	2	3	4	$\cdots$	j
1	2	4	8	16		2^j
2	4	16	65536	$\eta(5)$		$\eta(j+1)$
3	16	$\eta(17)$	$\eta(\eta(17)+1)$			
4	$\eta(17)$					

TABLE 13.1

The growth of $A(i,j)$, showing only entries than can be expressed conveniently.

Now we define the following functional inverse to $A(i,j)$: $\alpha(n) = \min\{ i \geq 1 \mid A(i,1) > \log_2 n\}$. This inverse function tells where the binary logarithm of its argument falls in the rapidly growing first column of Table 13.1. Since $A(i,1)$ grows so quickly, its inverse grows very very very slowly: for all $n < \eta(17)$, $\alpha(n) \leq 4$.

The worst-case complexity of weighted merging with path compression is $O(n\alpha(n))$ time. Thus, if we use both weighted merging and path compression on our union-find trees, the performance of the algorithm is linear for practical purposes. In the common online situation in which we must compute the answer to each $find(\ )$ as soon as it is performed, there are sequences of $union(\ )$s and $find(\ )$s that require $\Omega(n\alpha(n))$ time to compute; thus, this remarkable function is also a lower bound to the time required when union-find trees are used in most applications.

13.3
TOPOLOGICAL SORTING

A *partial order* on a set of elements is a relation $<$ with the following properties:

- *irreflexivity:* there is no element x such that $x < x$;
- *antisymmetry*: if a and b are two elements such that $a < b$, then it is *not* true that $b < a$;
- *transitivity*: if a, b, and c are three elements such that $a < b$ and $b < c$, then $a < c$.

Under a partial order, one of three possible relations holds between any two different elements a and b: $a < b$, $b < a$, or neither $a < b$ nor $b < a$ is true; in the third case, we say that a and b are *incomparable*. This contrasts with *total orders*, in which every pair of elements must be comparable; the familiar $<$ relation on integers is an example of a total order.

Mathematicians have studied partially ordered sets extensively to characterize their combinatorial properties. One natural application of partial orders is to plan the execution of a job that consists of a number of tasks. In this application, we read $a < b$ as "a must be completed before b is started."

As an example, consider Figure 13.5, which illustrates the connections among the steps in a simple recipe using a *directed acyclic graph* or *dag*. (The word "directed" refers to the directions implied by the arrows.) Each arrow in the dag represents a $<$ relation between two tasks: the task at the head of the arrow cannot be performed before the

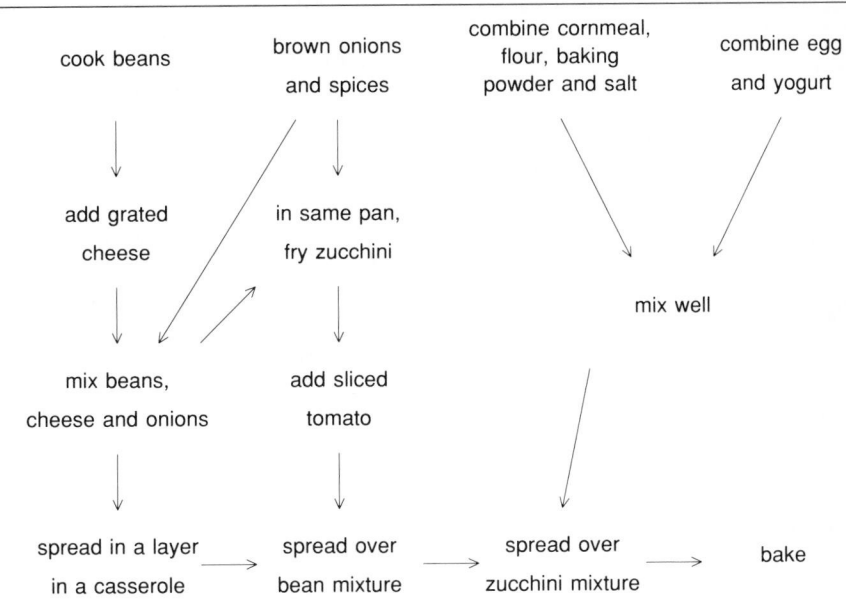

FIGURE 13.5

A partial ordering of the steps in the preparation of Frijoles con Queso, Etc. Casserole. (Source: M. Katzen, *The Enchanted Broccoli Forest*, Berkeley, Ca.: Ten Speed Press, 1982, 217.)

task at the tail of the arrow is completed. For example, the arrows along the bottom indicate that we must spread the three layers of the casserole in order before baking it. On the other hand, the four tasks along the top can be performed in any order.

Any partial order can be *extended* by adding more relations to it, so long as the added relations are consistent with the requirement that the entire set of relations continues to be irreflexive, antisymmetric, and transitive. We shall be interested especially in extending a partial order all the way to a total order, which is also known as *embedding* the partial order in a total order, or *topologically sorting* the partial order.

To see why you might want to sort a partial order topologically, imagine that you are alone in the kitchen and you have to prepare the recipe in Figure 13.5. Because you can do only one job at a time, you must find a total order for the tasks that is consistent with the partial order shown in Figure 13.5. Algorithm 13.2 is one way to perform this topological sorting. It repeatedly removes from the partial order those

/* Input: a set of ordered pairs that represent a partial order. */
/* Output: a total order in which the partial order is embedded. */
/* Data Structures: a dictionary of items (see caption) and a queue of items. */
Initialize Data Structures:
      For each ordered pair (a,b) in the input,
          add one to b's count of predecessors
          add b to a's list of successors
      Enqueue each item that has no predecessors
Construct Topological Order:
      While the queue is not empty
          for each successor of the item at the head of the queue,
             subtract one from its predecessor count
             if its predecessor count is zero,
                enqueue it
          dequeue and output the item at the head of the queue

---

ALGORITHM 13.2

This algorithm for topological sort assumes that we have a dictionary of the items being sorted, and that we can store with each item the number of its predecessors and a pointer to a linked list of its successors in the partial order.

---

items that have no predecessors, until no items remain in the partial order. Figure 13.6 shows the result of running Algorithm 13.2 on the partial order of Figure 13.5.

---

cook beans
brown onions and spices
combine cornmeal, flour, baking powder and salt
combine egg and yogurt
add grated cheese (to beans)
mix (cornmeal and egg mixtures) well
mix beans, cheese and onions
in same pan (as used for onions), fry zucchini
add sliced tomato
spread (bean mixture) in a layer in casserole
spread (zucchini mixture) over bean mixture
spread (cornmeal crust) over zucchini mixture
bake

FIGURE 13.6

Topologically sorted steps in recipe of Figure 13.5.

To prove that the output of Algorithm 13.2 is topologically sorted, let us say that an item is *living* until it is placed on the queue, at which point it becomes *dead*. An item is not placed on the queue until it has no more living predecessors, so all of the item's predecessors in the partial order are dead: they are either ahead of it on the queue or they have been output already. By definition of queue, the item cannot be output until all of its predecessors have appeared in the output, so the output is topologically sorted.

Suppose that there are n elements and m ordered pairs in a topological order, and that each dictionary operation requires $O(1)$ time. To initialize the data structures we examine each ordered pair once ($O(m)$ time) and each item once ($O(n)$ time). To construct the topological order, we examine each ordered pair once ($O(m)$ time) and output each item once ($O(n)$ time). Thus the time complexity of Algorithm 13.2 is $O(m+n)$.

13.4
SUMMARY AND PERSPECTIVE

We have seen data structures and algorithms that solve several problems on acyclic graphs. By referring to the methods in Parts I and II, we can state algorithms on graphs much more briefly than we could if we had to spell out every step.

One advantage shared by all kinds of acyclic graphs is implied by their defining property: if we start at a node and follow arrows, we shall eventually stop at a node; there is never any danger of retracing our steps or, worse, chasing forever around a cycle in the graph.

The algorithm to maintain disjoint sets is one of the most remarkable techniques in the field of data structures and algorithms. It is hard even to state its running time, much less to prove that the time bound cannot be improved from either above or below. Fortunately, despite its complicated analysis, Program 13.1 shows that it is simple to implement this algorithm, which performs very well in practice.

EXERCISES

1 Show that a rooted tree on n nodes has $n-1$ edges.

2 How many different binary trees are there with two nodes? How many different rooted trees?

3 Suppose that no node in a rooted tree has more than two children. What does the natural binary tree for this rooted tree look like?

4 Suppose that a rooted tree contains a node p with c children. If this tree is stored in its natural binary tree data structure, how long does it take to reach the youngest child of p starting at p? Show that in any data structure for rooted trees in which the number of pointers in each node is $O(1)$, it requires $\Theta(c)$ time to reach some child of p.

5 Show that preorder on a rooted tree and on its natural binary tree are the same.

6 Show that a postorder traversal on a rooted tree is equivalent to an inorder traversal of its natural binary tree.

7 Interpret the result of a postorder traversal of a natural binary tree in terms of the corresponding rooted tree.

8 Add Electra's children, Medon and Strophius, to the tree in Figure 13.1; to the data structure in Figure 13.3.

9 The family tree in Figure 13.1 shows only half of each parental relationship. Suggest a way to represent both parents of each child. How would your representation show that Pelops fathered Atreus and Thyestes by Hippodamia, and was also the father of Chrysippus and Troezen?

10 Zeus was Tantalus's father. Add him to the tree of Figure 13.1. Helen, the mother of Hermione, was Zeus's daughter. How would you add Helen to the tree of Figure 13.1?

11 Pelopea had a son, Aegisthus, by her father Thyestes. How would you add Aegisthus to the tree in Figure 13.1?

12 A simpler way to maintain disjoint sets than union-find trees is to store or label each element with the canonical element of its set. In effect, we keep union-find trees of height at most two. What is the worst-case time complexity of this approach? What is its best-case time complexity?

13 Give a sequence of operations that could give rise to the union-find tree in Figure 13.4 if both weighted union and path compression were used. Give a different sequence that gives rise to the same tree if neither weighted union nor path compression is used.

14 Show that weighted union alone uses $\Omega(n \log n)$ time in the worst case to perform $n-1$ $union(\ )$s and n $find(\ )$s.

15 Show that path compression alone uses $\Omega(n \log n)$ time in the worst case to perform $n-1$ $union(\ )$s and n $find(\ )$s. (*Hint*: Consider finding the lowest element in a binomial tree, and remember that $union(\ )$ operations need not be weighted.)

16 Explain how to construct a sequence of $n-1$ $union(\ )$ and n $find(\ )$ operations with which to test Program 13.1. The sequence should not be trivial, and any non-trivial sequence should have the property that all $n-1$ $union(\ )$ operations are properly formed.

17 Show that $\log_2^* n = o(\log_2^{(i)} n)$ for any i.

18 Can we always omit the base of the starred logarithm in asymptotic notation? That is, for the obvious definition of $\log_k^* n$, do we have $\log_k^* n = \Theta(\log_2^* n)$?

19 Show that $\alpha(n) = o(\log^* n)$.

20 Implement Algorithm 13.2. Discuss whether the assumption that dictionary operations can be performed in $O(1)$ time is reasonable.

21 The order of tasks given in Figure 13.6 is an unlikely order in which to prepare the recipe of Figure 13.5: it jumps too much among tasks on the different layers. Devise a topological sort that would produce a more natural order.

The *transitive closure* of a partial order is constructed by listing every binary relation that is implied by the partial order. For example, the dag in Figure 13.5 implies the relation *cook beans* < *bake*, even though that relation is not represented explicitly in the dag.

22 Construct the transitive closure of the partial order in Figure 13.5.

23 Devise an algorithm to construct the transitive closure of any partial order.

24 Describe what Algorithm 13.2 does when its input is not a partial order. That is, what happens when the input contains three elements a, b, and c such that $a < b$, $b < c$, and $c < a$; this violates the antisymmetry condition on partial orders.

REFERENCES

Chapter 2 of the following reference discusses trees extensively, and also mentions topological sorting:

    D. E. Knuth. *Fundamental Algorithms*. Vol. 1, *The Art of Computer Programming*. 2d ed. Reading, Mass.: Addison-Wesley, 1973.

The problem of maintaining disjoint sets received extensive attention in the late 1960's and early 1970's. This paper gives an upper bound of $O(n^{3/2})$ and a lower bound of $\Omega(n \log n)$ on simple union with path compression:

    M. J. Fischer. "Efficiency of equivalence algorithms." In *Complexity of Computer Computations*, ed. R. E. Miller and J. W. Thatcher, 153–167. New York: Plenum Press, 1972.

The following paper settled the complexity of weighted union with path compression:

    R. E. Tarjan. "Efficiency of a good but not linear set union algorithm." *Journal of the Association for Computing Machinery* 22 (1975): 215–225.

A shorter proof of this result appears in Chapter 2 of

    R. E. Tarjan. *Data Structures and Network Algorithms*. Philadelphia: Society for Industrial and Applied Mathematics, 1983.

14

Graphs

Chapter 13 barely hints at the rich variety of relationships that graphs can express. Indeed, graph theory and graph algorithms are subjects of study in their own right. This chapter introduces some ways to represent graphs and the solutions to some elementary graph problems. Even in this introduction, you will notice that we have to define many terms and prove carefully many facts about graphs. If you persevere, however, you will see several nice applications of the data structures and algorithms in Parts I and II.

14.1
TERMINOLOGY

We begin by defining some formal terms to augment our informal understanding of graph. A *graph G* is an ordered pair of sets (V,E); V is a set of *vertices*, and E is a set of *edges*. Each edge in E connects two different vertices in V. Figure 14.1 shows two examples of graphs.

One very basic distinction between graphs depends on the contents of the edge set E. If the edges have a direction, as depicted by arrows in Figure 14.1a, then the graph is *directed*. Each edge in a directed graph is an ordered pair of vertices (v,w), with $v \neq w$; the *tail* of the edge is v, and its *head* is w. We sometimes say that v is a *predecessor* of w, and that w is a *successor* of v; vertices v and w are *incident* to edge (v,w).

If the edges do not have directions, as in Figure 14.1b, then the graph is *undirected*. Each edge in an undirected graph is a set of two

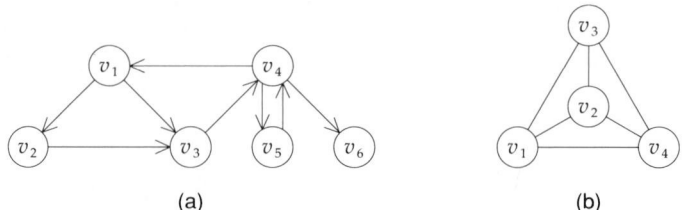

FIGURE 14.1

Examples of graphs: (a) directed; (b) undirected.

different vertices, $\{v,w\}$. Vertices v and w are said to be *adjacent* to, or *neighbors* of, each other; again, both v and w are incident to the edge $\{v,w\}$. The graph in Figure 14.1b is called the *complete graph* on four vertices, because an edge joins every pair of vertices.

These definitions exclude certain graph-like structures from being graphs. Since E is a set, our graphs cannot contain *multiple edges*. The two edges between v_4 and v_5 in Figure 14.1a do not violate this observation, because (v_4,v_5) and (v_5,v_4) are different ordered pairs, and hence different edges. Since each edge in a graph consists of two distinct vertices, our graphs cannot contain *self loops* either. To emphasize these restrictions, our class of graphs is sometimes called *simple*.

In this chapter we shall use n to denote the number of vertices in V and m to denote the number of edges in E. Because our graphs cannot contain multiple edges or self loops, we have

$$0 \le m \le n(n-1) = \Theta(n^2) \tag{14.1}$$

on directed graphs. Although we shall usually state the time complexity of algorithms in terms of both n and m, Equation (14.1) makes it possible to rewrite their time complexity in terms of n alone.

As we work with graphs, it is important to realize that a graph is an ordered pair of sets, and its representation as a drawing is merely a convenience. For example, Figure 14.2 shows another picture of the complete graph on four vertices: both it and Figure 14.1a contain the same number of vertices and the same edge connections; thus they depict the same graph. It is particularly important that the crossing of two edges in the middle of Figure 14.2 is only an incidental feature of this drawing, not a property of the complete graph on four vertices.

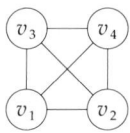

FIGURE 14.2

Another picture of the complete graph on four vertices, which is also shown in Figure 14.1b.

Applications of Graphs

Graphs can be used to model many physical and logical situations. We might abstract from a map to a graph; each vertex could represent a city, and each edge a road between cities. Many factories can be represented as graphs; each stage in a manufacturing process corresponds to a vertex, and the edges show how partially finished products progress through the stages. A graph can be used to represent an electrical circuit, with each vertex an active element and each edge a wire between elements. A computer program can also be represented as a graph; the vertices correspond to elementary pieces of the program, and the edges represent the flow of control among the pieces.

In these and most other applications of graphs, information is associated with the vertices or the edges of the graph, or both. For instance, in geographical applications of graphs, we might store the name of each city at the corresponding vertex, and we might label the edges with the distance or the cost of travelling between the cities at its endpoints. Any data structure for a graph must be able to store such information with the appropriate part of the graph.

14.2

DATA STRUCTURES

There is a variety of special classes of graphs for which particularly convenient representations can be defined. Indeed, the solutions to many problems in data structures can be regarded as finding a useful class of graphs whose representations permit certain operations to be performed efficiently. For general graphs, however, when we know of no special properties that the graph possesses, there are two principal representations.

$$\begin{pmatrix} 0 & 1 & 1 & 0 & 0 & 0 \\ 0 & 0 & 1 & 0 & 0 & 0 \\ 0 & 0 & 0 & 1 & 0 & 0 \\ 1 & 0 & 0 & 0 & 1 & 1 \\ 0 & 0 & 0 & 1 & 0 & 0 \\ 0 & 0 & 0 & 0 & 0 & 0 \end{pmatrix}$$

FIGURE 14.3

Adjacency matrix for the graph in Figure 14.1a.

Adjacency Matrix

The *adjacency matrix* for a graph on n vertices is an $n \times n$ matrix A of bits. We set $A_{ij} = 1$ if there is an edge from v_i to v_j, and $A_{ij} = 0$ if there is no such edge. Figure 14.3 shows the adjacency matrix for the graph in Figure 14.1a. Since we do not allow graphs to contain self loops, the adjacency matrix always has zeros on its main diagonal ($A_{ii} = 0$ for $1 \leq i \leq n$).

If we use the adjacency matrix representation when edges are labelled with information, then we can store the information for the edge from v_i to v_j at A_{ij}, and the information for vertex v_i at A_{ii}. In this case it is important that the graph not contain multiple edges. If a graph is undirected, we have a choice. A common approach is to represent each undirected edge $\{v,w\}$ as the pair (v,w) and (w,v) of directed edges. This leads to an adjacency matrix that is symmetric about its main diagonal ($A_{ij} = A_{ji}$ for $1 \leq i \leq j \leq n$). If space is at a premium, though, we can store just the lower triangle of A_{ij}: $\{A_{ij} \mid i > j\}$.

The adjacency matrix is a simple way to store a graph, but it has a couple of disadvantages. First, it takes $\Theta(n^2)$ space, even when $m = o(n^2)$; this is especially serious in a *sparse* graph, such as when $m = O(n)$. Second, it takes $\Omega(n^2)$ time to solve most graph problems when the graph is stored in an adjacency matrix.

Adjacency List

To store a graph in a linked structure, we store for each vertex a list of its successors. (Again, we usually represent an undirected graph by replacing each undirected edge by two directed edges.) Figure 14.4 shows the adjacency list representation for the graph in Figure 14.1a. Notice that vertices may appear on the adjacency lists in arbitrary order.

v_1: v_2, v_3
v_2: v_3
v_3: v_4
v_4: v_5, v_1, v_6
v_5: v_4
v_6:

FIGURE 14.4

Adjacency list representation for the graph in Figure 14.1a.

We can store information about the vertices with the list heads. We can store edge information in the nodes of the successor lists, since each node in an adjacency list corresponds to an edge. The association between nodes of the adjacency lists and edges of the graph shows that the adjacency list stores a graph in $\Theta(n+m)$ space.

14.3
SHORTEST PATHS

The edges of a graph represent ways we can travel through it. In many applications, each edge has a cost that reflects distance, time, or some other quantity that corresponds to the price we incur when we use that edge. In the graph in Figure 14.5, for example, we can go from v_1 to v_3 either directly, at a cost of 4, through v_2, at a cost of 3, or through both v_2 and v_4, at a cost of 2. In this section we shall discuss two problems that involve finding paths that cost as little as possible. Both problems can be posed on undirected graphs as well as on

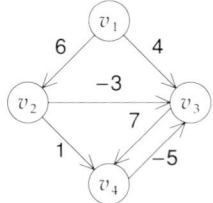

FIGURE 14.5

A directed graph whose edges are annotated with lengths.

directed graphs; to solve them in the undirected case we treat the undirected graph as a directed graph in the usual way.

Definitions

A *path* in a graph is a sequence of vertices $(v_0, v_1, \ldots, v_k)$ such that there is an edge that we can follow between each consecutive pair of vertices; that is, $(v_i, v_{i+1}) \in E$ for $0 \leq i < k$. We shall write $length(v, w)$ to denote the cost associated with edge (v, w), and $length(v_0, \ldots, v_k)$ to denote $\sum_{i=0}^{k-1} length(v_i, v_{i+1})$, the length of a path. A path is *simple* if it contains no repeated vertices; in other words, a simple path does not cross itself.

A *cycle* is a path that starts and ends at the same vertex (that is, $v_0 = v_k$). The length of a cycle is its length as a path. A cycle is *simple* if the only repeated vertex is v_0; we could also say that the cycle $(v_0, v_1, \ldots, v_k)$ is simple iff and only if $(v_0, \ldots, v_{k-1})$ is a simple path.

A *shortest path* from vertex v to vertex w is a path from v to w that is no longer than any other path from v to w. In the *single-source shortest-path* problem, we seek the shortest path from a designated *source* vertex s to every other vertex in the graph. In the *all-pairs shortest-path* problem, we seek the shortest routes between every pair of vertices.

Observations

Sometimes there is no shortest path from vertex v to vertex w. This obviously happens when there is no path at all from v to w; in Figure 14.5, for example, there is no path from v_3 to v_2 or v_1. A more insidious problem occurs when a graph contains a cycle ψ of negative length. If a path from v to w uses any part of ψ, then we can construct a shorter path by following it but going once more around ψ; thus, there are infinitely many paths from v to w, none of which is the shortest.

In our solutions to the single-source and all-pairs shortest-path problems, we shall consider missing edges to have infinite length. Thus, if there is no path from v to w in the graph, the shortest path from v to w has infinite length. Our algorithms will also have to cope with negative cycles.

At this point, it is hardly obvious what the set of shortest paths from a single source should look like, but we can make some elementary observations. Shortest paths should be simple: if a path includes a cycle, it is either negative and there is no shortest path at all, or it has nonnegative length and there is no reason to go all the way around it. Furthermore, if we have a shortest path between two vertices, then any subpath it contains must also be a shortest path between its endpoints. In fact, the set of shortest paths from a source vertex forms a tree, usually known as a *shortest-path tree*, but the only proof we shall offer of this fact is constructive: Algorithm 14.1 builds a shortest-path tree.

Our solutions to the single-source shortest-path problem use an important fact about shortest paths. Let T be a tree rooted at the source vertex s. Define $dist_s(v)$ to be the length of the path in T from s to v. Then we have the following characterization:

(∗) T is a shortest-path tree if and only if every edge (v,w) in G satisfies the inequality

$$dist_s(v) + length(v,w) \geq dist_s(w). \qquad (14.2)$$

The proof of the "only if" part of (∗) is simple: if there were an edge that violated Equation (14.2), then T would certainly not be a shortest-path tree, because the path in T from s to v, followed by the edge (v,w), would be a shorter path from s to w than the path in T.

To prove the "if" part of (∗), we prove by induction that if Equation (14.2) holds for every edge in G, then for any vertex w and for any path $(s, \ldots, w)$ that contains k edges, for any k, $length(s, \ldots, w) \geq dist_s(w)$; this establishes that the path in the tree from s to w is a shortest path. To prove the base case, $k = 1$, we must show that the path in T from s to any vertex w is no longer than the edge (s,w). Since $dist_s(s) = 0$ and Equation (14.2) holds, we have $length(s,w) \geq dist_s(w)$, as required. We take as our induction hypothesis that if a path $(s, \ldots, v)$ contains $k-1$ edges, then $length(s, \ldots, v) \geq dist_s(v)$. We shall prove that if a path $(s, \ldots, w)$ contains k edges, then $length(s, \ldots, w) \geq dist_s(w)$. Suppose that v immediately precedes w on the path $(s, \ldots, w)$. By definition we have

$$length(s, \ldots, w) = length(s, \ldots, v) + length(v,w);$$

by the induction hypothesis we have

$$length(s, \ldots, v) \geq dist_s(v);$$

and by Equation (14.2) we have

$$length(v,w) \geq dist_s(w) - dist_s(v).$$

We can combine these to complete the proof:

$$length(s, \ldots, w) \geq dist_s(w).$$

/* The algorithm uses a queue of vertices, which starts out empty.

    Each vertex has the following members:
        $dist_s$ — the length of the path in the tree from s to it (initially ∞);
        parent — its parent in the tree (initially NULL);
        inqueue — true if and only if it is on the queue.
    The queue operations enqueue and dequeue should set member inqueue.

    The result of queue operation head( ) is a vertex.
*/

$s.dist_s = 0$
enqueue(s)
while the queue is not empty
        for each successor w of head( )
            if $head( ).dist_s + length(head( ), w) < w.dist_s$
                $w.dist_s = head( ).dist_s + length(head( ), w)$
                w.parent = head( )
                if !w.inqueue
                    enqueue(w)
        dequeue

ALGORITHM 14.1

Breadth-first search to construct a shortest-path tree rooted at s.

A Breadth-First Algorithm

Algorithm 14.1 uses (*) directly to produce a shortest-path tree. We characterize its progress as *breadth-first* because after it explores the source vertex s, it explores the vertices one edge away from s, then those that are two edges away from s, and so on. Figure 14.6 shows the progress of Algorithm 14.1 on the graph in Figure 14.5 when v_1 is the source vertex. Notice that vertex v_3 is enqueued twice.

To analyze Algorithm 14.1, we divide the work it does into *passes*: pass 0 consists of the work done during the first execution of the *for*-loop, when s was at the head of the queue for the first time; pass k consists of the work done when the vertices enqueued during pass $k-1$ are next processed by the algorithm. An induction proof similar to the one above establishes that if there is a shortest path from s to w with k or fewer edges, then at the end of pass k, $dist_s(w)$ will be the length of this shortest path. Since no shortest path can contain more than $n-1$ edges, this implies that if a shortest-path tree exists, Algorithm 14.1 will find it. On the other hand, if the input contains a negative cycle, then Algorithm 14.1 will never stop.

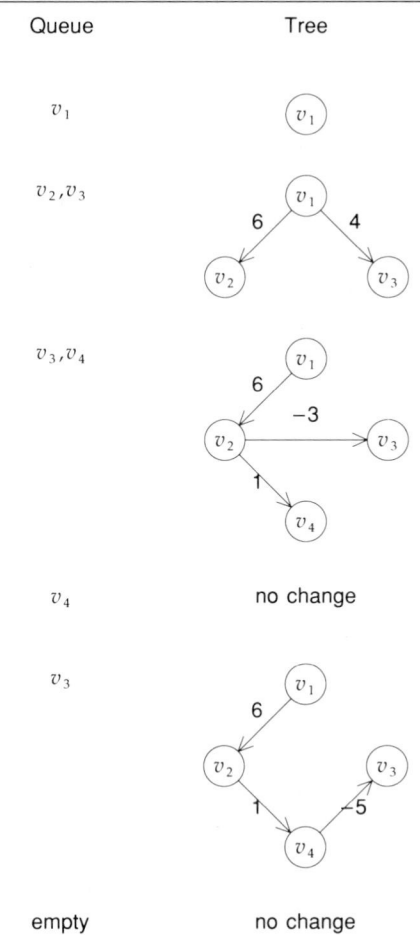

| Queue | Tree |

FIGURE 14.6

The progress of Algorithm 14.1 on the graph in Figure 14.5. Each line shows the contents of the queue when we begin processing the vertex at its head, and the status of the tree at that time. For example, the third tree results from processing v_2.

If a shortest-path tree exists, Algorithm 14.1 will find it in at most n passes. During a single pass, we look at each edge at most once, so we can perform a pass in $O(m)$ time. Therefore Algorithm 14.1 runs in $O(mn)$ time overall. We can also modify Algorithm 14.1 to count passes and to halt when it starts pass $n+1$, so that it will not run forever if no shortest-path tree exists.

A Greedy Algorithm

The idea of negative cycles may seem strange. Indeed, in many situations, no edge will have negative length. This makes it easier to compute a shortest-path tree, since we never need to worry that a negative edge will permit a path with more edges to cost much less than a path with fewer edges. We can grow the tree from the source, one edge at a time. Each time we choose an edge that leads to a closest vertex not yet in the tree, which ensures that the growing tree is a shortest-path tree on its vertices. This is called a *greedy* strategy because at each step we do what looks like it will get us closest to our goal. Algorithm 14.2 presents the idea formally, and Figure 14.7 shows its progress on a small directed graph.

Algorithm 14.2 can be implemented when the graph is stored in an adjacency matrix. In this case, each iteration of the outer *for*-loop uses $\Theta(n)$ time, and the entire algorithm runs in $O(n^2)$ time. Even if the graph is stored in a set of adjacency lists, the easiest way to implement Algorithm 14.2 is to examine every vertex during each iteration of the outer *for*-loop, which leads to a running time of $O(n^2)$. The exercises

---

```
/* Each vertex has the following members:
    parent — its parent, if it is in the shortest–path tree (initially NULL);
    dist — its distance from s, if it is in the tree (initially ∞);
    closest — the closest tree vertex if it is not in the tree.
*/

boolean intree(v)
    return v.dist < ∞

s.dist = 0        /* to make intree(s) == TRUE */
for w≠s
    w.closest = s
for (i = 1; i < n; i++)
    find v such that !intree(v) and v.closest.dist + length(v.closest,v) is a minimum
    v.parent = v.closest    /* Add v to the tree. */
    v.dist = v.parent.dist + length(v.parent,v)
    for all w such that !intree(w)
        if w.closest.dist + length(w.closest,w) > v.dist + length(v,w)
            w.closest = v
```

ALGORITHM 14.2

Greedy algorithm to compute a shortest-path tree from s when there are no negative edge weights.

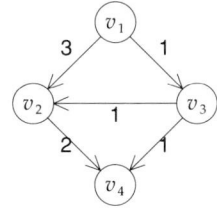

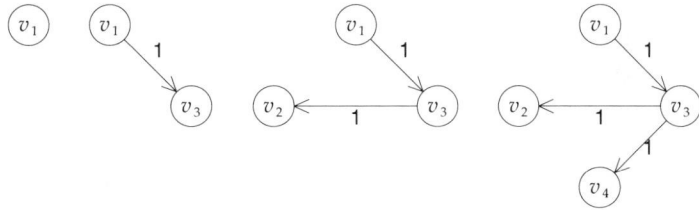

FIGURE 14.7

The greedy construction of a shortest-path tree from source v_1 on a graph that contains no negative edge weights.

suggest how one might use a priority queue to improve the running time to $O(m \log n)$.

The All-Pairs Shortest-Path Problem

Given the above solutions to the single-source shortest-path problem, we have several ways to compute the shortest paths between all pairs of vertices in a graph. We could run one of the above algorithms n times, using each vertex as source. To run the breadth-first algorithm n times requires $O(mn^2)$ time. To run the simple greedy algorithm n times requires $O(n^3)$ time; n runs of the more sophisticated greedy algorithm would require $O(mn \log n)$ time. Now we shall see a more direct solution to the all-pairs shortest-path problem; it is especially suitable when the graph is stored in an adjacency matrix.

Assume that A_{ij} is the cost of travelling from v_i to v_j. We shall modify the matrix so that at the end of the algorithm, A_{ij} is the cost of the shortest path from v_i to v_j. The exercises suggest the additional bookkeeping needed to recover the shortest paths themselves from the computation.

```
for (i = 1; i ≤ n; i++)
    A_ii = 0
for (k = 1; k ≤ n; k++)
    for (i = 1; i ≤ n; i++)
        for (j = 1; j ≤ n; j++)
            A_ij = min(A_ij, A_ik + A_kj)
```

ALGORITHM 14.3

Matrix algorithm to compute shortest distances between any two vertices in a graph.

Algorithm 14.3 considers all paths from v_i to v_j in an order defined by the vertex numbering. First it considers paths that pass only through v_1 on the way from v_i to v_j. Next it considers paths that pass only through v_1 or v_2 on the way from v_i to v_j. At the kth step, it considers paths that pass only through $v_1, \ldots, v_k$ as they go from v_i to v_j. Figure 14.8 shows the progress of this algorithm on the directed graph in Figure 14.7.

Since it consists of three nested for-loops that each iterate from 1 to n, Algorithm 14.3 runs in $O(n^3)$ time. It is so simple that a program that implements it may run in less time than a program that uses an asymptotically faster algorithm. It is especially useful when the edge lengths are either 1 or ∞; in this case, its output is the transitive closure of the input graph.

14.4
MINIMUM SPANNING TREES

In Section 14.3, each graph edge was labelled with the cost of travelling on it. A different, but equally natural, use of edge labels tells how much it costs to *construct* each edge. For example, we might have places that should be connected by a network, know the costs of connecting various pairs of places, and want to know the cheapest way to hook places together so that every pair of places can be joined by a path. This is the motivation for finding the *minimum spanning tree* in an undirected graph.

At start,

$$A = \begin{pmatrix} 0 & 3 & 1 & \infty \\ \infty & 0 & \infty & 2 \\ \infty & 1 & 0 & 1 \\ \infty & \infty & \infty & 0 \end{pmatrix}.$$

Nothing changes when $k = 1$.
After the iteration for $k = 2$, we have

$$A = \begin{pmatrix} 0 & 3 & 1 & 5 \\ \infty & 0 & \infty & 2 \\ \infty & 1 & 0 & 1 \\ \infty & \infty & \infty & 0 \end{pmatrix}.$$

After $k = 3$,

$$A = \begin{pmatrix} 0 & 2 & 1 & 2 \\ \infty & 0 & \infty & 2 \\ \infty & 1 & 0 & 1 \\ \infty & \infty & \infty & 0 \end{pmatrix}.$$

This is the final form of the shortest–distance matrix.

FIGURE 14.8

Progress of Algorithm 14.3 on the graph in Figure 14.7.

Definitions

A *subgraph* $G' = (V',E')$ of a graph $G = (V,E)$ is a graph such that $V' \subset V$ and $E' \subset E$; it is a *spanning* subgraph if $V' = V$. A *spanning tree* on a graph G with n vertices is a spanning subgraph T with $n-1$ edges and n vertices. In contrast to the trees of Section 13.1, a spanning tree has no root; it is sometimes called a *free tree*. In the minimum spanning tree problem, we seek a spanning tree whose cost is as small as possible.

Let $V = A \cup B$ with $A \cap B = \emptyset$; A and B form a *partition* of V. A *cut* is a set C of edges such that $\{v,w\} \in C$ if and only if $v \in A$ and $w \in B$; the edges in the cut connect across the partition defined by A and B.

Observations

Minimum spanning trees differ from shortest-path trees in several respects. They are defined only on undirected graphs. They are also free trees, while shortest-path trees are rooted. Finally, even if an undirected graph has a negative cycle, and hence no shortest-path tree, the graph still has a minimum spanning tree. Indeed, any undirected graph has a minimum spanning tree.

Both of the algorithms we shall consider to construct minimum spanning trees rely on the following property:

(∗) Let C be a cut of the vertex set of graph G. If c is an edge of minimum cost in C, then c is an edge in some minimum spanning tree of G.

To prove (∗), let $T = (V,F)$ be a minimum spanning tree of G. If $c \in F$, then there is nothing to prove. If $c \notin F$, then consider the graph $T' = (V,F \cup \{c\})$; T' contains a cycle, at least two of whose edges belong to C. Since c is an edge of minimum cost in C, we can remove one of the other edges in the cut C from T', leaving a spanning tree whose cost is no larger than the cost of T. Therefore it is a minimum spanning tree that contains c, and (∗) is established.

A Greedy Algorithm

One way to find a minimum spanning tree is to use a greedy strategy very similar to the one we used to find a shortest-path tree. We begin with some vertex v and grow a minimum spanning tree one edge at a

---

```
/* Each vertex has the following members:
      intree — TRUE if and only if it is in the minimum spanning tree (initially FALSE);
      closest — the closest tree vertex if it is not in the tree.
*/

v.intree = TRUE        /* v is arbitrary */
for w ≠ v
    w.closest = v
for (i = 1; i < n; i++)
    find v such that !v.intree and length(v,v.closest) is a minimum
    make { v,v.closest } an edge of the minimum spanning tree
    v.intree = TRUE
    for all w such that !w.intree
        if length(w.closest,w) > length(v,w)
            w.closest = v
```

ALGORITHM 14.4

Greedy algorithm to construct a minimum spanning tree.

time, selecting at each step the cheapest edge that connects the tree to a vertex not yet in the tree. At any step in this algorithm, we can apply observation (∗) to the cut defined by the vertices already in the tree and those not yet in the tree to show that the growing tree is a minimum spanning tree. Algorithm 14.4 presents the details. Figure 14.9 shows the progress of Algorithm 14.4 on a small undirected graph.

Algorithm 14.4 is very similar to Algorithm 14.2; the analysis of Algorithm 14.2 applies almost exactly to show that Algorithm 14.4 runs in $O(n^2)$ time. We can also use a priority queue to improve this running time to $O(m \log n)$.

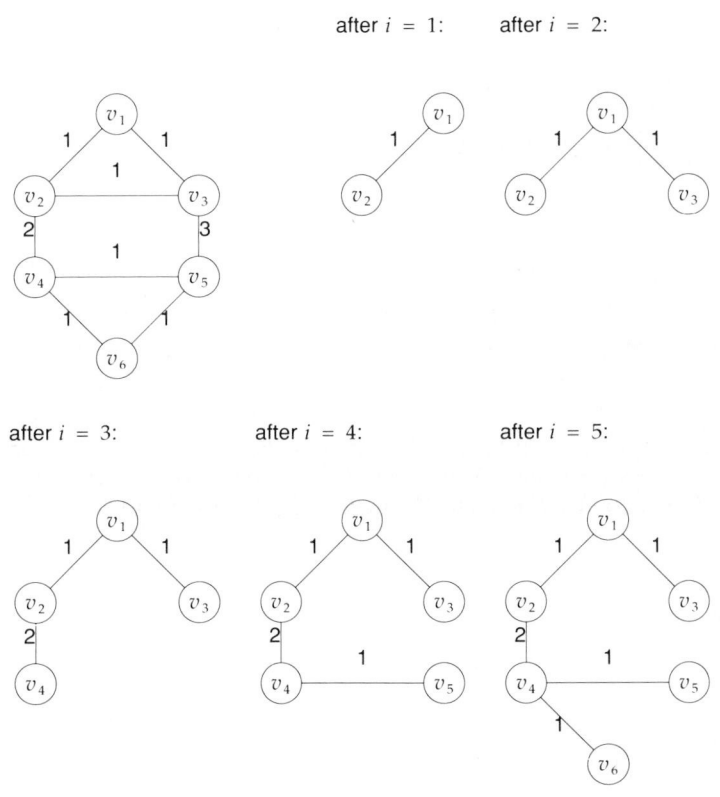

FIGURE 14.9

A small undirected graph, and the steps Algorithm 14.4 takes to construct a minimum spanning tree for it.

/* This algorithm uses a priority queue of edges, with cost as key,
   and union–find trees to maintain the forest of minimum spanning trees.
*/

Initialization:
     Place all edges into a priority queue by cost.
     Make each vertex the canonical element of its own set.
Construction:
     while there is more than one tree in the forest
         $e = findmin(\ )$ */* Say $e = \{v,w\}$. */*
         if $find(v) \neq find(w)$
              make e an edge of the minimum spanning tree
              union(v,w)
         deletemin$(\ )$

ALGORITHM 14.5

This algorithm grows the trees of a minimum spanning forest together.

Growing a Forest

Another way to construct a minimum spanning tree is to regard the vertex set V as a set of n trees in a forest to which we wish to add edges that connect them into a single tree. Algorithm 14.5 uses union-find trees to record when trees grow together and a priority queue so we can consider the tree edges in order from cheapest to most expensive. Because Algorithm 14.5 considers the edges in increasing order by cost, at any step we can apply observation ($*$) to the cut between the tree that contains v and the rest of the graph. Figure 14.10 shows the progress of this method on the graph in Figure 14.9.

If we store the priority queue of edges as a heap, then we can use bottom-up heap construction to build the heap in $O(m)$ time. It takes $O(n)$ time to make each vertex a singleton set. Therefore we can complete the initialization step in $O(n+m)$ time. The construction step uses $O(m)$ $find(\ )$ operations and $O(n)$ $union(\ )$ operations, which can be performed in $O(m\alpha(n))$ time if we use a forest of union-find trees, and $O(m)$ heap operations, which require $O(m \log n)$ time. Therefore Algorithm 14.5 uses a total of $O(m \log n)$ time. If $m = O(n)$, then this algorithm uses $O(n \log n)$ time, while the greedy method uses $O(n^2)$ time. On the other hand, when $m = \Omega(n^2)$, then this method uses $O(n^2 \log n)$ time. Thus, the choice between methods depends on how sparse the input graph is.

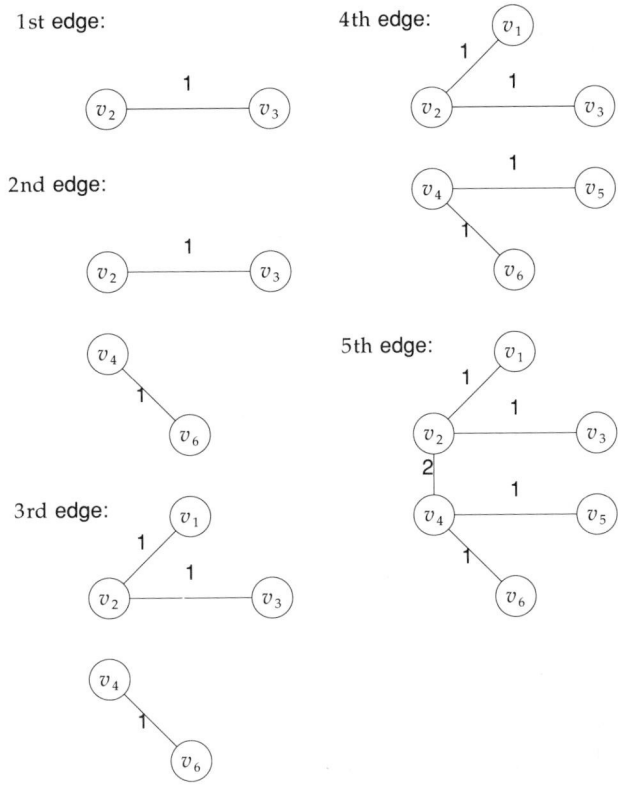

FIGURE 14.10

How Algorithm 14.5 grows trees together into a minimum spanning tree, assuming that the sorted order of edges is $\{v_2,v_3\}$, $\{v_4,v_6\}$, $\{v_1,v_2\}$, $\{v_1,v_3\}$, $\{v_4,v_5\}$, $\{v_5,v_6\}$, $\{v_2,v_4\}$, $\{v_3,v_5\}$. The graph is the same as in Figure 14.9. Note that the result is a different minimum spanning tree.

14.5

TRAVERSAL ORDERS AND GRAPH CONNECTIVITY

To cope with the possible existence of cycles in the input, a graph traversal algorithm must be able to mark vertices that have been visited. Algorithm 14.6 shows an important traversal algorithm known as *depth-first search*. The recursive function *traverse( )* implements the key idea of depth-first search: when you enter *traverse( )*, if you see an unvisited neighbor, go there and continue the traversal. By obeying

/* This function begins a graph traversal at vertex v. */
traverse(v)
    mark v as visited
    for each unvisited successor w of v,
        traverse(w)

Traversal Algorithm:
    Mark all vertices as unvisited.
    for (i = 1; i ≤ n; i++)
        if v_i has not been visited,
            traverse(v_i)

ALGORITHM 14.6

Algorithm to perform depth-first traversal of a graph. The representation of the graph is not specified, though the use of the term "successor" in *traverse(v)* suggests an undirected graph is represented by replacing each of its edges by two directed edges.

this rule we follow paths deep into the graph for as long as we can, hence the apposite description "depth-first."

If *traverse( )* is the workhorse of depth-first search, the top-level algorithm is what makes it a true traversal by ensuring that it reaches every vertex in the graph. On many graphs the top level algorithm will make very few calls to *traverse( )*: most of the vertices will be marked during recursive calls on *traverse( )*. For example, on the graph in Figure 14.1a, the top level will call *traverse(v_1)*, and then all other vertices will be visited during recursive calls to *traverse( )*; finally, the top level will test the other five vertices to be sure that they have already been visited.

Time Complexity of Depth-First Search

If a graph is stored as a set of adjacency lists, then depth-first search can reach all s of the successors of a vertex in $\Theta(s)$ time. Thus, the *for*-loop in *traverse( )* uses $O(m)$ time overall. Each vertex in the graph is marked unvisited once, marked visited once, and checked once in the top level. So long as each mark manipulation uses $O(1)$ time, all of the work on the vertices can be done in $O(n)$ time. It follows that depth-first search does $O(n+m)$ work overall; we say that its time complexity is linear in the size of the graph.

Ways to Mark Vertices

Algorithm 14.6 does not specify how vertices should be marked as visited. We can use this flexibility to our advantage as we tailor depth-first search to solve different problems. For example, to test whether a graph contains a cycle, we need only store at each vertex a boolean value that tells whether it has been visited: the graph contains a cycle if and only if during some call to *traverse*( ) we find that a neighboring vertex has been visited already.

Another natural way to mark vertices is to assign numbers to them. A vertex that has not been visited is numbered zero; when we visit a vertex for the first time we assign it a positive number. Such numberings are often used to express *equivalence relations* among the vertices or edges of a graph. An equivalence relation is a binary relation $\equiv$ on a set that has the following three properties:

- *reflexivity*: for all x, $x \equiv x$;
- *symmetry*: for all x and y, if $x \equiv y$, then $y \equiv x$;
- *transitivity*: for all x, y, and z, if $x \equiv y$ and $y \equiv z$, then $x \equiv z$.

An equivalence relation $\equiv$ on a set *induces a partition* of the set into subsets of elements that are equivalent under $\equiv$. The subsets in this partition are called *equivalence classes* or *components* of the set.

Connectivity of Undirected Graphs

Connectivity probably defines the most natural equivalence relation on the vertices of an undirected graph. Under the connectivity equivalence relation, two vertices are equivalent if and only if they can be joined by a path in the graph. This relation induces a partition of the graph into *connected components*.

We can use depth-first search to number the vertices of an undirected graph so that vertices have the same number if and only if they belong to the same connected component. We use a global counter that contains the number to be assigned to all vertices visited during recursive calls from a single call to *traverse*( ) at the top level. This counter starts at one, and increases by one after each top-level call to *traverse*( ).

This algorithm is especially useful whenever we want the input to consist of a single connected component. If an electrical circuit has more than one component, then only the component that is connected to power will do anything; the other components might as well not be present at all. A disconnected graph of highway connections means literally that for some places, "you can't get there from here (by car)."

Biconnectivity in Undirected Graphs

A graph can be connected but still vulnerable to becoming disconnected if a small part of it is removed. If two towns are connected by a single bridge, then they will be disconnected when that bridge closes. If several cities have flights to and from only a central "hub" airport, then they will be isolated when that airport closes.

An *articulation point* is a vertex such that if we remove the vertex and the edges incident to it, the resulting graph is disconnected. In the examples above, either endpoint of the bridge is an articulation point, and the hub airport is also an articulation point. If a connected graph has no articulation points, we say that it is *biconnected*. Since we can remove any vertex from a biconnected graph and still have a connected graph, the biconnected graph is less vulnerable to the failure of a single vertex than a mere connected graph: even after one vertex is removed, there will still be a path between any two vertices.

In a biconnected graph on more than two vertices, each pair of vertices can be joined by at least two paths that share only the two terminal vertices. Taken together, these two paths form a simple cycle. This suggests that we define the following equivalence relation of biconnectivity: two edges are equivalent if and only if they belong to a common simple cycle. The biconnected components of a graph are sets of edges.

We can use depth-first search to identify the articulation points in a connected graph. It is convenient to explain the algorithm in terms of a diagram that depicts the progress of depth-first traversal. Figure

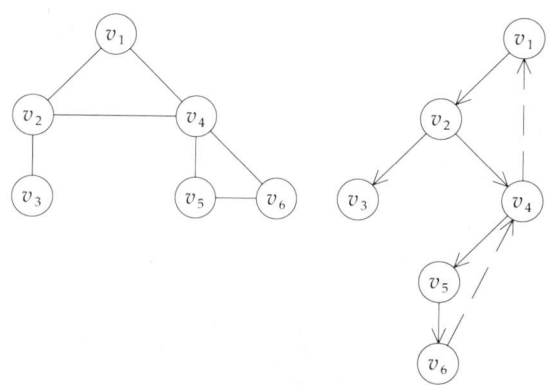

FIGURE 14.11

A small undirected graph and a depth-first diagram. Back edges are dashed.

14.11 illustrates a graph and a depth-first diagram. Each of the solid edges represents a recursive call to *traverse( )*; these solid edges form a tree since depth-first search never visits the same vertex twice. Each of the dashed edges corresponds to an edge that is not followed during depth-first search because it would take us to a vertex that has already been visited; these *back edges* always point from a vertex to an ancestor of that vertex. If we use the technique of representing an undirected graph as a directed graph by replacing undirected edges by pairs of directed edges, each tree and back edge will give rise to a trivial edge that points in the opposite direction; these edges are not part of the depth-first diagram, and in Algorithm 14.7 we assume that some provision is made to ignore them during processing.

In the algorithm to identify articulation points, we assign two numbers to each vertex. One, the *depth-first number*, is the number the vertex receives during a preorder traversal of the depth-first tree. It is simple to assign depth-first numbers by maintaining a global counter that starts at zero and increases by one whenever *traverse( )* is called. The other number, the *low number*, assigned to each vertex is the smallest depth-first number of all vertices that can be reached from the vertex by following zero or more tree edges and at most one back edge; the low number of a vertex tells how far any simple cycle that contains the vertex goes up the tree. Algorithm 14.7 computes the low number of each vertex during a postorder traversal of the depth-first tree. In Figure 14.11, the vertices are numbered in depth-first order; Figure 14.12 shows the depth-first diagram augmented by low numbers.

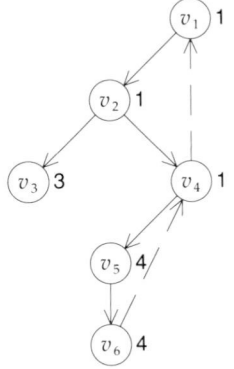

FIGURE 14.12

The depth-first diagram of Figure 14.11, showing low numbers of the vertices.

```
/* Each vertex contains these members:
     dfnum — the depth–first number; initially zero
     low — the low number.
*/

traverse(v)
     v.dfnum = v.low = ++globaldf
     for each successor w of v
          if w.dfnum == 0
               traverse(w)
          if w.low < v.low
               v.low = w.low
          if w.low ≥ v.dfnum
               v is an articulation point

Traversal Algorithm:
     globaldf = 0
     for (i = 1; i ≤ n; i++)
          vᵢ.dfnum = 0
     traverse(v₁)
```

ALGORITHM 14.7

Algorithm to report articulation points in a connected, undirected graph. Since the graph is connected we need only one call to *traverse( )* at the top level. When implementing this algorithm, recall that we must ignore the edge (w,v) when we process the edge (v,w).

Given the depth-first and low numbers of the vertices of an undirected graph, we can identify the articulation points. The root of the depth-first tree is a special case; it is an articulation point if and only if it has more than one child. If vertex v is not the root, then v is an articulation point if and only if a child w of v has a low number at least as large as v's depth-first number; if such a w exists, its low number tells us that no back edge from its subtree goes higher in the tree than v, so if we remove v then we would disconnect w and its descendants in the depth-first tree from the rest of the graph. In Figure 14.12, v_2 and v_4 are both articulation points.

Strong Connectivity in Directed Graphs

A directed graph is *strongly connected* if it contains a path between any two vertices. Strong connectivity in a directed graph is analogous to biconnectivity on an undirected graph. We define the following

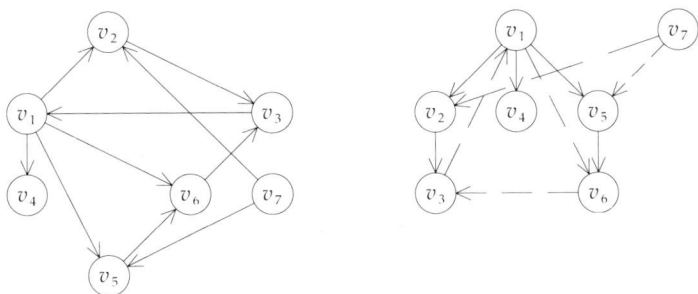

FIGURE 14.13

A small directed graph and its depth-first diagram. Note that the diagram contains two trees. Edge (v_1,v_6) is a forward edge; (v_6,v_3), (v_7,v_2), and (v_7,v_5) are cross edges.

equivalence relation of strong connectivity: vertices v and w are equivalent if and only if there is a path from v to w and a path from w to v. Any two vertices in a strongly connected graph lie on a common cycle (which need not be simple). The strongly connected components, or *strong components* of a directed graph are sets of vertices.

Our algorithm to find strong components also uses depth-first search. When we depict the results of a depth-first search on a directed graph, however, we can see that there are more kinds of non-tree edges than there were in the undirected case. Figure 14.13 shows a directed graph and its depth-first diagram. It contains tree edges and back edges, and also *forward edges*, which connect ancestors with descendants, and *cross edges*, which connect vertices that do not lie on the same path from the root. Note too that the depth-first diagram contains a forest of several trees.

To compute strong components using depth-first search, we assign two numbers to each vertex. One is the depth-first number we have seen before. The other number assigned to a vertex, the low number, is a variation on the low numbers assigned during Algorithm 14.7; the low number of a vertex is the smallest depth-first number of all vertices that can be reached from the vertex by following zero or more tree edges and at most one back or cross edge to a vertex whose strong component has not already been completed; the low number of a vertex tells how far up or over in the tree we can go and still find a cycle that contains it. We can compute the low numbers of vertices during a postorder traversal of the depth-first tree, as shown in Algorithm 14.8.

```
/*  This algorithm uses a stack of vertices.
    Each vertex contains these members:
       dfnum — the depth–first number (initially 0);
       low — the low number;
       onstack — TRUE iff is it on the stack.
*/

traverse(v)
    v.dfnum = v.low = ++globaldf
    push(v); v.onstack = TRUE
    for each successor w of v
        if w.dfnum == 0
            traverse(w)
            if w.low < v.low
                v.low = w.low
        else if w.dfnum < v.dfnum
            /* (v,w) is a back or cross edge */
            if w.onstack && w.low < v.low
                v.low = w.low
    if v.low == v.dfnum
        v is the root of a strong component
        do
            w = pop( ); w.onstack = FALSE
        while w ≠ v

Traversal Algorithm:
    globaldf = 0
    for (i = 1; i ≤ n; i++)
        if v_i.dfnum == 0
            traverse(v_i,v_i)
```

ALGORITHM 14.8

Algorithm to find the strong components of a directed graph.

Figure 14.14 shows the depth-first diagram of Figure 14.13 augmented by depth-first and low numbers.

By definition of low number, a vertex is the root of a strong component if and only if its low number is the same as its depth-first number. To see this, note first that a vertex's low number can be no larger than its depth-first number; if its low number is smaller, then it belongs to a cycle that includes vertices higher than it in the depth-first tree. We can use the low numbers to identify the strong components in the graph: two vertices belong to the same strong component if and

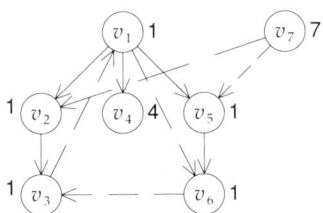

FIGURE 14.14

The depth-first diagram of Figure 14.13, augmented by low numbers.

only if they have the same low number. In Figure 14.14, vertices v_1, v_4, and v_7 are the roots of strong components.

14.6
SUMMARY AND PERSPECTIVE

Graphs are general, graphs are versatile, and graphs are common.

Because graphs are so general, it is harder to solve many graph problems than analogous problems on simpler structures. We already noted in Chapter 13 that the existence of cycles makes graph traversal challenging. And our recurring need to prove the conditions that mean a graph property is satisfied suggests the care with which we must define and solve problems on graphs. As further evidence for the difficulties of dealing with general graphs, notice how many of the problems studied in this chapter amount to finding some kind of acyclic subgraph of a general graph.

Because graphs are versatile, there are many ways to store and manipulate them. To cope with this versatility, we need to have on hand a variety of tools from Parts I and II. This chapter contains no running program, because it seemed less useful here than anywhere else: we have built up many of the necessary computational tools already, but we would have to build several more structures to write a program that uses graphs. The appropriate structure seems to depend strongly on the application: it is hard to define an appropriate data type "graph."

Graphs are common because they can represent so many kinds of important situations. Many graph problems have been studied and their solutions are well understood. Unfortunately, many other graph problems have been studied extensively and have no good solutions.

EXERCISES

---

1 For each of the applications of graphs mentioned at the end of Section 14.1, discuss whether a directed or undirected graph would be appropriate.

2 Describe some other applications of graphs.

3 Explain why $m \leq n(n-1)/2$ in simple undirected graphs.

4 How would you represent a graph with multiple edges in an adjacency matrix?

5 Show how to address the element A_{ij} when the lower triangle of the adjacency matrix is stored in an array of $n(n-1)/2$ entries.

6 Describe an algorithm to detect multiple edges and self loops in a graph that is stored as a set of adjacency lists. What is the time complexity of your algorithm?

7 What do the sets of adjacency lists look like when they represent a tree? a directed acyclic graph?

Two graphs $G = (V,E)$ and $G' = (V',E')$ are *isomorphic* if there is a one-to-one and onto function $f:V \rightarrow V'$ such that $(v,w) \in E$ if and only if $(f(v),f(w)) \in E'$. In general it seems to be hard to decide whether two graphs are isomorphic without trying all possible isomorphism functions f. For some special cases, however, better methods are known.

8 Given two trees, show how to test whether they are isomorphic.

9 Show that if there is a shortest path between two vertices then there is a simple shortest path between them.

10 Show that any subpath of a shortest path is a shortest path.

11 Label the vertices on the queue with their pass numbers in Figure 14.6.

12 Prove for Algorithm 14.1 that if there is a shortest path from s to w with k or fewer edges, then at the end of pass k, $dist_s(w)$ will be the length of this shortest path.

13 Implement Algorithm 14.1, modified so that it reports when a negative cycle exists.

14 Show how to find a negative cycle if Algorithm 14.1 runs for more than n passes.

15 Show that the output of Algorithm 14.2 satisfies 14.3(∗).

16 What happens when Algorithm 14.2 is run on input that contains edges with negative lengths?

17 Implement Algorithm 14.2 to run when the graph is stored as an adjacency matrix.

18 Implement Algorithm 14.2 to run in $O(n^2)$ time when the graph is stored as a set of adjacency lists.

19 Two steps are needed to improve the running time of Algorithm 14.2. We need a data structure in which we can quickly find the

closest vertex that is not yet in the tree at each step; a priority queue is a good choice for this. When we update the *closest* members of vertices, we should consider only successors of v that are not yet in the tree, not all non-tree vertices; the adjacency list representation makes this natural. With these two changes, implement Algorithm 14.2 to run in $O(m \log n)$ time.

20 Show how to detect a negative cycle in Algorithm 14.3.

21 To recover shortest paths from Algorithm 14.3, we store shortest-path trees for each vertex; since each vertex has a parent in each tree, we need to store n parents for each vertex. Show how to maintain these trees during Algorithm 14.3. Show that they obey 14.3(∗).

22 Construct a minimum spanning tree on an undirected graph that is not a shortest-path tree for any vertex in the graph.

23 Prove or disprove: in an undirected graph with non-negative edge weights, a shortest-path tree is a minimum spanning tree.

24 Explain why the time bound for the priority queue operations in Algorithm 14.5 can be written as $O(m \log n)$ and not $O(m \log m)$.

25 What is the result of a depth-first traversal of a complete graph?

26 Prove that the cycle-finding algorithm in Section 14.5 works.

27 Prove that the algorithm in Section 14.5 to label vertices with their connected components works.

28 A *bridge* in an undirected graph is an edge whose removal disconnects the graph. Show how to find all bridges in a graph.

29 Show that depth-first search on an acyclic graph visits the vertices in topological order.

30 Modify Algorithm 14.6 to mark edges as they are traversed. Show that it traverses each edge of the input graph once.

31 Here is an idea for a garbage collection algorithm: Perform a depth-first traversal of the heap by starting at each static, external, or automatic pointer variable, marking all nodes reached during the traversal; scan through memory and collect all unmarked nodes. A recursive implementation of this *mark-and-scan* algorithm requires a deep stack at exactly the time when memory is in short supply. Suggest a non-recursive way to perform a depth-first traversal.

32 Prove that in a biconnected graph on more than two vertices, each pair of vertices can be joined by at least two paths that share only the two terminal vertices.

33 Prove that the stated "equivalence relation of biconnectivity" really is an equivalence relation.

34 A graph is *Hamiltonian* if all of its vertices lie on a single simple cycle. Show that a Hamiltonian graph is biconnected. Construct a biconnected graph that is not Hamiltonian.

35 Show that the back edges in the depth-first diagram of an undirected graph always point from a vertex to an ancestor of that vertex.

36 Show that Algorithm 14.7 calculates low numbers as defined in the text.

37 Implement Algorithm 14.7, taking care to cope correctly with trivial edges.

38 Show how to recover the biconnected components of a graph during a depth-first traversal.

39 Show that a cross edge in the depth-first diagram of a directed graph always goes from a vertex with a higher depth-first number to a vertex with a lower depth-first number.

40 Show that Algorithm 14.8 calculates low numbers as defined in the text.

41 Implement Algorithm 14.8 so that it reports the vertices in a strong component when it identifies the root of the component in the depth-first diagram.

42 Show that Algorithm 14.9 produces strong components.

The *underlying graph* of a directed graph is the undirected graph we obtain by ignoring the directions on the edges. If the underlying graph of a directed graph is biconnected, the directed graph is sometimes said to be *weakly connected*.

43 Give an example of a weakly connected graph that is not strongly connected.

44 Give an example of a strongly connected graph that is not weakly connected.

45 Describe the following equivalence relation in terms of equivalence relations we have seen already: two edges v and w are equivalent if they belong to a common simple cycle.

Given a directed graph, we can define the corresponding *reduced* graph by the following operations: collapse each strong component into a sin-

---

Assign depth–first numbers to the vertices in postorder.
Form the reversal *of the graph by reversing the direction of each edge.*
for $(i = n; i \geq 1; i--)$
    if v_i *has not been visited,*
        start a depth–first search in the reversal at v_i
        the depth–first tree rooted at v_i *is a strong component*

ALGORITHM 14.9

Another algorithm to find strong components.

gle super-vertex; replace multiple edges that travel between components by single edges.

46 Show that the reduced graph is directed and acyclic.

47 Show that Algorithm 14.3 produces the strong components in topological order.

REFERENCES

The statement in Section 14.2 that most graph problems require quadratic time to solve when the graph is stored in an adjacency matrix was known as the Aanderaa–Rosenberg conjecture before it was proved:

> R. L. Rivest and J. Vuillemin. "On recognizing graph properties from adjacency matrices." *Theoretical Computer Science* 3 (1975): 371–384.

Algorithm 14.2 appears in:

> E. W. Dijkstra. "A note on two problems in connexion with graphs." *Numerische Mathematik* 1 (1959): 269–271.

Algorithm 14.3 appears in

> R. W. Floyd. "Algorithm 92: shortest path." *Communications of the ACM* 5 (1962): 345.

Its specialization to transitive closure is often known as Warshall's algorithm:

> S. Warshall. "A theorem on Boolean matrices." *Journal of the ACM* 9 (1962): 11–12.

Most authors attribute Algorithm 14.4 to R. C. Prim or E. W. Dijkstra, and Algorithm 14.5 to J. B. Kruskal. The following article shows that both were discovered early in the twentieth century by Czech and Polish authors:

> R. L. Graham and P. Hell. "On the history of the minimum spanning tree problem." *Annals of the History of Computing* 7 (1985): 43–57.

Asymptotically faster algorithms for finding shortest-path trees ($O(n \log n + m)$) and minimum spanning trees ($O(m \log^* n)$) appear in:

> M. L. Fredman and R. E. Tarjan. "Fibonacci heaps and their uses in improved network optimization algorithms." In *Proc. 25th Ann. Symp. on Foundations of Computer Science* (1984): 338–346.

Many applications of depth-first search are described in

> R. E. Tarjan. "Depth-first search and linear graph algorithms." *SIAM Journal on Computing* 1 (1972): 146–160.

Algorithm 14.9 is credited to S. R. Kosaraju in Chapter 6 of

> A. V. Aho, J. E. Hopcroft, and J. D. Ullman. *Data Structures and Algorithms*. Reading, Mass.: Addison-Wesley, 1983.

Appendixes

A

C
for
Programmers

This appendix is meant to tell enough about C to let someone familiar with elementary programming begin reading and writing C programs. Some details have been omitted from the descriptions of many features of C; they should not matter for the example programs.

A Sample Program

We use a simple, rather contrived program to illustrate basic features of C. Program A.1 produces the small table of squares and cubes shown in Figure A.1.

Functions

A program is a collection of functions. The general form of a function definition is

type_name function_name (*argument_list*)
function_body

Program A.1 defines two functions; cube() and main().

Function cube() takes one argument, x, that is declared to be of type double; it uses the return statement to return a value of type double to the function that called it.

Function main() takes no arguments, but its definition includes an empty set of parentheses. In general, when a function is defined or called, its name must be followed by parentheses.

```
#include "ourhdr.h"

#define sqr(x) ((x)*(x))

double cube(double x)
{
    double y = x*x*x;
    return y;
}

int low = 1, high = 9;

main()
{
    int i;
    for (i = low; i <= high; i++) {
        double value;
        value = (double) i/10;
        if (i%2)
            printf("%g %g %g\n", value, sqr(value), cube(value
    }
    exit(0);
}
```

PROGRAM A.1
A C program that produces the table in Figure A.1.

In Program A.1, main() calls three other functions, cube(), printf(), and exit(). Appendix B describes the arguments to the latter two functions.

```
0.1 0.01 0.001
0.3 0.09 0.027
0.5 0.25 0.125
0.7 0.49 0.343
0.9 0.81 0.729
```

FIGURE A.1
The output of Program A.1.

When a program is run, `main()` is the first function called. A program without a function `main()` may define functions and declare variables, but it cannot be executed.

Statements

Simple statements are composed of expressions, including function calls; they must be terminated by a semicolon. This contrasts with languages that use the semicolon to separate statements, such as Pascal.

A *compound statement* is a sequence of variable declarations followed by statements, all surrounded by braces (`{}`). (Here and in all later uses, the unqualified term *statement* means either a simple or a compound statement.) Program A.1 includes three compound statements. One is the object of the `for`-statement in `main()`. The other two are the bodies of `cube()` and `main()`. The body of any function is a compound statement.

Statements are executed in the sequence in which they appear, starting with the first statement in `main()`.

Variables

Variables can be declared at the beginning of any compound statement. In Program A.1, `i` is declared in the body of `main()` and `y` is declared in the body of `cube()`; `value` is declared in the compound statement that is the object of the `for`-loop.

A variable declaration may include an *initialization*, which gives the variable a value. In Program A.1, variables `low` and `high` are initialized when the program starts executing. Variable `y` in `cube()` is initialized whenever `cube()` is called. See Section 6.2 for more about variable initialization.

Types

In this appendix we discuss only the built-in arithmetic types. There are four integer types: `char`, `short`, `int`, and `long`. The size of integer that can fit into variables of the various integer types depends on the compiler; the only guarantee is that any valid `short` value will fit into an `int`, and any valid `int` value will fit into a `long`. In any implementation, a `char` variable will be big enough to contain a character. Programs in this book declare most integer variables to be of type `int`, but to use those programs with compilers that store `int`s in 16 bits one might need to change those declarations to `long`.

There are two floating-point types: `float` and `double`. The precisions available in the two floating-point types also depend on the implementation; they may be the same.

If a function does not return a value, it can be declared to be of the special type `void`.

Chapter 3 discusses arrays, pointers, `typedef`s, and user-defined structures. Chapter 6 discusses `union`s.

Storage Classes

Besides a type, a variable also has a *storage class*. We shall discuss here only the four classes `auto`, `static`, `extern`, and `register`. By default, a variable declared inside a compound statement has storage class `auto`; it exists only when the compound statement is being executed, and is lost irretrievably when execution leaves the statement. All of the variables declared inside functions in Program A.1 are automatic variables. A `static` variable declared inside a compound statement exists and retains its value between executions of the compound statement. Program 12.2d includes an example of a static variable declared in a function.

The treatment of variables declared outside any compound statement depends on the compiler. A variable declared outside any compound statement is certainly known to all functions that follow it in the same file. If the value of the variable should be available to all functions in the whole program (whose text may span several files), then its storage class should be `extern`. If access to its value should be limited to functions that are contained in the same file, then its storage class should be `static`. The distinction between `static` and `extern` does not matter for programs that are contained entirely in a single file.

The declaration that a variable is of storage class `register` offers the compiler a hint that the variable will be used frequently in the compound statement in which it is declared. Not all variables can be stored in registers, and some compilers ignore this hint completely.

Constants

A sequence of digits that does not begin with zero is interpreted as a decimal constant. If it fits into an `int` it is of type `int`, otherwise it is of type `long`.

A sequence of digits that includes a decimal point is interpreted as a floating-point constant. Floating-point constants may also include the letter e or E followed by an integer; the expression xen means $x\times10^n$.

A single character that appears between single quote marks is a character constant; for example, 'a' is a character constant whose value depends on the computer's character set. Some useful characters are named by two-character backslash expressions:

\n (newline),

\t (tab),

\' (single quote), and

\\ (backslash itself).

A sequence of characters that appears between double quote marks is a string constant. A double quote mark in a string constant should be preceded (escaped) by a backslash. A character between double quotes is a string constant, not a character constant.

Expressions

The name of a variable is an expression whose value is the value stored in the variable. We can also use operators to compose expressions out of several variables and constants. Parentheses override the default precedence of operators.

Unary Operators

Unary operators take a single argument. They include

− (unary minus),

! (logical not),

++ (increment), and

−− (decrement).

Program A.1 uses an increment operator as part of the control of the for-loop.

Unary minus and logical not affect the value of an expression but they do not change the value of their argument. The increment and decrement operators change their arguments in one of two possible ways. Consider the increment operator, which adds one to its argument. Whether it adds one before or after the value of the expression is computed depends on where the ++ appears: if it comes before the argument, the argument is incremented first; if it comes after the argument, the argument is incremented after the value is computed. For example, if the value of x is 5, then the value of x++ (post-increment) is 5 while the value of ++x (pre-increment) is 6; after the expression is evaluated, the value of x is 6 in both cases. The decrement operator, which subtracts one from its argument, works in a similar fashion.

Binary Operators

Binary arithmetic operators include

+ (addition),
− (subtraction),
* (multiplication),
/ (division), and
% (integer remainder function).

Program A.1 uses binary arithmetic operators to compute y in cube() and value and the if-condition in main().

Binary relational operators include

< (less than),
> (greater than),
<= (less than or equal),
>= (greater than or equal),
== (equal), and
!= (not equal).

An expression that uses binary relational operators has value 1 (true) if the relation holds and 0 (false) if it does not. Program A.1 uses the binary relational operator <= as part of the control of the for-loop.

The relational operator for equality is a double equals-sign; if you use a single equals-sign, the resulting program will compile and execute, but give strange results.

Logical binary operators include

&& (logical and), and
|| (logical or).

Both are evaluated in a short-circuit fashion: operands are evaluated only until the value of the result becomes known. For example, if the first operand of && is false, the entire expression must be false, so the second operand is never evaluated. Programs 5.1c and e rely on short-circuit boolean evaluation.

Bitwise operators work only on integer operands. They include the unary

~ (one's complement),

and the following binary operators

& (and),
^ (inclusive-or),
| (exclusive-or),
<< (left shift), and
>> (right shift).

Assignment

The symbol for assigning a value to a variable is =, as in Fortran and in contrast to Pascal. Assignment is used in Program A.1 as part of the control of the for-loop and to give a value to value. Binary arithmetic and bitwise operators are available in the form of *assignment operators*. For example, the statement x+=2 adds two to x. Assignment operators make it clear that the value of a variable is involved in the expression that updates it.

Types of Compound Expressions

Expressions that involve only integers are performed in integer arithmetic. Expressions that involve both integer and floating-point numbers are performed in floating-point arithmetic. The defaults can be overridden by *casting* the expression to have a different type than its default. Program A.1 uses a cast to force the division of i by ten to be performed in floating-point arithmetic.

Zero is False

When an expression is used as a condition that determines whether another statement is executed, it is considered to be *true* if it is not zero, and *false* if it is zero. It is common for C programs to rely on this and not state explicitly that a variable or function returns a value that is interpreted as true or false. Program A.1 includes an example: i%2 is zero (false) on even i and one (true) on odd i; therefore the object of the if-statement is executed only when i is odd.

Conditional Execution

The conditional statement has two forms.

```
/* action only on true */
if ( condition )
    statement
```

Program A.1 uses this simple form, which executes *statement* only when *condition* is true.

```
/* general form */
if ( condition )
    statement₁
else
    statement₂
```

This form executes *statement*₁ when *condition* is true, and *statement*₂ when *condition* is false. Program 2.1 includes an example of this kind of if-statement.

The following expression

$$condition\ ?\ expression_1\ :\ expression_2$$

has the value *expression*₁ if *condition* is true, and *expression*₂ if *condition* is false. Program 5.1g uses such an expression.

Indefinite Iteration

There are two forms of conditional iteration.

```
/* test before first iteration */
while ( condition )
    statement
```

In the while-statement, *condition* is tested before each iteration of the loop, and *statement* is executed if and only if *condition* is true; thus it is possible that *statement* is not executed at all. Program 3.5 uses a while-statement.

```
/* test after first iteration */
do
    statement
while ( condition )
```

In the do-statement, *condition* is tested after each iteration of the loop, and execution leaves the loop if and only if *condition* is false; *statement* is executed at least once. Program 8.2 uses a do-statement.

Definite Iteration

The for-statement:

```
for ( expression₁ ; expression₂ ; expression₃ )
    statement
```

is an abbreviation for the following common form of while-statement:

```
expression₁ ;
while ( expression₂ ) {
    statement
    expression₃ ;
}
```

Program A.1 uses a for-loop.

The *statement* in a for-loop may change the value of the variables that are involved in *expression₂*: C enforces no restrictions on assignment to the loop control variable, in contrast to Pascal.

Early Loop Termination

There are two ways to leave loop bodies early, without waiting for the condition to be tested at the top or bottom of an iteration.

The continue-statement terminates a single iteration. The following two while-loops are equivalent:

```
/* using continue */
while ( condition ) {
    statement₁
    if ( expression )
        continue;
    statement₂
}

/* using goto */
while ( condition ) {
    statement₁
    if ( expression )
        goto end;
    statement₂
    end: ;
}
```

The break-statement completely terminates the loop. The following two while-loops are equivalent:

```
/* using break */
while ( condition ) {
    statement₁
    if ( expression )
        break;
    statement₂
}

/* using goto */
while ( condition ) {
    statement₁
    if ( expression )
        goto out;
    statement₂
}
out: ;
```

Program 12.1f uses both kinds of loop termination.

Selecting Among Cases

The switch-statement selects among several cases according to the value of an integer variable:

```
switch ( expression ) {
case expr₁:
    code for expr₁
    break;
case expr₂:
    code for expr₂
    break;
default:
    code for default case
    break;
}
```

If *expression* is equal to *expr₁*, the code for *expr₁* is executed. If *expression* is equal to *expr₂*, the code for *expr₂* is executed, and so on. If *expression* is not equal to any of the *exprᵢ*, the code for default is executed; a switch-statement that does not contain a default case does nothing if no case matches *expression*. Programs 5.1 and 8.2 show switch-statements with and without default cases. If the code for different cases is not separated by break-statements, execution falls through from one case to the next.

Preprocessor Features

Program A.1 directs the compiler to include the text of file `ourhdr.h`, which is listed in Appendix C. In general, the text of a file named in a `#include`-statement replaces the statement itself.

Program A.1 also defines a *macro* `sqr(x)` that has one argument. Wherever the expression `sqr(y)` occurs in the succeeding program text, it is expanded into the expression $((y) * (y))$.

EXERCISES

1 Would it matter if we used pre-increment in the `for`-loop in Program A.1?

2 Consider the following revised definition of macro `sqr`:

```
#define sqr(x) x*x
```

What is the value of the expression `sqr(x+y)`? `sqr(i++)`?

3 Why does the expression −1<5<4 have value 1?

REFERENCES

The authoritative reference on the C language is the combined textbook and reference manual

B. W. Kernighan and D. M. Ritchie. *The C Programming Language*. 2d ed. Englewood Cliffs, N.J.: Prentice-Hall, 1988.

The types of arguments in "old C" functions are declared after the function's signature, for example:

```
double cube(x)
double x;
```

While this style of function declaration is still permitted, most compilers cannot subject programs that use it to the same careful type-checking that the standard style encourages.

B

Library Functions

The function library that comes with most versions of C should include some version of most of the functions described in this appendix. The following is neither a complete listing of library functions nor a complete description of the functions that are included. It should, however, include library functions that are used in the programs in this book. It also notes when a function belongs to the standard library.

Random Number Generation

```
int rand(void)
```

The call `rand()` returns a uniform pseudo-random integer x in the range $0 \leq x \leq \text{RAND\_MAX}$, where `RAND_MAX` is at least $2^{15} - 1$. This is a standard library function.

```
double frand(void)
```

The call `frand()` returns a uniform pseudo-random number x in the range $0 \leq x < 1$.

```
int nrand(int val)
```

The call `nrand(val)` returns a uniform pseudo-random integer x in the range $0 \leq x < \text{val}$.

Numeric Conversion

```
int atoi(char *s)
```

The call atoi(s) returns the value of the integer digit sequence in string s. This is a standard library function.

```
double atof(char *s)
```

The call atof(s) returns the value of the floating-point digit sequence in string s. This is a standard library function.

Program 3.11 uses both of these functions.

String Manipulation Functions

All of the functions described here assume that their arguments are null-terminated. Some libraries, including those that comply with the standard, also include variant functions that accept an additional parameter as a bound on the length of all string arguments: look for functions named strncmp(), strncpy(), and strncat().

Section 3.2 describes strcmp(), strcpy(), and strlen() further.

```
int strcmp(char *s1, char *s2)
```

The call strcmp(s1, s2) returns a value that is negative, zero, or positive depending on whether s1 is lexicographically smaller than, equal to, or greater than s2. This is a standard library function.

```
char *strcpy(char *s1, char *s2)
```

The call strcpy(s1, s2) copies the string in s2 into the string s1, destroying whatever was there before. This is a standard library function.

```
int strlen(char *s)
```

The call strlen(s) returns the number of non-null characters that precede the first null character in string s. This is a standard library function.

```
char *strcat(char *s1, char *s2)
```

The call `strcat(s1, s2)` catenates string s2 onto the end of string s1. It assumes that there is room for s2 at the end of s1. This is a standard library function.

```
char *strdup(char *s)
```

The call `strdup(s)` returns a pointer to freshly-allocated space that contains a copy of string s.

File Manipulation

In many environments, including those that comply with the standard, C programs can rely on the operating system to open three files named `stdin` (standard input), `stdout` (standard output), and `stderr` (standard error output). When a program must manipulate other files, however, it can use the functions described here.

```
FILE *fopen(char *name, char *type)
```

The call `fopen(name, type)` opens the file whose name is stored in string name. If `type` is r, the file will be opened for reading; if `type` is w, the file will be created for writing; if `type` is a, the file will be opened for writing at its end. The function returns a pointer to the FILE, or NULL if it was unable to open the file as requested. This is a standard library function.

```
int fflush(FILE *stream)
```

The call `fflush(stream)` flushes the output buffer associated with the FILE pointer `stream`. That is, all characters the program has sent to the file are written to the physical file. This is a standard library function.

```
int fclose(FILE *stream)
```

The call `fclose(stream)` flushes the output buffer and closes the file associated with FILE pointer `stream`. This is a standard library function.

Character Input and Output

```
int getc(FILE *stream)
```

The call getc(stream) reads and returns the next character from stream, or EOF if it reaches the end of file. This is a standard library function.

```
int getchar(void)
```

The call getchar() is the same as getc(stdin). This is a standard library function.

```
int putc(char c, FILE *stream)
```

The call putc(c, stream) writes character c to stream. This is a standard library function.

```
int putchar(int c)
```

The call putchar(c) is the same as putc(c, stdout). This is a standard library function.

String Input and Output

```
char *fgets(char *s, int n, FILE *stream)
```

The call fgets(s, n, stream) reads a single line of at most n−1 characters from file stream into string s, including the newline character, then appends a null character to s. The function returns NULL when it reaches the end of file. This is a standard library function.

```
char *gets(char *s)
```

The call gets(s) stores characters from the standard input up to, but not including, a newline into string s, then appends a null character to s. It returns NULL when it reaches the end of file. Many system administrators removed gets() from the C libraries in their charge early in November, 1988.

```
int fputs(char *s, FILE *stream)
```

The call fputs(s, stream) writes the null-terminated string s to file stream. This is a standard library function.

```
int puts(char *s)
```

The call puts(s) writes the null-terminated string s to the standard output and appends a newline character. This is a standard library function.

Formatted Input

The formats in the following are strings that control how characters are interpreted. The ellipses represent arguments that point to variables where the data interpreted using format can be stored. Conversion specifications introduced by a % character in the format string tell how to interpret sequences of input characters. Among the conversions included in implementations of the scanf() family that comply with the standard are

%c (char),
%d (int),
%f (float),
%lf (double), and
%s (string).

Input strings are terminated by spaces or newlines, unless the % and s are separated by a bracketed set of characters that must be included or excluded from the string (see Program 12.1e).

```
int scanf(char *format, ...)
```

The call scanf(format, ...) interprets characters from the standard input according to format and returns the number of arguments that were successfully matched. This is a standard library function.

```
int fscanf(FILE *stream, char *format, ...)
```

The call fscanf(stream, format, ...) does the job of scanf() on characters from stream. This is a standard library function.

```
int sscanf(char *s, char *format, ...)
```

The call sscanf(s, format, ...) does the job of scanf() on characters in string s. This is a standard library function.

Formatted Output

The `formats` in this section are strings that tell how variables in the argument list are to be interpreted for printing. The ellipses represent expressions that are to be interpreted using `format`. Conversion specifications introduced by a `%` character in the `format` string tell how to interpret variables. Among the conversions included in implementations of the `printf()` family that comply with the standard are

`%c` (`char`),

`%d` (`int`),

`%e`, `%f`, or `%g` (`float` or `double`),

`%s` (`string`), and

`%%` (percent itself).

The `%` may be followed by a conversion specification that tells how wide the output field should be. Here are some examples of conversion specifications:

`%10d` (print an integer right-justified in a field 10 characters wide);

`%12.2f` (print a floating-point value right-justified in a field 12 characters wide, with 2 characters after the decimal point);

`%-20.10s` (print 10 characters from a string, right justified in a field 20 characters wide).

```
int printf(char *format, ...)
```

The call `printf(format, ...)` prints the expressions on the standard output in accordance with `format`. This is a standard library function.

```
int fprintf(FILE *stream, char *format, ...)
```

The call `fprintf(stream, format, ...)` writes the characters that would be produced by `printf()` onto the file pointed to by `stream`. This is a standard library function.

```
int sprintf(char *s, char *format, ...)
```

The call `sprintf(s, format, ...)` writes the characters that would be produced by `printf()` into string `s`. This is a standard library function.

Memory Management

The next functions are used for dynamic storage allocation. See Section 6.3 for a more detailed description. In "old C," void * was not a valid type; hence the generic pointer type was char *. The type size_t is defined in standard library stddef.h; for most purposes one can think of it as unsigned.

```
void *malloc(size_t n)
```

The call malloc(n) returns a pointer to a contiguous block of at least n bytes. This is a standard library function.

```
void free(void *p)
```

The call free(p) frees a block allocated by malloc(). This is a standard library function.

```
void *realloc(void *p, size_t n)
```

The call realloc(p, n) changes the size of the block to which p points to be at least n bytes long, and leaves the contents unchanged up to the smaller of the old and new sizes. This is a standard library function.

```
char *calloc(size_t n, size_t size)
```

The call calloc(n, size) allocates space for an array of n elements of size bytes each; the space is initialized to contain all zeros. This is a standard library function.

Program Termination

Both of these functions make a program stop executing.

```
void abort(void)
```

The call abort() sends a signal to the operating system that usually causes a core dump. This is a standard library function.

```
void exit(int status)
```

The call exit(status) sends the value of status to the operating system; usually zero means normal termination and non-zero means abnormal termination. This is a standard library function. An alternative to calling exit() is for function main() to return a value.

REFERENCES

The dangers of gets() are mentioned in

E. H. Spafford. "Crisis and aftermath." *Communications of the ACM* 32 (1989): 678–687.

C

Our Header File

Here is a listing of the file ourhdr.h, which is #included by every program in the book:

```
#include <stdio.h>
#include <stdlib.h>
#include <string.h>

extern *strdup(char *);

#define demand(fact, remark) {\
    if (!(fact)) {\
        fprintf(stderr, "demand not met:  " #fact "\n");\
        fprintf(stderr, #remark "\n");\
        abort();\
        exit(1);\
    }\
}

typedef int boolean;
#define FALSE 0
#define TRUE !FALSE
```

An alternative to demand() is the assert() macro defined in the standard library, which will print the fact that failed to be true along with the name of the source file and the line number at which the failed assertion occurred, then call abort().

D

Solutions to Selected Exercises

Chapter 1

10 Program 1.1 processes five transactions, since `scanf()` consumes numbers without regard to white space.

11 Program 1.2 processes one transaction, since `gets()` reads the entire line into a buffer, and then the program processes the first transaction.

14 Program 1.6 installs the sought account name at the end of the array, so it is guaranteed to be found if it is not already present. Therefore, the `while`-loop need not test to avoid running off the end of the array. The last array slot must always be unoccupied, however, so Program 1.6 has room for one fewer accounts than Program 1.2.

18 We could give all instrumentation statements a distinctive comment, so that they can be found easily when we need to remove them. We could also place the instrumentation statements into a macro that includes or excludes them as desired.

20 This diagram should explain why six is a triangular number:

```
 .
 . .
 . . .
```

Chapter 2

1 If we do not save the value of $x^{\lfloor n/2 \rfloor}$, then $power_2(x, n)$ will use n multiplications.

9 Both variants of $power_1(\ )$ have multiplication complexity $\Theta(n)$.

12 The second derivation is correct (compare Exercise 1.19). The error in the first is that the constant hidden by the $O(1)$ is n.

16 It is straightforward to verify that $mult_2'(n)$ behaves as shown. To avoid unnecessary overflows and underflows, $power_2'(\ )$ should check whether $i = 1$ before squaring z.

20 This follows directly from Stirling's approximation: $n! = ((n/e)^n \sqrt{2\pi n})(1 + O(1/n))$. Roughly, $n!$ grows as fast as $(n/e)^n$, which is faster than k^n.

Chapter 3

4 The time complexity of `ourstrcpy()` is $\Theta(|src|)$.

7 The time complexity of the sequence of catenations is $\Theta(\sum_{i=1}^{k}(k-i+1)|s_i|)$. When all of the s_i are equal in length, this is asymptotically $\Theta(k^2|s_1|)$.

10 The expression `*pm.name` dereferences member `name` of variable `pm`. When `pm` is a pointer, it *has* no members.

Chapter 4

3 This requires three changes: $push(\ )$ should increment T after storing x in $stack[T]$, $top(\ )$ should return $stack[T-1]$ if the stack is not empty, and $empty(\ )$ should be true if $T \le 0$.

6 Here is a modified version of $top(\ )$:

thing $*top(\ )$
    demand(!*empty*$(\ )$, *top of empty stack*)
    return &*stack*→*thisone*

10 If $enqueue(\ )$ did not set $new \rightarrow next$ to $NULL$, some garbage in the $next$ member of the newly allocated node could be interpreted by $dequeue(\ )$ as a pointer to another queue node.

14 On the author's computer, the integer remainder operator can return a negative value that is not suitable as an index into the queue array. Adding N forces the result to be positive.

20 Since it pushes and pops each addend digit exactly once, each digit of the sum is pushed and popped exactly once, and the sum has at most $\max(m,n)+1$ digits, Program 4.1 adds an m-digit number to an n-digit number in $O(m+n)$ time.

27 The only permutation of 1, 2, 3 that cannot be realized using one stack is 3, 1, 2. In words, we cannot get 3 to come out first without reversing the order of 1 and 2.

Chapter 5

1 Since C arrays are indexed from zero, the function could return a negative number to indicate that the item was not found.

6 The complexity of Algorithm 5.6 is $\Theta(\max(|s_1|,|s_2|)^2)$.

14 This function could be used to dump the doubly linked list:

```
dump (node *p)
{
    printf ("%d ", p->value);
}
```

18 Each node must contain its row and column index, as well as the value stored in the matrix at that location.

Chapter 6

6 This could happen if there would be room to grow the dynamically allocated space only after the original space was de-allocated.

8 Since *expand( )* is a system call, it is expensive to make. Moreover, there is unlikely to be a corresponding function that we can use to return small hunks of memory to the operating system as we finish with them.

11 The time and space complexity are both $O(n)$ for a list of n items.

14 The nodes on a circularly linked list will not be collected by a reference-count garbage collector, because every node is pointed to by some other node.

Chapter 7

5 (b) To achieve the claimed time bound, search repeatedly for the last two elements on the list. Transpose interchanges them at every search, but they never come closer to the front.

15 The lesson of Equation (7.5) is that you must look for the largest possible solution to a system of recurrence inequalities, consistent with other knowledge. For example, we know that $T(n) = O(n)$ in Equation (7.5), because the binary tree cannot be taller than $n - 1$.

16 For $n = k^c$, $T(n) = c + 1 = 1 + \log_k n$. In words, $\log n$ is the number of times we must divide by a constant before we reach one.

26 The following algorithm labels a tree in level order:

```
/* This algorithm uses a queue of tree nodes. */
enqueue(root)
while !empty( )
    p = dequeue( )
    make p's label be i++
    enqueue(left child of p)
    enqueue(right child of p)
```

29 For even n, the sequence $1, n, 2, n-1, \ldots, n/2, n/2+1$, generates a long, skinny binary tree.

31 Not all binary trees are equally likely to be produced by inserting a random permutation of n elements into a binary search tree.

32 There are $n+1$ null pointers in the simple representation of a binary tree with n nodes.

Chapter 8

3 The proposal is equivalent to treating the keys as array indexes. The size of array needed grows quickly with the key length; for example, a four-digit string of lower-case characters represents a number (in base 26) between 0 and $26^4 = 456976$. If most of the strings can be expected to appear, then this is not a bad solution. If only a small fraction of the possible strings will appear, however, this wastes a lot of space.

4 The incrementation function $incr( ) = -(2M+1)$ may cause the program with the simpler statement to fail on some computers, because try will be assigned a negative value.

8 In Program 8.3, try always points to a place that contains a pointer to an item. It begins by pointing to a slot in the hash table; as it traverses the list headed at that slot, it points to the next member of the predecessor of the current node in the traversal. It calls calloc() because it is important that the newly allocated node have a null next member.

Chapter 9

2 If an AVL tree on n nodes is h tall, then Equation (9.2) shows that $n = \Omega(\phi^h)$, where $\phi = (1+\sqrt{5})/5$. Therefore $h = O(\log_\phi n)$.

3 There are 2^i nodes at depth i from the root of the complete, infinite binary tree. Since $\sum_{i=0}^{k-1} 2^i = 2^k - 1$, a complete binary tree does not have n nodes until it has $\lceil \log_2 n \rceil$ levels. Since any binary tree on n nodes must be at least as tall as the complete binary tree on n

nodes, we conclude that the height of a binary tree on n nodes is $\Omega(\log n)$.

4 The insertion could only increase the height of one of the two subtrees of the subtree of height $h+2$ in Figure 9.8a. If both subtrees have height $h+1$ after the insertion, then the tree was unbalanced before the insertion occurred.

9 This answer applies to Figure 9.21a; a similar explanation can be given for Figure 9.21b. The colors of f, g, and h are known because we performed a color flip at g; the color of e must be red because we are assuming that the color flip led to a violation of the red rule. Before we performed that color flip, the tree was red-black. Since e is red, c and d must be black. If b were also red, then we would have performed a color flip at c, on the way down to g, and before we ever reached it. Therefore, b must be black.

14 If we tried to build a,b trees with $2a > b+1$, then we would not be able to perform a legal split of a $(b+1)$-node.

Chapter 10

11 Morse code is interpreted by people who listen for spaces between characters. Thus, it is really a ternary (or base three) code, not a binary code at all.

16 Program D.1 is a tree-printing function.

17 The Huffman tree must be stored along with the Huffman-coded contents of the file. If the file is short, then the compression produced by the Huffman code may not compensate for the extra space needed to store the tree. Can you show that *any* scheme for data compression must cause some files either to grow or to stay the same size?

22 The root of B_k has k children. For $k \geq 1$, the tree is of height k. Tree B_k contains 2^k nodes. All of these quantities can be verified by induction.

23 The binary representation of n is unique. Since a binomial forest cannot contain two trees of the same size, it must contain a B_i tree if and only if the ith bit of n's binary representation is one.

27 To perform *deletemin*( ) on a binomial queue of n nodes,

find the smallest item in the root of one of the B_k;

remove it, producing one each of $B_{k-1}, \ldots, B_0$;

use Exercise 25 to merge the products of the *deletemin*( ) with the remainder of the queue.

Each of these steps takes $O(\log n)$ time.

```c
void printtree(node *t, int indent)
{
    int i;
    if (!t)
        return;
    if (isleaf(t)) {
        for (i = 0; i < indent; i++)
            printf("\t");
        printf("%d %c\n", t->freq, t->let);
        return;
    } else {
        printtree(t->left, indent+1);
        for (i = 0; i < indent; i++)
            printf("\t");
        printf("%d\n", t->freq);
        printtree(t->right, indent+1);
    }
}
```

PROGRAM D.1

A program to print a tree.

30 In the tallest leftist tree on n nodes, no node has a right child; the tree has height $n-1$. A tree on n nodes in heap shape is a leftist tree; its height is $\lceil \log_2(n+1) \rceil$.

Chapter 11

2 Suppose that every item in the input array is out of place. Since each swap can put at most two elements back into place, we shall need at least $\lceil n/2 \rceil$ swaps to sort the array.

4 Binary insertion sort uses $\Theta(n \log n)$ comparisons, and $O(n^2)$ swaps.

17 If we start with an array of n items, the smaller subarray has at most $\lfloor n/2 \rfloor$ items. The number of times we can halve the size of the subproblem before we reach an array of size one is $\lceil \log_2 n \rceil$.

18 Each step of the quicksort-based algorithm need process only the subarray that is known to contain the median; the other subarrays can simply be ignored. Since the partition step takes linear time and we expect the subarrays to be halved in length each time, this algorithm takes linear expected time. It can be modified to find the kth largest item in the same time bound.

26 Before the ith step, the integers are sorted by their last i digits; afterwards, they are sorted by their last $i+1$ digits. This algorithm runs in $O(nk)$ time.

35 Algorithm 11.6 uses as many comparisons as selection sort and as many swaps as pure insertion sort (Algorithm 11.1). It moves elements more often than Program 11.1.

Chapter 12

1 From the balance-sheet equation, we know that

$$ASSETS + EXPENSES = NET\ WORTH_n + LIABILITIES + INCOME$$

always holds, so it holds at the end of accounting period n. At the start of period $n+1$, $ASSETS$ and $LIABILITIES$ are the same as they were at the end of period n, so

$$NET\ WORTH_{n+1} = ASSETS - LIABILITIES.$$

After we replace $ASSETS$ and $LIABILITIES$ in the balance-sheet equation and rearrange it, we arrive at the equation claimed in the exercise.

2 The net worth carried over from Figure 12.3 is $1500 + 400 - 5850 = -3950$.

Chapter 13

2 There are two binary trees with two nodes: a root with a left child, and a root with a right child. There is only one rooted tree with two nodes: a root with a child.

12 In the worst case, the ith operation is $union(i, i+1)$, for $1 \le i < n$, and $union(\ )$ merges the first set into the second; thus, the ith operation relabels $i-1$ elements, and the $union(\ )$s take $\Theta(n^2)$ time. In the best case, the operation sequence is the same, and $union(\ )$ merges the second set into the first; the ith operation relabels one element, and all of the $union(\ )$s and $find(\ )$s together take $\Theta(n)$ time.

16 Construct a random permutation ρ of $1, 2, \ldots, n-1$. For $1 \le i \le n$, the $(2i-1)$th operation is $find(\ )$ on a randomly chosen element of $1, \ldots, n$. For $1 \le i < n$, the $2i$th operation is $union(\rho_i, \rho_{i+1})$. This ensures that the two arguments to $union(\ )$ never belong to the same set.

21 Depth-first search (Algorithm 14.6) visits the nodes in topological order.

24 When its input is not a partial order, Algorithm 13.2 reaches a state in which the queue is empty and every remaining node has a predecessor. It halts without producing some of the nodes as output.

Chapter 14

3 In the directed case, each vertex can have at most $n-1$ edges that point out of it. Therefore there can be at most $n(n-1)$ edges overall. If we apply this analysis to an undirected graph, we count each edge twice; therefore an undirected graph contains at most $n(n-1)/2$ edges.

4 If only the numbers of edges between vertices mattered, we could store the edge multiplicities in an array of integers. If the edges were labelled with data, we could represent the matrix as a two-dimensional array of linked lists of edges.

7 The adjacency list of a directed acyclic graph naturally corresponds to a set of ordered pairs that define a partial order; it is an ideal form of input to Algorithm 13.2.

10 If a subpath π' of a shortest path π were not a shortest path between its endpoints, then we could shorten π by replacing π' by the shortest path between its endpoints.

24 Since $m = O(n^2)$ (Equation (14.1)), we have immediately that $\log m \le 2 \log n + c = O(\log n)$.

25 A depth-first traversal of the complete graph on n vertices yields a depth-first tree of height $n-1$ with a lot of back edges.

35 A back edge points from a vertex v to a vertex w that has already been visited. If the graph is undirected, then v and w belong to the same connected component. Since w has already been visited and belongs to the same component as v, w must be an ancestor of v in the depth-first tree.

39 All nodes that can be reached from a vertex v and that have higher depth-first numbers than v are descendants of v in the depth-first diagram.

45 The edges that are equivalent under the stated relation form subgraphs that are both weakly and strongly connected.

Appendix A

1 No. Program 2.2 contains an example in which the use of pre-increment would change the output.

2 The expression `sqr(x+y)` expands to `x+y*x+y`. Since multiplication has higher precedence than addition, this is evaluated as

x+(y*x)+y. The value of sqr(i++) is i*(i+1), and after the expression is evaluated, i is two greater than it was before.

3 The binary relational operators associate left-to-right, so this expression is interpreted as (-1<5)<4. The inequality -1<5 is true, so it has the value one. The inequality 1<4 is also true, so the entire expression is true.

Index

To avoid cluttering the index with astronomical, biblical, culinary, historical, and mythological names, index entries related to such examples are collected under the heading "Examples."